COLLINS HISTORY CONNECTIONS

3

Britain 1750–1900

The 20th Century World

Christopher Culpin
Peter Fisher

Collins
Educational
An Imprint of
HarperCollins*Publishers*

Contents

Britain 1750–1900

attainment target

This symbol appears with questions which are targeted at the attainment target for history. At the end of Year 9 you will be given a level in history on the basis of how well you have answered these questions.

Some questions are about how much you know about different periods in the past: how people lived and what they believed. Others are about how things change through history and why these changes happen.

People are always trying to describe the past and sometimes they say different things. You will be asked about these differences and why they occur.

We find out about the past from historical sources. You will be asked about how we can use these sources to reach conclusions about the past.

Introduction

The huge machine in this picture is a steam-hammer. It was invented in 1840 by James Nasmyth, who also painted the picture of it. Since the iron age people have known that if you hammer iron when it is white-hot you get wrought iron, which is strong and pliable. Until the 19th century, making wrought iron from small iron bars was a job done by village blacksmiths.

Nasmyth's steam-hammer, as you can see, could hammer a bar of iron as big as a tree trunk. A steam-engine replaced the muscles of a blacksmith to power the hammer. By the 1840s, wrought iron was needed in vast quantities for railway locomotives and tracks, mining equipment, shipbuilding and many kinds of industrial machinery. Wrought iron was not only used in Britain: it was traded all over the world.

There are also clues in the picture about how industry changed people's lives. The village blacksmith probably lived next to the forge and worked alone or perhaps with one assistant. In this picture the iron is being made in a large ironworks. Lots of people, working together, were needed to work in factories like this one and they usually lived nearby in large towns or cities.

In this book you will see in overview how industry changed people's lives, in Britain and across the world, in the years from 1750 to 1900. You will be able to investigate some of the topics in depth.

This book deals with the years 1750 to 1900. During these years the British people were swept up in extraordinary changes because Britain was the first country to INDUSTRIALISE. In fact, the changes were so great that they are often called an INDUSTRIAL REVOLUTION. In this unit we will find out in outline what this means and why it happened. We will find out that the Industrial Revolution changed not only people's working lives but also where they lived. The unit therefore ends with outline and depth studies of life in cities.

Industry and cities

Look at Sources 1 and 2. What is going on in each painting? What things are the same in each? What is different?

Britain in 1750

Despite the smart clothes the artist has given them, the people in Source 1 are farmworkers. Britain in 1750 was a land where farm work was the most common job. It was also a land where:
- most people lived in the countryside
- the total population was only 10.7 million people
- the fastest means of transport was still, as it had been for thousands of years, the speed of a galloping horse.

Britain in 1900

The people in Source 2 worked in the huge factories behind them in the painting. They lived in an industrial town, Wigan, in Lancashire. Britain in 1900 was a land where most people worked in industry. It was also a land where:
- most people lived in cities
- the total population was 40 million
- the fastest means of transport was an express train capable of travelling at over 70 miles (110 kilometres) per hour.

SOURCE 1
'The Haymakers' by George Stubbs, a painting from the late 18th century.

SOURCE 2
Factory girls in their lunch break, Wigan, Lancashire – a painting of the late 19th century.

Moving to the factory system

Think of the last time you went shopping. Wherever you live the shops are full of enormous amounts of things for sale. Many of the same things can be seen in shops all over the country. This is because Britain, like most of the other countries which supply goods to our shops, is industrialised. Industrialised countries have FACTORIES which can make large quantities of goods and transport them over a wide area.

It hasn't always been like this. Take cloth for example. Everyone had to wear clothes, so plenty of cloth was needed. The main cloth-making areas were East Anglia, the West Country, Yorkshire and Lancashire.

Up to the 18th century cloth was made in people's homes. This is called the DOMESTIC SYSTEM. Families often had a bit of land and a few animals but these did not take up all their time. Women collected raw wool, SPUN it on spinning wheels (see Source 3) and passed the YARN they made to the WEAVERS. Weavers, usually men, wove the yarn into cloth on LOOMS in their own homes. Some homes were built with especially large windows to give more light for this job, see Source 4. Quite young children were expected to help.

Under an industrial system cloth is made in factories. Britain was the first country in the world to industrialise. Source 5 shows how amazed people at the time were by the change to the factory system. It is this change which led to all the other changes described above. It is this change, and how it affected people's lives, which is the overview theme of this unit.

SOURCE 4
Weavers' cottages with large windows.

SOURCE 3
Women working at home, spinning and winding yarn, 1814.

Discuss these questions in pairs.

1 Describe the workers and workplaces shown in Sources 1 and 2.

2 What differences do you think there would be in the lives of the people shown in each source?

3 Do you think the domestic system was a good thing? Think about: children working, health risks, dirt and pollution in the home, control of the quality of goods.

A cotton-spinning factory offers a remarkable example of the use of very great power. Often we can see, in a single building, a steam engine set in motion 50,000 spindles. The whole factory requires but 750 workers. But the machines, with the assistance of that mighty power, can produce as much yarn as formerly could hardly have been spun by 200,000 men, so that each man can produce as much as formerly required 166! In 12 hours the factory produces 62,000 miles of thread, which would encircle the earth two and a half times!

SOURCE 5
From *History of the Cotton Manufacture in Great Britain*, by Edward Baines, published in 1835.

Case study: why did the cotton industry grow?

Let us take one industry and see what we can learn from it about why industrialisation happened. Source 6(a) shows the enormous growth of the cotton industry from almost nothing to a multi-million pound business. By 1850 over one third of a million people worked in it. The description 'Industrial Revolution' seems to apply to the cotton industry above all others. Why did it happen? There could be several reasons.

Idea 1: perhaps the rising British population all wanted to wear cotton clothes? No, because although the population was rising, it was nothing like as fast as the growth of the cotton industry.

Idea 2: perhaps the cotton was sold abroad? Yes, most of it was. In 1850 over half of the value of all British exports came from cotton goods. This meant they had to be cheap. Look at Source 6(b): the price of cotton fell. So something happened which enabled cotton to be made in large quantities, much cheaper than before.

Idea 3: under the domestic system (see page 5) there was always a shortage of yarn for the weavers. It took up to 10 spinners to keep a weaver supplied with yarn. This was especially so after the invention, by John Kay in 1733, of the flying shuttle which enabled weavers to work even faster. Inventors put their minds to making new machines to spin more yarn.

a Value of cotton cloth sold		b Price of a length of cotton cloth	
1770	£600,000	1780	£2.00
1820	£18,500,000	1812	65p
1860	£33,000,000	1860	25p

SOURCE 6
Value and price of cotton sold.

Hargreaves' Spinning Jenny, 1764

Hargreaves' first machine could spin eight spindles at once. Later versions could spin up to 80 spindles. It was worked by hand and spun a fine but weak thread.

Arkwright's Frame, 1769

This invention produced a strong, coarse thread. Arkwright insisted that only large versions of it should be made, driven by horse- or water-power. Spinning now had to be done in factories. (You can read more about Arkwright on pages 18 to 19.)

Crompton's Mule, 1779

This machine produced a strong, fine yarn. It too had to be powered by water or steam so was only used in factories. Mules with 400 spindles were soon being made; in 1825 a mule which could spin 2,000 spindles was built.

Cartwright's Power Loom, 1785

Weaving was so complicated that it seemed unlikely that it could ever be done by a powered machine. Cartwright's invention did not work well and it was not until the 1820s that successful power looms began to be used in factories. However, by 1860 there were 400,000 of them in use.

Factories

Most of the new inventions which transformed the cotton industry could only be used in factories. They were too large to be used in people's houses. Most of all, their huge increase in output came from using stronger power than human muscles could provide. Factories already existed in the textile industry: Source 8 shows a silk factory in Derby. New industrialists like Richard Arkwright and Jedediah Strutt copied the idea: Source 9 shows Strutt's factory at Belper. By 1850 there were nearly 2,000 cotton factories in Britain.

SOURCE 7
A 96-spindle water-frame, from Arkwright's mill, now in Helmshore Museum, Lancashire.

SOURCE 8
The Lombe brothers' silk mill at Derby, built about 1717.

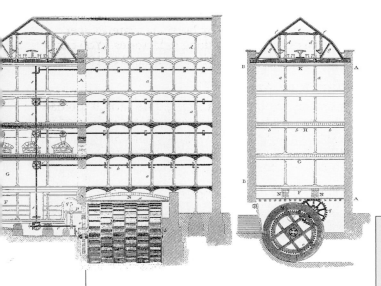

SOURCE 9
Diagram of Jedediah Strutt's cotton mill at Belper, Derbyshire, in 1819.

The following factors all helped the cotton industry to grow.

1 New technology: the introduction of machines meant that each worker could produce much more, at a lower cost.

2 Power: the huge waterwheel that powered Strutt's factory at Belper can be seen in Source 9. Later factories used steam power. For more on this factor see pages 8 to 9.

3 Capital (money): Strutt's factory (Source 9) cost £5,000 to build, £5,000 to equip with machines and another £5,000 to buy the material to get it started up. The total of £15,000 was an enormous amount of money at that time.

4 Entrepreneurs: these are the people who organised it all: buying land, designing buildings, hiring workers, selling the products. For a depth study of one of the most successful entrepreneurs, see pages 18 to 19.

5 Transport: all the raw materials and finished goods being carried about needed better transport. For more on this factor, see pages 10 to 11.

6 Exports: over half the cotton goods made were exported. This ability to sell beyond the limits of Britain's home population was vitally important to the success of the industry. For more on this factor see unit 2.

---

attainment target

1 What reasons were there for the fall in the price of cotton shown in Source 6(b)?

2 How do the inventions described on these pages explain the figures in Source 6(a)?

3 How do you think an invention like the frame in Source 7 would affect the lives of hand-spinners: after six months? After five years?

4 Which do you think was the most important cause of the rise of the factory system: all the new inventions? One of the new inventions? The need for power?

5 Draw a diagram showing the links between the factors for growth in the cotton industry listed above.

6 Turn your diagram into a piece of extended writing.

ACTIVITY

You could make a depth study of another industry, perhaps a local one, and see if the same factors applied.

What made the wheels go round?

For centuries the only forms of power for those who needed more than humans or animals could provide came from wind or water. Windmills gave only about 15 HORSE-POWER, and could only work irregularly. Waterwheels, however, were used in great numbers, all over Britain. The need for more power for factories and ironworks led to a marked improvement in waterwheel design. John Smeaton, at the Carron Ironworks in Scotland, made larger and more efficient wheels. Many early cotton factories found them quite good enough. (See Source 10 and also the huge wheel in Source 9 on page 7.)

The Cyfarthfa Ironworks in Wales used a wheel 50 feet (over 15m) in diameter. These giants could produce up to 200 horse-power, far more than any early steam-engine; the motion was steady and constant, unlike the jerky movement of steam-engines. Only after about 1850 did steam-power really overtake water-power.

SOURCE 10
Waterwheel at the cotton mill at Cromford, Derbyshire.

I had two motives in offering you my assistance, which were love of you and love of a money-getting idea.

I realised that your engine would require money, accurate workmanship and good selling to make the most of it. The best way of doing this was to keep it out of the hands of ordinary engineers who would be liable to produce inaccurate workmanship. My idea was to set up a factory near to my own by the side of our canal where I would erect all necessary for the completion of the engines and from which we would serve the world with engines.

SOURCE 11
Extract from a letter from Matthew Boulton to James Watt, 1769.

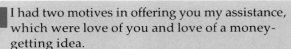

'Mr Wilkinson has improved the art of boring cylinders so that a 72-inch [1.8m] cylinder is no further from absolute accuracy than the thickness of a thin sixpence.'

SOURCE 12
Extract from a letter from James Watt to John Smeaton, 1776.

Steam-engines

Thomas Newcomen had invented a workable steam-engine back in 1712. It was enormous, slow and inefficient.

- IRONFOUNDERS could not make the cylinder accurately enough to prevent it leaking steam.
- It could only provide an up-and-down motion.
- The cylinder had to be continually heated and cooled, so it used huge quantities of coal. It was used to pump water out of coalmines but did not seem to have any use in factories.

In 1764 James Watt, a scientific instrument maker at Glasgow University, was asked to repair a model of a Newcomen engine. He saw that it would be improved if the steam could be drawn off into a separate cylinder, or condenser, and cooled there: the main cylinder would stay hot, the condenser would stay cool.

Watt had no money of his own, so he teamed up with Matthew Boulton, who ran an ENGINEERING works in Birmingham. Boulton's motives for doing this are described in Source 11. Boulton was friendly with an ironmaster, John Wilkinson, who had a machine for boring accurate holes to make cannon. At last Watt could get his cylinders made accurately. He wrote enthusiastically to Smeaton about it (see Source 12) and Boulton and Watt began making engines in 1775. Further improvements turned the up-and-down motion into a round-and-round motion. The engines were now suitable for driving machines and removed the jerkiness (Source 13).

SOURCE 13
A Watt engine of 1788, in the
Science Museum, London.

SOURCE 14
Steam-powered calico-printing
machines, 1834.

Steam-power in industry

Owners of ironworks, coalmines and Cornish tinmines took up Boulton and Watt's engine in a big way. The first all-steam cotton factory was started at Papplewick, Nottinghamshire, in 1785, but steam-power was generally slow to catch on in the cotton industry.

By about 1820 steam-engines were being more widely used to drive large new mules and power looms. The effects of this are described on page 6. They were also used for other processes in the cotton industry, such as printing patterns on cloth (Source 14). By 1851, seven out of eight cotton factories were powered by steam.

Steam-power also came late to the woollen industry of Yorkshire. When it did, huge new mills were built for them, like the one described in Source 15.

Any industry requiring large amounts of power was using steam by 1850. Steam-engines were used for sawing wood and stone, pressing oilseed, grinding cutlery, rolling metal sheets or tubes, twisting ropes and drawing wire. They were used to pump water in mines, breweries, tanneries, soapworks and ironworks.

'When the works are finished 4,500 hands will be required to keep them going. The weaving shed will contain 1,200 looms. The steam-engines to work them are equal to 1,250 horse-power.'

SOURCE 15
Description of the opening of Titus Salt's new woollen mill at Saltaire, near Bradford, from the *Illustrated London News*, of 1 October 1853.

1 Read Source 11. What did Matthew Boulton and James Watt each contribute to the success of their partnership?

2 How did changes in the iron industry help to make better steam engines?

3 What links are there between iron, coal and steam engines?

4 The machines in Source 13 replaced hand-printing. How would this change affect the skilled workers who used to do this job?

Why did transport have to improve?

It is not true that people did not move around the country in the past. Travel was very difficult, however, because the roads were so bad. As Source 16 shows, even the queen could get stuck in the mud. Most people who could afford it rode around on horseback. Those who could not walked. Goods were carried around the country in slow lumbering wagons. Where hills made it impossible to use wheeled vehicles, packhorses were used. The expanding industries of the late 18th century needed to be able to sell their products over a wide area. They needed:

- fast transport for business people
- cheap transport for bulky goods such as coal, iron, clay and stone. Carrying coal by road could cost 10d (4p) per tonne. At this rate, the price of the coal doubled in 10 miles (16 kilometres).

Would better roads solve the problem?

The reason roads were so bad is that no one bothered to repair them properly. Everyone was supposed to work for six days a year on the roads. Often all they did was tip some stones in the worst of the ruts.

One answer was for local business people and landowners to set up a 'turnpike trust'. A turnpike is a section of road with gates across it. All road users had to pay a toll to pass through the gates. The money was used to improve the roads. The first turnpike was set up in 1663 but the number increased after 1750. By 1830 about 35,000 kilometres of road were operated by turnpike trusts.

From the 1770s three famous engineers began to make real improvements in road design:

- John Metcalf who worked in the Pennine area in the late 18th century.
- Thomas Telford who worked in Scotland and on the London to Holyhead road (now the A5) in the early 19th century. He built well-drained roads with easier gradients.
- John McAdam worked for over 50 different turnpike trusts in southern England in the early 19th century. He built smooth roads at a cheaper cost than those built by Telford.

	1760	1830	1851
Bath	30 hrs	12 hrs	2.5 hrs
Manchester	46 hrs	19 hrs	5 hrs
Edinburgh	160 hrs	43 hrs	11.5 hrs

SOURCE 17
Journey times from London for 1760, 1830 and 1851.

'We set out at six in the morning and did not get out of the carriages (except when we were overturned or stuck fast in the mud), till we arrived at our journey's end 14 hours later.'

SOURCE 16
Queen Anne describes a journey from Windsor to Petworth, a distance of 40 miles (64 kilometres), in 1704.

Better road surfaces meant that coaches could go at faster speeds (see Source 17). At every 'stage' the four horses pulling the coach were changed, usually at an inn. By using fresh horses, speeds of 10 miles (16 kilometres) per hour were kept up. However, road transport was not the answer to industry's problems: it was very expensive and quite unsuitable for heavy goods.

Cheap transport: canals

Even on a smooth road a horse can only pull a weight of half a tonne; it can pull about 30 tonnes on water. For this reason, waterways were used for freight wherever possible.

The great age of canal-building began with the Duke of Bridgewater's canal, completed in 1761. The Duke owned a coalmine at Worsley, only 8 miles (13 kilometres) from the growing city of Manchester. His problem was that the cost of carrying coal by packhorse into Manchester made it too expensive. The Duke hired James Brindley to make a canal link. Brindley proved to be a canal-building genius and the price of the Duke's coal fell from 3p to 1.5p per hundredweight (50 kilograms).

Further canals were built to link major British rivers like the Trent, the Mersey, the Severn and the Thames (see Source 18). The early Industrial Revolution, from the 1770s to the 1840s, was based on canal transport. However, although they were cheap, canals were very slow. A heavy frost or a long drought could bring the whole system to a halt. Different canals were owned by different companies so cross-country journeys could often be delayed and expensive.

Railways: fast and cheap

One horse can pull a load of 8 tonnes on a smooth track. By 1810 there were 300 miles (480 kilometres) of iron tracks, called 'plateways' in Britain. They were mainly in the coalfields along the River Tyne.

Early steam engines, as we saw on page 8 were huge. What was needed was one light enough to travel on rails but strong enough to pull wagons. The first locomotive to do this was built by Richard Trevithick in South Wales in 1804. By 1823 there were 20 such locomotives in use on Tyneside. George Stephenson became skilled in designing, building and driving them.

He was then asked to design a line from Stockton to Darlington. It opened in 1825 and used horses, locomotives and stationary steam-engines. Stephenson compared them and showed that the locomotive was by far the best form of power. This led business people in Liverpool and Manchester to plan a railway. Stephenson laid out the line and then won a competition, with his famous 'Rocket', to

You have five loads to carry. These are:
a   ten tonnes of coal
b   a large catch of herrings
c   a small case of letters, some containing money
d   four large boxes of china plates and cups
e   two busy business people.

The journey distance is 200 miles (320 kilometres). In 1750 you can use a horse, packhorse, wagon or river-barge. In 1850 you can use a stagecoach, canal-barge or railway. Which mode of transport would you choose for each load at each time and why?

provide locomotives for it. The line opened in 1830 and was a great success (see Sources 19 and 20).

Other railways followed rapidly: 2,000 miles (3,200 kilometres) by 1842, 7,000 miles (11,200 kilometres) by 1852 and 20,000 miles (32,000 kilometres) by 1892. All major cities and industrial areas were linked. For people, railways were cheaper and faster than stagecoaches, which went into rapid decline. For all kinds of goods railways were as cheap as canals but much faster. Canals went into a long, slow decline.

SOURCE 19
Trains on the Liverpool–Manchester railway, 1830s.

'Before the Liverpool–Manchester railway stagecoaches could carry 688 persons per day. The railway, from its beginning, carried an average of 1,070 per day. The fare by coach was 50p inside and 25p outside; by railway it is 25p inside and 17p outside. The time of the journey by coach was four hours; by railway it is one and three-quarter hours. All the coaches but one have ceased running. Goods delivered in Manchester are received the same day in Liverpool; by canal they were never delivered before the third day.'

SOURCE 20
Effects of the Liverpool–Manchester railway on coach and canal transport, described in 1832.

SOURCE 18
Double lock on the Regent's Canal, 1801, Islington Tunnel in the distance.

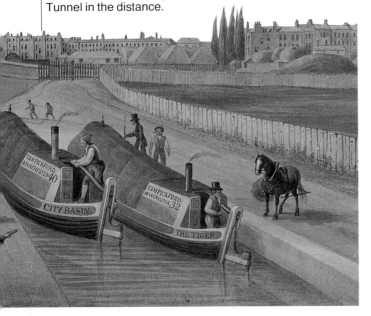

How were people's working lives affected?

New machines in factories put an end to many old skilled jobs. On pages 8 to 9 we saw that there was a time-lag between new inventions in cotton spinning and cotton weaving. For a while hand-loom weavers grew rich, weaving all the yarn produced in factories. But when steam-powered looms were introduced, the hand-loom weavers suffered because machines could weave the cloth much faster and more cheaply. The only way they could compete was to take cuts in their wages. Soon they were in dire poverty (see Source 21). The only alternative was to go and take a factory job.

'Many of the weavers cannot provide for themselves and their families sufficient food of the plainest and cheapest kind. They are clothed in rags, they have scarcely any furniture in their houses. Despite their poverty they have full employment; in fact their labour is excessive, often 16 hours a day.'

SOURCE 21
From a Report to Parliament about hand-loom weavers, 1835.

'Be at the works the first in the morning to encourage those who come regularly to time, distinguishing them from the less orderly parts of the work-people by presents or other marks.'

SOURCE 22
Josiah Wedgwood's instructions to his foremen.

Factory discipline

It must have been very hard for people used to working on their own at home, at their own speed, to fit into factory work. The powered machines went on and on, hour after hour, and workers had to keep up with them. Owners of the first factories had strict rules to enforce discipline (see Sources 22 and 23).

Wages, hours and conditions

Wages were usually better than in farmwork but only when the factory was working. If business became slack, workers were laid off, with no income at all. To the new factory-owners the workers were 'hands', labourers to be hired and fired when needed. Hours were long and the only day off was Sunday.

Working conditions were often unpleasant. See Source 24 for one of the jobs in the iron industry. Cotton factories were usually kept hot and humid to prevent the threads from breaking

1 The door of the lodge will be closed ten minutes after the engine starts every morning, and no weaver will be admitted until breakfast time. Any weaver absent during that time shall forfeit 3d [1p] a loom.

2 Weavers leaving the room without the consent of the overlooker shall forfeit 3d.

9 All shuttles, brushes, oilcans, windows etc. if broken shall be paid for.

11 If any hand is seen talking to another, whistling or singing he will be fined 6d (2½p).

SOURCE 23
Factory Rules, extracts, 1844.

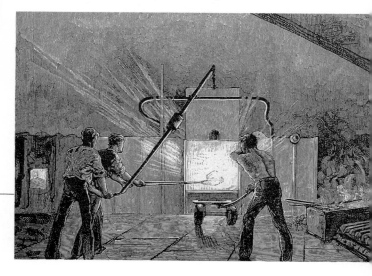

SOURCE 24
Working Cort's puddling furnace: the two men had to stir 28 lb (12.7 kg) of metal, then lift it out in four huge balls of hot iron.

SOURCE 25
Men, women and children, working in a cotton-mill in the 1840s.

Children

Children had always worked with their families. Some early factories took on large numbers of poor and orphaned children who were made to live in the factory. Many were badly treated and this system was stopped in 1802. In early factories mothers, fathers and children often worked together (Source 25). However, later factories only needed unskilled workers to look after the machines and tie up the threads. Factory-owners could get children to do these jobs for the lowest wages. Parents, often unemployed themselves, were glad of the money. Source 26 shows that these child-workers had no protection from bad conditions.

Dangers

It is clear from many of the pictures in this unit that early factory machines were often dangerous. There were no safety laws and no protective guards on dangerous machines. Some dangers, such as those described in Source 26, were obvious. Others, such as the dangers to health from lead in the paint used to decorate pottery, were not understood.

'A boy aged 16 working at Hemingsley's nail factory at Wolverhampton. Accidents happen there every week, very near; finger ends are continually pinched, sometimes pinched off, or cut off.'

SOURCE 26
Accidents in nail factories, from a Report to Parliament on children's work, 1843.

attainment target

Moving from the domestic system to the factory system changed workers' lives.

1 What changes were there in the places where people worked?

2 What other changes were there in people's working lives?

3 Which aspects of the changes do you think workers would dislike most? Explain your answer.

4 Do you think working in factories was more or less dangerous than working in the domestic system?

People on the move

We have no accurate figures for the population of Britain before 1801. Since then a CENSUS has been made every ten years. Historians make estimates for the years before 1801. Their estimate for Britain in 1750 is about 10.7 million. Source 27 shows that the population then rose steeply. In fact, it was the fastest population rise in the history of Britain: it rose by at least 10 per cent every ten years from 1780 to 1911. From 1811 to 1821 it rose by 17 per cent. Nowadays the rise is nearer 4 per cent every ten years.

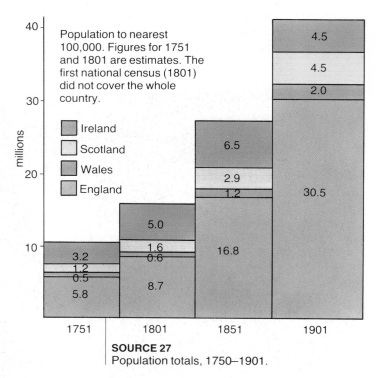

SOURCE 27
Population totals, 1750–1901.

	1750	1851
London	657,000	2,491,000
Liverpool	22,000	376,000
Glasgow	23,000	345,000
Manchester	18,000	303,000
Birmingham	24,000	233,000
Leeds	10,000	172,000
Bristol	50,000	137,000
Newcastle	28,000	88,000
Preston	5,000	70,000
Norwich	35,000	68,000
Brighton	5,000	66,000

SOURCE 28
Town growth, 1750–1851.

Why did the population rise?

There are only three possible answers: more people came to live here; fewer people died; more people were born.

People did move to Britain, but many EMIGRATED, so that cannot be the reason. Nor did death become less common. As we shall see in this unit, killer diseases took their toll throughout this period. It is possible that people were better fed (see page 15) so more resistant to illness, but that was only a minor factor.

The main factor seems to be that more people married and married younger. The number of unmarried people fell from 15 per cent to 7 per cent of the population. The average age of marriage fell from about 27 to about 24. These changes led to more babies being born.

Why did these changes happen?

One reason was that there were better harvests in the 18th century, so food was cheaper. Wages went further and people could afford to get married. However, the main reason was that men and women, particularly young people, were moving to towns to work in industry. They could earn good wages and were free to make their own decisions. Back home, parents might interfere; many farming jobs meant living in the farmer's house as a single person. Factory-owners took no such interest in their employees' personal lives. In fact, the average age of marriage in industrial areas was nearer 20. Married couples in industrial cities may have chosen to have big families as children could earn money working in the factories (see page 13).

The results of this move to the cities can be seen in Source 28. From 1750 to 1851 the population of rural Britain rose by 88 per cent; the population of URBAN areas rose by 129 per cent. Many of the places listed grew even faster than that. By 1851, for the first time, more British people lived in urban areas than in the countryside.

attainment target

1 Why were cities attractive to young people?

2 How do you think the increase in the number of people would affect:
the need for food?
the demand for goods such as clothing?

3 Did the population rise cause the growth of cities, or did the growth of cities cause the rise in population?

SOURCE 29
Prize bulls of improved breeds with their herdsmen.

How were these people fed?

When you studied 'Medieval Realms' you probably found out about the way the land was farmed in the Medieval village. Things hadn't changed much by the early 18th century. There were still strips in the open fields. Wheat and barley were grown for two years and then the exhausted land was left to lie fallow. The only fertiliser was animal manure. Crop yields were very low under this system but farmers were locked into it: they could not grow more crops because the land became exhausted; they could not make it more fertile by keeping more animals because they had no winter fodder for them.

When you studied 'The Making of the United Kingdom' you found out that Royalists fled abroad after the Civil War. Many went to Holland. The Dutch grew turnips and clover on their farms to provide winter fodder for animals and to make the soil more fertile. After 1660 British farmers also began to grow these crops: more fodder meant more animals; more animals meant more manure; more manure meant more fertile soil and better crop yields.

Farmers also found it worthwhile to use 'selective breeding': they bred carefully from selected animals to produce certain qualities, such as more meat or longer wool. Some of the results can be seen in Source 29.

Enclosure

It was hard to introduce new crops or better animals with the open fields system. Strips were mingled together across the fields and all the village animals grazed together. Enclosure simply means dividing up open land into small fields and putting hedges round them. Farmers could then do what they liked on their own fields. Source 30 shows some enclosed land: the hedges run across the old strips, which can still be seen.

Sometimes all the villagers agreed to enclose their open fields. Commons or greens could also be enclosed in this way. If they did not agree an Act of Parliament could be passed to enclose the open fields if the owners of four-fifths of the land wanted it. There was a huge increase in the number of enclosures: nearly three million hectares of land were enclosed in this period.

Enclosure was expensive. It cost money to pass an Act of Parliament, to hire a surveyor to map the fields and then to plant the hedges. Better-off farmers and landowners gained most; poorer farmers lost out and often had to sell up.

SOURCE 30
Aerial photograph showing enclosure hedges of 1795 lying across the old open field strips.

Results

Unlike industry, improvements in farming before 1850 did not mean that people were replaced by machines. In fact the number of people working in farming rose from 1.7 million in 1801 to 2.1 million in 1851. However the population was rising much faster than this, so workers were available to go to towns to work in factories. Better farming meant that all those extra mouths could be fed and fed cheaply. Cheap food meant that industrial wages did not have to be high, which pleased industrialists. In this way, the changes in farming were essential for the Industrial Revolution.

SOURCE 31
The walking city: Sheffield in about 1850.

Living in cities

The population was rising fast (see pages 14 to 15). Improvements in farming brought some new jobs, but not enough. Farming wages were low and irregular. The new factories created by the Industrial Revolution needed thousands of workers. The move to the cities became a flood.

At first people did not move far: perhaps 10–15 miles to the nearest town. But they were mainly young, and felt free to move on again if better prospects turned up elsewhere. They were joined by people from other parts of Britain, Ireland and the rest of Europe. Teeming masses of people, most of them born in the country, caused cities in the early 19th century to grow rapidly.

Cities at this time had no public transport to speak of. People had to live within walking distance of their work. This produced the close-packed landscape of houses, factories, shops and churches you can see in Source 31. This was called 'the walking city'. Workers woke to the sound of the factory bell or hooter. Their houses were blackened by smoke from factory chimneys.

Housing

With so many people wanting to live and work in cities, housing was in great demand. Large, old houses were split up, with families sharing a flat or even a room. Builders realised that there were profits to be made from building cheap houses quickly. Thousands of small houses were built in this way, usually in TERRACES.

SOURCE 32
Back-to-back houses near Halifax, Yorkshire.

SOURCE 33
Houses with separate cellar-dwellings in Merthyr Tydfil, Wales.

'Most of those districts lived in by the millworkers are newly built. The houses are ill-drained, often ill-ventilated, unprovided with toilets. As a result, the streets, which are narrow, become the resting place of mud, refuse and disgusting rubbish. In Parliament Street there is one toilet for 380 inhabitants.'

SOURCE 34
Description of Manchester in 1832.

Source 32 shows a common way of getting a lot of houses into the space available: back-to-back. Source 33 shows another way of cramming in more families. In 1840, a government report found 15,000 people in Manchester and 39,000 in Liverpool living in one-room cellars. Sources 34 and 35 describe some of the results of this overcrowding.

Health

Overcrowding was just one side of a serious health problem in cities. At that time no one understood the need for clean water, good drainage, SEWAGE systems and refuse disposal. There were no planning laws.

Water was often not piped to poor people's houses. It had to be bought from water-carriers or carried from standpipes in the street. Drains and sewers were not provided either and there was no system of refuse disposal. Dirty water, sewage and rubbish therefore piled up in the streets or in overflowing pits.

The effects of this situation on health can be seen in Source 36. Typhus, diphtheria and tuberculosis were common. There were also cholera epidemics. Children and babies were most at risk: the death rate of working-class under-fives in Preston in 1851 was 63 per 1,000. In Britain today it is 16 per 1,000.

'Between the backyards of the two rows of cottages, a cesspool extends the whole length of the street which receives the contents of the privies [lavatories] and drains . . . The contents of the cesspool belong to the landlord and are taken out twice a year.'

SOURCE 35
Description of cottages in Preston, Lancashire, in 1844.

ACTIVITY

Work in groups of four. Using the information and sources on these pages, put together a report on living conditions in 19th century towns. In your report, you can write up interviews with eye-witnesses who saw what conditions were like, as well as adding notes and sketches of your own. The final report can be in the form of a booklet, to be sent to the government to demand some improvement.

	Wiltshire	Liverpool
Gentry, professional people and their families	50	35
Farmers, tradesmen and their families	48	22
Labourers and their families	33	15

SOURCE 36
Average ages of death, 1842.

Look at Source 36.

1 What do these statistics tell us?

2 Suggest reasons for the differences between the figures for Wiltshire and Liverpool.

3 Suggest reasons for the differences between the figures for the different classes.

4 If cities were so unhealthy, why did people move to them?

Arkwright – father of the Industrial Revolution?

The Victorian writer Thomas Carlyle was amazed by the life story of Richard Arkwright (Source 37). He wrote: 'Oh reader, what a historical phenomenon is that bag-cheeked, pot-bellied, much-inventing barber.' It is certainly a classic story of 'rags to riches'. When you have read these two pages you can make up your own mind about him. Was he a hero? A villain? A con man? A clever business man?

Richard Arkwright was born in 1732 in Preston, Lancashire, the youngest of 13 children. His family was poor and when he grew up he became a barber. Many people at that time wore wigs and he went into business buying people's hair and turning it into wigs. As he travelled round Lancashire from his home in Bolton he heard a lot about cotton MANUFACTURING. He realised that there was money to be made if someone could invent a machine to spin more yarn.

Soon he was spending all his time and money trying to make spinning machines. Eventually his wife, in disgust, smashed his models and left him. Arkwright PATENTED his 'Frame' in 1769. (If you patent a new invention you register it with the government. No one else is allowed to use it unless they pay you money, called a ROYALTY.) This 'Frame' spun the cotton into yarn by passing it through four pairs of rollers moving at increasing speeds. It is doubtful that the idea was Arkwright's. As early as 1738 Paul and Wyatt had suggested the roller method of spinning. John Highs then took up the idea, but did not complete the machine. The rest of the story is told, in its different versions, in Sources 38, 39 and 40.

SOURCE 37
Sir Richard Arkwright (1732–1792).

'After many years' intense and painful application I invented about the year 1768 the present method of spinning cotton built upon very different principles from any invention that had gone before it.'

SOURCE 38
Arkwright's own description of the invention of the 'Frame'.

In 1767 Arkwright fell in with Kay, a clockmaker at Warrington. Kay told him of Highs' scheme of spinning with rollers. Arkwright persuaded him to make a model of Highs' machine. He also persuaded Kay to work for him. There is no evidence to show that Arkwright had ever thought of making such a spinning machine before his interview with Kay at Warrington. Kay appears not to have been able to make the whole machine and therefore applied to Peter Atherton, an instrument maker, to make it.

SOURCE 39
Description of the invention of the 'Frame' by Edward Baines, an admirer of Arkwright, written in 1835.

'Mr Arkwright roundly asserts that he invented the frame round about 1768 . . . What effrontery! His abilities consisted solely in having cunning enough to pump a secret out of a silly, talkative clockmaker and having sense enough to know when he saw a good invention.'

SOURCE 40
Description of the invention of the 'Frame' by another historian of the cotton industry, Richard Guest, written in 1823.

Arkwright and factories

Arkwright insisted that the only versions of the 'frame' which could be made were large. They were too large for people's homes and required power to drive them. Anyone wanting to use a frame had to build a factory.

Building a factory cost a lot of money. Arkwright was not rich but went into business with John Smalley, Samuel Need and Jedediah Strutt. Their first factory, in Nottingham, was small and the frames were driven by horses. In 1771, Arkwright opened a large factory at Cromford, Derbyshire, powered by water (Source 41). Soon he was the owner of ten factories and was making huge profits from them. His first factory employed 300 workers but his second factory at Cromford had 800 'hands' by 1783.

Arkwright the entrepreneur

On page 7 we saw that the success of these new industries depended on entrepreneurs. These were the people who ran the whole business, often controlling it with an iron hand. Arkwright was a tough, hard-working, ruthless entrepreneur. He regularly worked from 5 a.m. to 9 p.m., travelling on relays of horses between his factories. In several places he built good houses in order to attract workers (see Source 42). He built pubs and chapels for them and gave prizes to good workers. He also had very strict discipline in his factories. He employed children and young women because he could discipline them more easily and pay them less. They also had to work long hours.

Arkwright became a rich man. He lived in Willersley Castle, was made High Sheriff of Derbyshire in 1785, and was knighted in 1786. He died in 1792.

SOURCE 41
Arkwright's factory at Cromford, Derbyshire, painted by Joseph Wright of Derby (1734–1797).

SOURCE 42
Houses in North Street, Cromford, built by Arkwright.

> **attainment target**
>
> 1 What truths, untruths and opinions can you find in Sources 38, 39 and 40?
>
> 2 What was Arkwright's contribution to:
>   **a** new processes in the cotton industry?
>   **b** the factory system?
>   Use the sources to explain your answer in both cases.
>
> 3 'A great entrepreneur who showed that anyone can go from rags to riches.'
>   'A cunning operator who rose to wealth and power on other people's ideas and money.'
>   Which description do you think best fits Sir Richard Arkwright? Give reasons for your opinion.

This depth study is about later 19th century cities and how they changed from those described on page 16. You could follow this study by looking at a town or city near where you live.

Suburbs

By the later 19th century better public transport was putting an end to 'the walking city' and leading to the rise of SUBURBS. Horse-drawn trams were introduced in 1860 and electric trams from 1885. By 1914 there were 2,500 miles (4,000 kilometres) of tram routes in British cities, providing cheap transport for millions. Railway companies bought land beside rail routes and built houses on it, encouraging people to move out of the city. Some ran 'workmen's specials' with cheap tickets for working people on early morning trains. In London the working-class suburb of Willesden rose in population from 3,000 in 1851 to 114,000 in 1891. West Ham's population rose from 19,000 to 267,000 over the same period.

Source 43 describes the growth of different suburbs for different kinds of middle-class commuters. The horse-drawn tram in Source 44 would take you into central London for one penny. So began the process of moving out of the city, which has been going on ever since.

The railways have set us all moving far away from London – that is to say the middle class of Londoners, people ranging from three to five hundred a year. They betake themselves to far-off spots like Richmond, Watford, Croydon or Slough. The smaller fry content themselves with semi-detached boxes at Putney, Kilburn, New Cross or Ealing but the wealthier are found to go daily to the capital from as far as Reading or Brighton.

SOURCE 43
Description of the growth of London's suburbs, written in 1873.

SOURCE 44
Horse-drawn tram in a suburban road in north London.

SOURCE 45
Interior of a Victorian house. Typical features are the tiles, plantpot, oriental carpet and heavy drapes.

Suburban houses

There was space in the suburbs to build large detached or semi-detached houses for middle-class commuters. These were sometimes called villas. Builders were helped by the advances of the Industrial Revolution. Bricks and glass could now be produced cheaply in large quantities in factories, rather than by hand. Welsh or Cornish roofing slates could be brought cheaply by rail.

Source 45 shows what the inside of a Victorian villa was like. Industrial Britain was prosperous and the middle classes had money to spend on making their houses fashionable. Factory-made tiles, stained glass, mirrors, ornaments, curtains and heavy furniture were reasonably priced. British trading links across the world (see unit 2) brought all kinds of goods from abroad, such as the eastern carpet in Source 45, brass from India, mahogany from Africa and so on. People could live at a standard of luxury which only the rich could have afforded a hundred years earlier. Servants were cheap so cleaning and dusting masses of ornaments was not a problem.

William Morris hated factory-made goods and admired eastern designs. He wanted to return to hand-made processes. His own designs for curtains, wallpaper and fabrics are still popular today (see Source 46).

Owners of these suburban villas expected them to include the latest in hygienic inventions, too. Source 47 shows a selection of flush toilets, made in the factories of 'the Potteries'. Their glazed finish meant that germs, discovered in 1861, could be kept at bay.

For those who lived there, the suburbs were pleasant, leafy, quiet places to live. Nineteenth century suburban villas were planned with large gardens, ideal for the friendly tennis party shown in Source 48.

SOURCE 46
Wallpaper designed by William Morris.

SOURCE 47
Museum display of flush toilets.

SOURCE 48
Painting of a tennis party in the garden of a middle-class villa in Leamington.

1 Suggest reasons why middle-class Victorians preferred living in the suburbs.

2 Why was a good public transport system essential for the growth of suburbs?

3 What items which were probably made in a factory can you see in Sources 45, 47 and 48?

4 Do you live in a suburb? What are the advantages and disadvantages of living there?

The City Fathers

Early 19th century cities sprang up with no planning or controls. This was not because local councils did not care what happened; it was because they believed it was not their job to interfere in things like housing or hygiene. They thought that governments only make things worse and that people will sort things out for the best, on their own. This was called 'LAISSEZ-FAIRE' and some ideas about what governments should and should not do can be seen in Source 49.

Municipal Corporations Act, 1835

Many cities had grown so fast that they hardly had any local government. Some towns had local councils, called corporations, but they were often not elected and usually did very little. The Municipal Corporations Act of 1835 set up new corporations in 178 towns or cities. By 1903 another 135 towns or cities had gained the same rights. These included places as large as Birmingham, Manchester, Huddersfield, Bradford, Halifax and Rochdale.

These new corporations were intended to be more democratic, following the changes made to Parliamentary voting by the 1832 Reform Act (see unit 3). In fact, only better-off males could vote at

'What are the duties of the government? To restrain crime, to protect property, to pass laws to protect order and justice, to conduct relations with other countries.

It is not the duty of government to feed or clothe people, to build houses for them, to regulate their work or their families, or supply them with teachers, doctors or books.'

SOURCE 49
'Laissez-faire', as explained by Edward Baines in a letter written in 1846.

first, about 5 per cent of the adult population. Later in the century, the right to vote was widened. The new corporations also had few powers at first. Many things which local councils do now, such as street cleaning and lighting, were still looked after by other people.

However, as the 19th century went on, it became clear that 'laissez-faire' was not providing answers to the terrible problems of the cities. The middle-class voters who controlled the new corporations wanted to take action. Gradually, their powers were increased. This was the great age of city corporations. Joseph Chamberlain, Mayor of Birmingham 1873–1876, carried out several improvements in the city. Led by him, the city bought up and demolished 16 hectares (40 acres) of slums near the city centre and built impressive new roads. This kind of bold action was the opposite of 'laissez-faire' and gained the name 'MUNICIPAL SOCIALISM'.

City corporations could raise money from local taxes, called rates. They were not afraid to spend to solve their problems. Health was a major concern, and many towns spent heavily on putting in drains, sewers and a good water supply. From 1860 to 1900 Bradford spent £1.5 million on street improvement, £300,000 on drains and £3 million on the water supply. Source 50 shows new sewers being built in London.

To the 'City Fathers', as the councillors were often called, health meant fresh air too. Rapidly growing, unplanned cities had few open spaces for the public. Municipal parks, with flowerbeds, paths, seats, a boating lake and a bandstand were provided in many cities (see Source 51). The rising population meant that the old graveyards became full. New municipal cemeteries were laid out on the edge of the city. Municipal baths and wash-houses were built, too.

SOURCE 50
Sewers being built in London, 1862.

SOURCE 51
Bandstand in the People's Park, Halifax, Yorkshire.

The City Fathers were proud of their city and wanted buildings to be proud of. In many northern cities the corporation controlled the market and built new market halls (see Source 52). They also wanted the city to be more than just a place of business and industry. City art galleries, museums, libraries, concert halls and lecture rooms were built.

At the centre of it all was a new town hall. It had to have offices for the people running all the new things the city was taking on, a chamber for council meetings, and a grand hall for concerts, dances and lectures. Its architecture also had to express the pride people were beginning to take in their city (see Source 53).

SOURCE 52
Inside the Market Hall, Bolton, Lancashire.

SOURCE 53
Painting of Rochdale Town Hall.

ACTIVITY

1 Get into groups of four. You are councillors in a city in the north of England in 1876.
Councillor Accrington supports 'laissez-faire' and wants to keep the rates down.
Councillor Bacup is keen on parks and sport.
Councillor Congleton feels that the council's priority should be better drains and cleaner streets.
Councillor Dewsbury wants to offer the people of the town more culture by building an art gallery and buying modern pictures for it.
Discuss what each of you wants for the town and try to reach a decision.

2 There is to be a grand opening of the new park by the Mayor, with bands, a circus and free ice-cream for the children. Design a poster advertising the event; suggest some of the things the Mayor should say in his speech.

The people

By the end of the 19th century, city life for working people had improved a little. New laws, such as the 1875 Artisans' Dwellings Act, meant that better housing was being built (see Source 54). Improvements to public health (see pages 62 to 65) brought real benefits. By this time cities had facilities to meet all kinds of interests, from dance halls to chapels.

People joined together in a wide range of clubs and societies. There were 691,410 ALLOTMENTS by 1881. Allotment holders held competitions for chrysanthemums, marrows, leeks. Enthusiasts, usually men, took time and trouble over breeding canaries, pigeons or whippets.

Choirs were very popular, usually as part of church or chapel life. Many played in brass bands, often sponsored by a factory-owner. By the end of the century, cycling had become a popular hobby with both sexes.

Thousands began to spend their Saturday afternoons watching sport. Various kinds of football had been popular for centuries. They were crude, rough games, with few rules which varied from place to place. In late 19th century Britain, people were more in touch with each other and a common set of rules was needed. In 1863 the Football Association was formed and agreed the rules. The FA Cup started in 1872. The leaders in this move were upper-class men from public schools. However, football was becoming increasingly popular in working-class northern towns. In 1883 Bolton Olympic beat Old Etonians in the Cup Final and the game changed forever. Big grounds were built in many cities. Fans could travel by train to away matches. Soccer hooliganism began, with attacks on referees and opposing teams.

SOURCE 54
Late 19th century terraces, Manchester. By this time laws had been passed which said that houses had to be a certain distance apart and courtyards had to be open at one end. Compare with Source 54, page 62.

Street life

Many city families were still desperately poor. The children in Source 55 look cheerful but there are signs of their families' poverty. These children, from overcrowded homes, lived on the streets. Source 56 explains how interesting the streets were. Much shopping was still done from market stalls. All kinds of goods were sold from barrows or trays.

There were differences between the sexes in how leisure time was spent. For women, making the money last the week was almost a full-time occupation. A loan from the PAWNSHOP was often the only way of making ends meet. Caring for the children was also mainly women's responsibility. Meeting friends and neighbours in the street helped make these tasks bearable.

SOURCE 55
Children in Liverpool, circa 1900.

First thing in the morning the lamplighter came round with his long pole, turning out the streetlamps and in the evening lighting them again. There were hawkers singing their wares, gypsies to tell your fortune, the cats'meat man with his one-wheel barrow, the milkman ladling milk from a churn on a barrow. Sunday was the day of the muffin man. He came round balancing a large tray on his head, packed with muffins, and ringing a bell, calling out 'Muffins!'. In the afternoon there would be the winkle man calling out from his barrow of winkles, shrimps and cockles. There was a ballad-singer who sang a popular song and sold copies of it for a penny. There was the hurdy-gurdy man, an Italian with a small organ on a short pole and a monkey trained to turn the handle.

SOURCE 56
Childhood memories of Albert Jacobs, born in London in 1889.

SOURCE 57
A city pub: The Vine, Stepney, London.

For men, the most attractive escape from a crowded, shabby house was the pub. With their bright lights, mirrors, polished wooden bars, frosted glass and plush seats they were a little taste of luxury (Source 57). Pubs were the centre of social life, too. Sports teams were run from pubs. Some city pubs had entertainment rooms, which were the origins of the music halls (see Source 58).

Other pubs had meeting rooms for serious occasions. Some Chartists met in pubs (see page 52) and so did some TRADE UNION branches (see page 54).

Opposition to pubs came from the powerful TEMPERANCE movement. They blamed alcohol for violence, the breakdown of family life, poverty and the decline of religion. Their attitude to pubs can be read about in Source 59.

SOURCE 58
Acrobats at the Alhambra Music Hall, London.

ACTIVITY

You could follow up this depth study with some local study work. There are plenty of ideas on these pages which you could follow up by studying your nearest large town or city. Follow them up in two ways: first by going and looking, and second by using the local library and record office.

'Over the door were three enormous lamps. They were in full glare this Sunday evening, and through the doors of these infernal dens of drunkenness and mischief, crowds of miserable wretches were pouring in, that they might drink and die.'

SOURCE 59
A pub described in a temperance magazine, 1836.

attainment target

1 Compare the housing in Source 54 with the housing in Source 32 on page 16 and Source 33 on page 17. In what ways were these better houses? In what ways would this housing be healthier to live in?

2 Many people found late 19th-century cities interesting and exciting places to live in. What did people from different classes enjoy about city life?

UNIT 2

AIMS

In unit 1 we saw how Britain became the first industrialised nation in the world. In this unit we shall see how Britain's trade helped to make these changes happen.

In overview, we shall see that Britain was involved in trade all over the world. Merchants sold British-made goods, bought raw materials and made money which they invested in factories, mines and machines. We shall see that from 1750 to 1900, Britain moved from trading with the world to ruling large parts of it as the British EMPIRE.

The unit goes on to a depth study of one of Britain's most important trading enterprises, the slave trade.

Trade and the empire

Think of the food you have eaten over the last few days: how much of it was grown or produced in this country? How much of it came from abroad? What about the things you own: were they made in Britain or overseas? We expect to see goods from all over the world in our shops, but they only get here because Britain is a trading nation. British trade means selling things made in Britain to foreign countries (exports) and bringing goods from abroad which British people need and want to buy (imports). In the Middle Ages, as you may remember from when you studied 'Medieval Realms', Britain traded with Europe. By 1700 foreign trade was more than just Europe-wide, it was becoming worldwide. The voyages of 16th and 17th century European seamen brought most of the world into contact with Europe. British merchants, along with French, Spanish, Portuguese and Dutch merchants, bought and sold goods in a worldwide market centred on Europe.

Look at Source 1. It shows the kind of merchant ship involved in this trade. What goods might this ship have been carrying? If it were bound for Britain from overseas, the cargo might have been tea from China, tobacco from North America, sugar from the West Indies, silk or spices from the East Indies or cotton from India. This import trade was worth £8 million a year by the 1770s. If the ship were bound for overseas, from Britain, it might have been carrying any of the goods listed in Source 2.

SOURCE 1
This painting of a merchant ship was made by Thomas Whitcombe at the end of the 18th century.

'Woollens, linen, silk, iron, brass, leather, glass, china, clocks, watches, jewels, gold and silver, lace, medicine, gunpowder, bricks, paint, candles, swords, books, toys, stationery, cutlery, HABERDASHERY, household goods, furniture, clothes . . . in short all things necessary for life and almost the whole is British manufacture.'

SOURCE 2
Goods bought by Europeans in the West Indies, 1763.

Trading wealth

To foreign observers, like the author of Source 3, trade was the main source of Britain's wealth. Many people were involved. There were probably 6,000 merchants and 100,000 seamen in Britain. Ports on the west coast, such as Liverpool, Glasgow and Bristol, grew. There are several clues to the origins of Bristol's prosperity in Source 4.

British trade was two-way, as we have seen. In the slave trade, for example, goods from Britain and India such as cloth, metal items and guns were sold to buy slaves in Africa. The slaves were then transported across the Atlantic to America where they were sold. Returning ships were then loaded with sugar, tobacco or cotton which could be sold at a good profit in Britain. (You can read more about the slave trade in the depth study on pages 34 to 41.)

You can see from the dates of the sources you have seen so far in this unit that Britain had an important foreign trade before the Industrial Revolution really got started. This meant that:

- rich merchants had money to invest in new industrial enterprises (these could be expensive, see page 7).
- raw materials from abroad such as cotton were readily available in Britain.
- a trading network was already in place to sell British industrial goods abroad.

'The natural products of Britain do not at most amount to a quarter of her riches. The rest she owes to her colonies and her people, who by the transport and exchange of the riches of other countries, continually add to their own.'

SOURCE 3
The French writer Le Blanc, describing the importance of trade to Britain, writing in 1747.

SOURCE 4
Bristol harbour in 1720.

Why did the slave trade develop?

The first colonies in America did not have slaves. Colonists used native American workers or white workers shipped out from Europe, often as an alternative to prison. However, growing and processing crops such as cotton, tobacco and sugar needed large numbers of workers. Native Americans were dying of European diseases by the thousand. The colonists' answer to the shortage of workers was to import black slaves from West Africa. Over 10 million black slaves were taken from Africa to work on PLANTATIONS in America before the trade was abolished in the 19th century.

> As the slaves come down to Fida from the inland country they are put into a prison near the beach. When the Europeans are to receive them they are brought out on to a large plain, where the ship's surgeons examine every part of them. Such as are declared good and sound are marked on the breast with a red-hot iron, imprinting the mark of the French, English or Dutch companies. The branded slaves are then returned to their former prison where they await shipment, sometimes 10–15 days.

SOURCE 6
Description of slaves on the coast of Africa, written in the 18th century.

> 'She had taken in 336 males and 226 females. The space between decks was so low that they sat between each other's legs, so close that there was no possibility of their lying down or changing their positions day or night. This was when the thermometer was standing at 89 degrees [89° Fahrenheit = 32° Celsius].'

SOURCE 7
Captain Newton's description of conditions on board his slaveship.

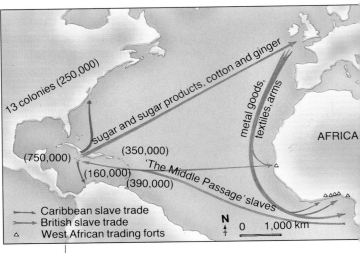

SOURCE 5
Map of the 'triangular trade', showing numbers of slaves TRANSPORTED.

The map (Source 5) shows the three stages of the 'triangular trade', as it was called. Manufactured goods, such as cloth and guns, were used to buy slaves from their African masters. What happened at a slave-dealing fort on the West African coast is described in Source 6. Slaves were then loaded on to ships and taken across to the Caribbean islands or to North or South America. This was the dreaded 'middle passage', on which up to a million slaves may have died. To the slaveship-owners, slaves were just goods to be sold. The more they could cram into the holds of their ships the bigger their profit. Conditions on a slaveship on the 'middle passage' are described in Source 7. Irons such as those in Source 8 had to be used to stop slaves attacking the crew.

On arrival, the slaves would be sold by auction (see Source 9). Meanwhile the merchant ships would be loaded with valuable cargo for the trip back to Europe.

Slaves resisted this treatment in a number of ways. Many committed suicide. Runaway slaves in Jamaica, called MAROONS, set up little communities in the hills. There were slave rebellions and communities of runaway slaves in several colonies. Some slaves managed to buy their freedom or were given freedom by their owner.

SOURCE 8
Irons used on slaves.

Britain and the slave trade

Britain was well placed to take part in this trade. There were plenty of merchant ships; industry was producing the goods to sell in West Africa; there was an increasing demand for colonial products such as sugar. In 1713, Britain gained the right (called an **asiento**) to supply 4,800 slaves a year to the Spanish colonies in America. As demand for colonial products grew, so did the slave trade. By the later 18th century 60,000 slaves a year were being carried, half of them in British ships. The slave trade was tremendously profitable. In the 1730s Bristol slaveships regularly showed a profit of £8,000 per trip. Liverpool had over 100 slaveships by the second part of the 18th century, employing half the sailors in the port and bringing in £1 million a year.

The British slave trade was abolished in 1807 and slavery was abolished in British territories in 1833. For more on the slave trade and abolition see pages 34 to 41.

One of the other results of the slave trade was that an increasing number of black people came to live in Britain. There were black communities in London and other British ports by the 18th century. A black sailor in the Royal Navy can be seen in Source 10.

SOURCE 9
A slave auction in Virginia, USA.

ACTIVITY

Divide into groups of three. Each group is an anti-slavery society. Prepare a leaflet to persuade people that slavery is wrong and should be abolished. Your teacher is a firm believer in the slave trade and makes quite a lot of money out of slave-worked plantations. Try to persuade her/him to change her/his mind.

SOURCE 10
Picture of the death of Admiral Nelson, 1805, showing a black sailor on 'HMS Victory'.

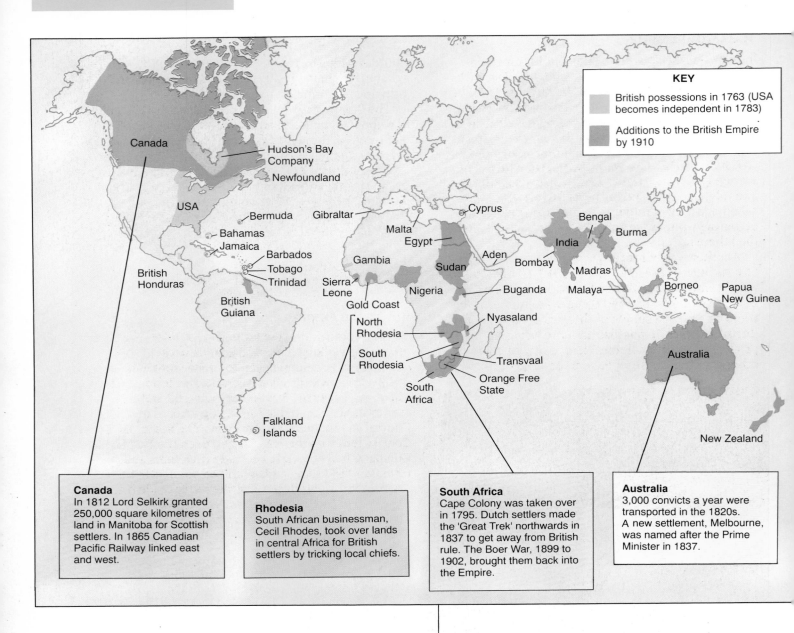

Canada
In 1812 Lord Selkirk granted 250,000 square kilometres of land in Manitoba for Scottish settlers. In 1865 Canadian Pacific Railway linked east and west.

Rhodesia
South African businessman, Cecil Rhodes, took over lands in central Africa for British settlers by tricking local chiefs.

South Africa
Cape Colony was taken over in 1795. Dutch settlers made the 'Great Trek' northwards in 1837 to get away from British rule. The Boer War, 1899 to 1902, brought them back into the Empire.

Australia
3,000 convicts a year were transported in the 1820s. A new settlement, Melbourne, was named after the Prime Minister in 1837.

SOURCE 11
The British Empire in 1763 and 1910.

Why did Britain gain an empire?

The British Empire of the 18th century was a trading empire. This had two main features. First, as you can see from Source 11, it did not consist of much territory. The only large area of British territory overseas in 1763 was the 13 colonies in America (until they became the independent USA in 1783). The rest of the empire consisted mainly of trading posts. Second, trading companies, not the British government, ran many of the colonies. The Hudson's Bay Company, set up in 1670, ran much of northern Canada. The Royal Africa Company, founded in 1672, dealt with West Africa. Most important of all, the East India Company, set up in 1600, ruled an increasing part of India.

In fact, British politicians of this time did not want an empire. They reasoned that governing far-off lands was unnecessary and expensive. They knew the importance of trade; however, and were prepared to go to war to expand it. The Seven Years' War (1756 to 1763) was fought by Britain and Prussia against France and Austria. The war resulted from commercial and colonial rivalry. By the end of the war Britain had gained several sugar plantation islands in the Caribbean and extended its influence in India. The French had also been removed from most of North America including Canada.

The British Empire

So how did Britain come to rule the vast territories shown in Source 11? In the second half of the 19th century British attitudes towards the idea of empire began to change. In 1850 Lord Russell spoke of the 'high and holy work' of extending British influence across the world. The idea that the British were a superior race, with a mission to bring other races 'up' to Britain's standards, was gaining strength. David Livingstone believed that British science, medicine and religion were benefits he had to bring to what he called 'the dark continent' (Africa). He made a series of journeys across Central Africa (see Source 12) and died there in 1863.

Another reason for the growth of empire was EMIGRATION. Between 1815 and 1912, 10 million people emigrated to British territories overseas. Businesses also supported the idea of empire. They could be sure of a supply of cheap raw materials from British colonies. It was also easier to sell their products to British colonies than to compete with other countries in the open market.

SOURCE 12
David Livingstone's PADDLE-STEAMER on the River Shire, 1858.

Ruling the empire

Trading companies were for trading, not for governing millions of people. Gradually the government in Britain began to believe that East India Company officials or NABOBS, like John Mowbray – Source 13, were too powerful and corrupt. The India Act, 1784, set up a Board of Control to supervise the Company. The Board of Control removed the MONOPOLY which the East India Company had enjoyed over trade with India and China. In 1857 thousands of Indian soldiers MUTINIED against British interference in their way of life (the First War of Independence). In 1858 the British government took over running India from the East India Company, see Source 14.

SOURCE 13
British merchant, John Mowbray, in 1790, with his Indian servant and business agent.

SOURCE 14
A British official working in a Punjab court room drawn by a British artist in 1888.

How important was trade to British industry?

The tremendous increase in Britain's trade is shown in Source 15. Clearly, all these goods coming into and going out of the country meant that much larger docks and harbours were needed. Source 16 shows one of London's great 19th century docks: the West India Docks, begun in 1802. The dock on the left is a timber dock; the other two are surrounded by warehouses, for exports (left), and imports (right). Other huge docks were built at Liverpool, Swansea, Cardiff, Bristol and Glasgow.

	Exports	Imports
1720s	£7.5 million	£7.0 million
1760s	£15.0 million	£10.5 million
1800s	£37.5 million	£28.5 million
1840s	£141.5 million	£79.5 million

SOURCE 15
Values of British imports and exports.

SOURCE 16
West India Docks, London, in the 19th century.

Imports

How could increasing imports benefit Britain? Firstly, by providing jobs. There were thousands of dockers employed at the great docks such as those in Source 16. Most imports, like tobacco, sugar, cotton, tropical timber or cocoa, went to factories. Here they were made into the things people would buy. All these processes provided jobs. In 1753, for example, there were 120 sugar refineries in Britain. Another example is cocoa, which was becoming a popular drink in the 19th century, especially among those who opposed the sale of alcohol. Cadbury's and Fry's factories turned the raw cocoa into drinking or eating chocolate.

Secondly, industrialists benefited from the supply of cheap raw materials for their factories. Some of them supported the growth of the British Empire and set up their own plantations to produce these raw materials. Source 17 shows one of the tea plantations in Ceylon (now Sri Lanka) belonging to Lipton's, a Scottish tea importer.

Thirdly, imports also provided cheap food. The larger ships, and refrigerated ships, being built by the late 19th century brought meat from South America, grain from North America, butter and cheese from Australia and New Zealand. Bananas and pineapples were a common sight in British shops by 1900. Industrialists wanted cheap food in Britain: this would lower the cost of living and mean that they would not have to pay high wages.

Exports

British settlers in the colonies were a ready market for British goods, see Source 2 on page 27. But booming British industry needed big markets. By 1850, Britain was producing two thirds of the world's coal, half the iron, five sevenths of the steel, half the cotton goods and two fifths of the hardware. Britain could not use all this at home; only a growing empire could keep up with growing British industry. It was essential to sell abroad. By the 1850s the most valuable British export was cotton cloth, worth £35

SOURCE 17
Lipton's tea plantation,
Ceylon (now Sri Lanka).

SOURCE 18
British-built railway in Ceylon, 1893.

million a year. Next came manufactured metal goods of all kinds, from guns to clocks, worth £15 million. Exported woollen cloth brought in £9 million and iron (either in its raw form, as pig-iron or as iron bars) £5 million. Coal exports, mainly from Wales, increased in the 19th century from 0.2 million tonnes to 3.2 million tonnes. In the second half of the century, railway engines, rolling stock and all kinds of equipment became important exports: Source 18 shows a British-made railway in Ceylon.

Cotton exports

In unit 1 it was the cotton industry that gave us the most remarkable example of industrial change. It is worth looking at cotton again to see how it fitted into British trade. All the raw material for the cotton industry was imported, mostly from the USA. Once turned into cloth, two thirds of it was exported, mostly to Africa and the slave plantations of the West Indies. India had a thriving cotton industry when the British arrived. Her cotton goods were imported into Britain until this was stopped in 1700 to protect the British cotton industry. From 1813, cheap Lancashire cotton goods were sold in India. The Indian cotton industry could not compete and collapsed. India became just another huge market for British-made goods.

Investment

We saw in unit 1 that new industries often needed large amounts of money (capital) to get started. Merchants, having made money in foreign trade, were often looking for ways of investing it. Many new industrial enterprises were helped by receiving capital investment from merchants. Abraham Darby,

who set up a pioneering ironworks at Coalbrookdale in 1709, was helped by capital from Bristol merchants. Anthony Bacon, a London merchant involved in many trading ventures including the slave trade, set up the Cyfarthfa ironworks at Merthyr Tydfil in South Wales in 1765. Anthony Crawshay, another London merchant, also played a large part in developing the South Wales iron industry. Capital from slave traders went into James Watt's steam engines and the Liverpool to Manchester railway.

> **attainment target**
>
> 1 Which British industries needed imports from the colonies?
>
> 2 Which British industries exported their goods?
>
> 3 How did imports from abroad affect the things British people ate and drank in the years 1750 to 1900?
>
> 4 Cheap raw materials   Cheap food
> Money to invest   Large export market
> Choose two of these factors and show how they assisted the British Industrial Revolution.
>
> 5 Which of the four factors in question 4 affected the cotton industry?
>
> 6 Explain what the British Empire has to do with all four of the factors in question 4.

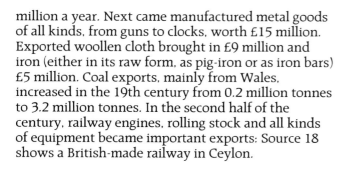

How did the slave trade work?

Jam pudding, trifle, ice-cream, treacle tart, spotted dick, apple pie . . . think of any traditional British pudding and one of the main ingredients will be sugar. It is the same with drinks: from the middle of the 17th century British people began to change from drinking ale or cider to tea, coffee or hot chocolate, all sweetened with sugar. Between 1700 and 1709 the average Briton consumed 1.8 kilograms of sugar per year; by 1800 to 1809 the annual average was 8 kilograms.

The British were just as addicted to tobacco. They smoked it in pipes, chewed it or sniffed it. In the 1630s half a million kilograms of tobacco were imported from Virginia to Britain; by 1775 Virginia and Maryland together sent 100 million kilograms of tobacco.

Sugar and tobacco were produced by slaves. In one of the great crimes against humanity, about 10 million human beings were taken from their homes in Africa to work as slaves in the Americas.

SOURCE 20
Olaudah Equiano, 1745 to 1797. He was born in what is now called Nigeria, kidnapped into slavery at the age of 11 and sold in Barbados. He became servant to a ship's captain and sailed to England with him where he learnt to read and became a Christian. He eventually bought his freedom and campaigned against the slave trade. This portrait was made while he was living in London in the 1780s.

a 'When a trader wants slaves he applies to a chief for them, and tempts him with his wares. Such a mode of obtaining slaves in Africa is common and I believe more are procured this way, and by kidnapping, than by any other.'

After being kidnapped Equiano was taken on board a slaveship:
b 'I was soon put down under the decks . . . with the loathsomeness of the stench, and crying, together I became so sick and low that I was not able to eat, nor had I the least desire to taste anything.'

On arrival in Barbados he was sold by the method known as a 'scramble':
c 'On a signal given (the beat of a drum) the buyers rush at once into the yard where the slaves are confined and make a choice of that parcel they like best. The noise and clamour increase the terror of the Africans. In this manner are relations and friends separated, never to see each other again.'

SOURCE 19
Extracts from Olaudah Equiano's autobiography, published in 1789.

The case of the *Zong*

In 1781 the slaveship, the *Zong*, from Liverpool, sailed from West Africa with 470 slaves and a crew of 17. By the time the *Zong* was nearing Jamaica, 60 slaves and seven crew members were dead. Many of the surviving slaves were ill. The captain, Luke Collingwood, knew that he would be unable to sell many of the slaves in such poor health. He therefore ordered his crew to throw the sick slaves overboard, so that the ship owners would be able to claim the insurance. A further 131 slaves met their death in this way. In fact the insurance company refused to pay and the case went to court. The lawyer acting on behalf of the ship owners said in court, 'What is all this talk of human people being thrown overboard? They are goods and property'.

This was the attitude which made the slave trade possible: those involved regarded slaves as nothing more than goods to be found, traded, sold and forced to work. Violence and cruelty marked every stage.

SOURCE 21
A 19th century painting of slave-merchants on the coast of Africa.

SOURCE 22
Plan of slaves crammed into one deck on a slaveship, the *Brookes* of Liverpool. The complete plan shows 454 slaves on this 320 tonne ship.

The slavers

Slavery had existed in Africa long before the Europeans came. However, the demand for more and more slaves led to the growth of a slave-trading network across West and Central Africa. Slavers either kidnapped their victims (see Sources 19) or got them by making war and taking prisoners. The slaves were chained together and marched to the coast where European slaveships were waiting. Slaveship captains made deals with the slavers. In 1680, for example, a slave cost three pieces of printed silk, or 12 gallons (55 litres) of brandy. In the 18th century the slavers wanted guns and up to 400,000 were traded every year. The guns allowed the slavers to capture more slaves. Source 21 shows the scene on the coast, where deals were made and slaves branded, chained and whipped on to the ships.

The 'middle passage'

Source 22 shows what it was like on board ship. The normal height between decks was 1.5 metres, but this was halved by putting in shelves to hold more slaves. The slaves were chained in pairs; diseases like dysentery were rife; food was supplied in buckets to be shared by ten people. The stench of a slaveship could be smelt hundreds of metres away (see Source 19b). The slaves were allowed on deck in small groups in calm weather to take exercise; in storms they stayed below in complete darkness.

The sale

As they arrived in the New World slaves were made ready for sale. White hair was dyed, the slaves' food was improved and their bodies were oiled. Slaves with dysentery sometimes had their anus stopped up by the ship's surgeon. On landing, buyers examined the slaves as if they were animals, before taking them off to an unknown fate on the plantations (see Source 19c).

1 There are many accounts of the slave trade written by white people but very few by slaves themselves. The extracts in Source 19 are therefore especially useful. What things do you think it would tell us which other accounts do not?

2 'Slaves were treated as objects, not human beings.' Give examples of this from these pages.

3 Which part of the slave trade described here do you think was the most terrible: being enslaved? The middle passage? The sale? Give reasons for your answer.

SOURCE 23
A 19th century photograph of a slave-hut on Barbados.

SOURCE 24
Sunbury plantation house, Barbados.

Slaves at work

The slaves' huts (see Source 23) were kept at some distance from the plantation house (see Source 24). The slaves had to leave their huts for work at 6am. They were divided into three 'gangs': the first gang was made up of the fittest young men and women. They did the hardest work of all. People in the second gang were older or younger or had been disabled by accidents. Members of the third gang could only do light tasks. In all three cases they were urged on by the whip of the overseer (see Source 25). They worked until 6pm, with a break for breakfast at 9am and a two-hour break in the middle of the day. Their daily routine, and their existence, revolved around working on the plantation, see Source 26.

On sugar plantations all the processes had to be done quickly, before the cane lost its sweetness. Cutting the tough cane was hard work; it was then milled (Source 25) and the syrup boiled. Slaves who worked in the boiling rooms suffered from the incessant heat.

Cotton, most of it destined for the cottonmills of Lancashire, see unit 1, had to be picked over and over again as it ripened at different times, see Source 27.

Women worked alongside men in the fields but were also used as house-slaves. Here their lives were easier but they were subject to regular sexual harassment from male members of the plantation owner's family.

After arriving on the plantations, the life expectancy of a slave was about eight years. Diseases – yaws, yellow fever, leprosy, dysentery and tuberculosis – were common. Punishments were harsh, including regular beatings. One female slave had her ear nailed to a tree for breaking a plate.

SOURCE 25
A sugar-mill in Barbados. The slaves are feeding sugar-cane between two wind-powered rollers which crush the cane to extract the juice. Note the white supervisor and black overseer with a whip.

'Negroes are the sinews of a plantation and it is as impossible for a man to make sugar without the assistance of Negroes, as to make bricks without straw.'

SOURCE 26
John Pinney, a plantation owner on Nevis, writing in 1764.

SOURCE 27
A 19th century photograph of slaves harvesting cotton in the southern USA.

Leisure

Slaves worked a six-day week. On Sundays and in the evenings they could work in their little garden-plots. The produce was sold in the markets which flourished on Sundays. Sundays were also days for parties: music, dancing and drinking; remembering their homes in Africa and forgetting their present plight (Source 28).

In the early years of slavery no effort was made to introduce slaves to Christianity. To do so would be to admit that they were people. Slaves held to their African religion and the 'OBEAH MEN' who interpreted it. This had to be done in secret as whites feared the influence of these obeah men who were often the driving force behind revolts. From about 1750 Methodists and Baptists began to work among slaves. Many slaves were converted to Christianity and some became preachers and religious leaders. They were also natural leaders of resistance.

> **attainment target**
>
> 1 Choose two sources from Sources 23, 24, 25, 26, 27 and 28 which you found told you most about the life of slaves. Explain your choice.
>
> 2 Draw up a list of other questions you would like to ask about the life of slaves. What type of historical source would help you answer them?
>
> 3 What problems do you think historians have in finding out about the life of slaves?

SOURCE 28
Slaves in their best clothes at a celebration.

How did slaves resist slavery?

Black people did not just sit and accept slavery. The chains, the whips, the violence which went with slavery were all necessary to stop resistance. This resistance could take many forms. Some slaves committed suicide as a last act of defiance, depriving their owner of the profit they would have made from their unpaid labour. On the ships there was the ever-present danger of mutiny. The number of slaves so outnumbered the crew that, if they could just get hold of some weapons, the ship could be taken over. It happened many times and ships' captains could only resort to the kind of harshness described in Source 29.

Runaways

Slaves were always running away from their masters. It is hard to say just how many but between 1732 and 1782 5,600 advertisements giving details of runaway slaves appeared in South Carolina newspapers. Most plantations always had between five and ten per cent of their slaves missing. Some just went off for a while to see friends, lovers or relations on other plantations. Others tried to stay free by living rough. The usual punishment on Barbados for running away was 40 lashes and a branded 'R'. Sometimes the slaves themselves hid runaways. In one story, Sam, a 20-year-old slave had been hidden by his father for 16 years. He had been 'stolen by his parents' (whatever that means!) at the age of six, when he was sent to another plantation.

> I put them all in leg-irons; and if these be not enough why then I handcuff them; if the hand-cuffs be too little, I put a collar round their neck, with a chain locked to a ring-bolt on the deck; if one chain won't do I put two, and if two won't do I put three.

SOURCE 29
A comment made by a slaveship captain.

Maroons

Several islands had communities of maroons – escaped slaves living independently. There were maroons in Honduras, Dominica and Saint Vincent, the island refuge for runaways from Barbados. However the largest maroon communities were in Jamaica (see Source 30). The high mountains, deep valleys and impenetrable forests of the island made it impossible for white authorities to catch the escaped slaves. From 1729 to 1739 the First Maroon War was waged against them (see Source 31). In the end the British had to make a treaty with the maroon leader, Cudjoe, allowing them to hold certain lands (Source 32). There was a Second Maroon War in 1795, when 300 maroons and 200 more recently escaped slaves held off 5,000 British troops.

SOURCE 30
Trelawney town – a maroon town in Jamaica.

SOURCE 31
A maroon ambush.

SOURCE 32
British army officers
and maroons signing
a treaty.

Rebellions

The one great fear of the white community was a slave rebellion. The population figures given in Source 33 show why. Rebellions were always put down with terrible savagery: for example a rising in 1712 in New York was followed by 21 executions. To desperate slaves, however, any fate seemed better than enduring slavery.

Rebel leaders, and often most of their followers, were usually recent arrivals from Africa. This was the case with the rebellion of 1735 to 1736 in Antigua and Tacky's rebellion of 1760 in Jamaica. The events of the 1790s in the French colony of Saint Domingue horrified white planters everywhere. Inspired by the ideals of the French Revolution, the slaves rose in successful revolt. Their leader, Toussaint L'Ouverture, claimed Liberty, Equality and Fraternity for black people as well as white. Despite the best efforts of the armies of France, Spain and Britain, the independent black state of Haiti was proclaimed in 1804. Now there was an example to follow and it took many years and many troops before British control of its West Indian colonies was secure. Major rebellions took place in 1816 in Barbados and in 1823 in Demerara. Then, in 1831, there was a huge rising in Jamaica led by a Baptist preacher named Sam Sharpe. Property costing over £1 million was destroyed; 14 white people and over 500 slaves were killed; many other slaves were privately executed afterwards in an orgy of revenge. The rebellion, and planter violence, helped to bring about the end of slavery in British territory, see pages 40 to 41.

	black	white
Jamaica	250,000	30,000
Barbados	62,000	16,000
Grenada	24,000	1,000
Saint Vincent	12,000	1,450
Dominica	15,000	1,240

SOURCE 33
Black and white populations of British West Indian islands, 1791.

attainment target

1 What do these pages tell you about
  a slaves' attitudes towards slavery?
  b white planters' attitudes towards slavery?

Start this question by making a list of points. Find sources or other information to support the points you want to make. Write it up as a series of paragraphs.

How was slavery abolished?

There was quite a sizeable black population in Britain in the 18th century, see Source 34. Some were servants – it was very fashionable to have a black servant – some were free, doing all sorts of jobs, and some were slaves.

How was it possible to be a slave in Britain, a country that prided itself on its freedom? Granville Sharp set out to show that slavery was against the laws of Britain. He helped black people in London and defended those facing forced removal back to the colonies when their masters returned. In the so-called Somerset Case, 1771 to 1772, the judge decided that a slave could not be removed by force from Britain. The black community celebrated with a party in a Westminster pub: admission tickets cost five shillings. Freed slaves, like Olaudah Equiano (see page 34), worked with Sharp. In fact it was Equiano who brought the *Zong* case to his attention.

Abolitionists

In 1787 twelve people, some of them Quakers, began a campaign to abolish slavery. For this to succeed they had to convince Parliament. The MP William Wilberforce began to make speeches in Parliament against slavery. He was in poor health so much of the work of obtaining facts about the slave trade was

SOURCE 34
Drawing of a mixed gathering of blacks and whites in London in the early 19th century.

'If the minds of Africans were unbroken by slavery, if they had the same opportunities as other people, they would be equal . . . The argument that states them to be an inferior link in the chain of nature and so designed for slavery . . . is wholly false.'

SOURCE 35
An extract from a book by Thomas Clarkson.

done by Thomas Clarkson. Clarkson exposed the racism of slavery (Source 35). He went to Bristol and Liverpool and talked to slaveship crews. He saw the slave-irons and torture implements on sale in harbourside shops. He was often threatened by people involved in the slave trade.

Several arguments were used by those in favour of slavery, see Source 36. One was that the slave trade provided sailors for the navy. Clarkson showed that the death rate on slaveships was so high that it actually killed off more sailors than it trained. He argued that wage-workers were much better employees than slaves, a point taken up by the great economist Adam Smith (see Source 37).

The anti-slavery campaign had widespread support, including such famous figures as the pottery owner Josiah Wedgwood (see Source 38). Many thousands of ordinary working people also gave it their support. Mass petitions were handed to Parliament. It was one of the first mass movements. It was also the one issue in industrial areas on which both employers and workers could agree. The slave trade was abolished in 1807 but the campaign to free all slaves continued. The West Indian sugar plantations were in decline by this time anyway, in the face of competition from Cuba and Brazil.

Parliament tried to make slave-owners treat their slaves better after 1807. Harsh punishments were banned, slaves were encouraged to go to church. The failure of this policy was shown up in the violent slave revolts of 1831 and the savage way they were put down. Slavery in British territory was abolished in 1833, with slave-owners receiving compensation of £38 per slave.

> The experience of all ages demonstrates that the work done by slaves, though it appears to cost only their maintenance, is in the end the dearest of any. Whatever work a slave does is squeezed out of him by violence only.

SOURCE 37
An extract from Adam Smith's *Wealth of Nations*, 1776.

SOURCE 38
Plaque made by Josiah Wedgwood.

SOURCE 36
Three comments made by opponents of abolition.

a 'It would be ruinous to the colonies and people of this country.' MP for Plymouth.
b 'Damnable doctrine of Wilberforce and his hypocritical allies.' Lord Nelson.
c '[In the West Indies, without the slave trade] crops will decline, the population and the produce will be at an end.' William Beckford (poet, travel writer and slave owner, 1790).

attainment target

| Black abolitionists like Equiano | White abolitionists like Wilberforce and Clarkson | Popular support for anti-slavery | Failure of economic arguments for slavery (see Source 37) | Competition for British slave plantations |

1 Above are some reasons why slavery was abolished. Choose three of these and explain how they helped to bring about the abolition of slavery.

2 The most common explanation for abolition has usually been the work of white abolitionists like Wilberforce. Why has this interpretation been commonly held? Do you think it is accurate?

AIMS

In this unit you will find out how
the British people reacted to the
changes you read about in unit 1.
You will see in outline how the
American and French Revolutions
encouraged demands for change.
You will see that the reform of
Parliament, when it did come,
disappointed many people. You can
see what else working people did to
try to improve their lives, and how
the law affected working
conditions, through depth studies.
The unit ends with a depth study
on women's lives and roles.

Popular responses

In unit 1 we saw that industrialisation affected the lives of most of the
people of Britain, often for the worse. Their grievances usually came
down to one thing: it was a struggle to live. Their working hours were
long, hard and sometimes dangerous. Children had to work to help
families make ends meet. People had to put up with poor living
conditions. What could they do?

They certainly could not expect the government to help. In a modern
election everyone over 18 can vote. They can elect people to do what they
think needs doing. It was not at all like this in the 18th century. As you
saw when you studied 'The Making of the United Kingdom' the conflicts
of the 17th century left Parliament in control of the country, and
landowners in control of Parliament. They believed that only those with a
stake in the country by owning land could vote. Only four per cent of
men had this right; no women could vote. Parliament admired the
so-called 'Glorious Revolution' of 1688 which had settled these rights.
Lord Justice Braxfield said in 1793 that 'The British constitution is the
best that ever was since the creation of the world and it is not possible to
make it any better'.

SOURCE 1
The Declaration of Independence of the USA in 1776 began 'We hold these truths to
be self-evident, that all men are created equal, that they are endowed by their
creator with certain inalienable rights and that among these are life, liberty and the
pursuit of happiness'.

Tom Paine

The revolution in the American colonies which led to the foundation of the USA (Source 1), and the revolution in France (Source 2), gave hope to many British people. Tom Paine (pictured in Source 3) took part in both revolutions. His ideas inspired British reformers for many generations.

He was born to Quaker parents in Thetford, Norfolk in 1737. In 1774 he emigrated to America and fought for the American colonists against the British in the War of Independence. He then worked for the new US government but returned to Britain in 1787. In 1792 he published *The Rights of Man* in which he laid out his criticisms of the British constitution (see Source 4). The book was tremendously popular, selling 200,000 copies.

The spread of Paine's ideas

Paine was attacked by the government and fled to France. There he was made a French citizen and member of the National Convention (Parliament). He lived in France until 1802 but then returned to the USA and died in 1809.

All over Britain Corresponding Societies were set up to meet and discuss the ideas of Paine, Volnay (see Source 5) and events in France. The king was openly criticised (see Source 6). The British government was terrified of a revolution here on the French model. RADICALS were arrested, printers closed down and societies banned. However, hope for radical reform was not crushed and *The Rights of Man* remained on many cottage bookshelves to convince anyone who read it that the system must be changed.

SOURCE 2
Execution of King Louis XVI of France in 1793 in the name of the revolutionary ideals of 'Liberty, Equality, Fraternity'.

SOURCE 3
Tom Paine.

'I disapprove of monarchic and aristocratic forms of government. . . . Hereditary distinctions of any kind must work against human improvement. Hence it follows that I am not among the admirers of the British Constitution.'

SOURCE 4
An extract adapted from Tom Paine's *Rights of Man*.

'People: What work do you do in this society?
Privileged class: None. We are not made to work.
People: How then have you acquired your wealth?
Privileged class: By governing you.
People: By governing us! We toil and you enjoy. We produce and you spend. Wealth flows from us and you absorb it.'

SOURCE 5
An extract from Volnay's *Ruins of Empire* which was published in the 1790s.

A sullen silence hung over the crowd. No hats were pulled off and frequently a cry of "Give us bread!", and once or twice "No King!" with much hissing and groaning.

SOURCE 6
Crowd reactions to King George III in 1795.

Popular protests

Luddites, 1811 to 1812

Groups of skilled textile workers smash the machines which were making goods cheaper than they could.

'Peterloo', 1819

A demonstration at St Peter's Fields, Manchester, calling for votes for all adult males. The demonstrators are charged by soldiers and 13 are killed.

Captain Swing riots, 1830

Agricultural labourers, losing work because of threshing machines, destroy the machines and attack farmers' property.

Emigration

The failure of Chartism and the suppression of early trade unions led many people to emigrate (see Source 9). From 1851 to 1920 4.7 million people emigrated from Britain to the USA, 2.9 million to Canada, 2.1 million to Australia and another 1.6 million elsewhere.

Co-operatives, 1844

A small group of weavers in Rochdale got together to buy food and household items wholesale and sell them, at fair prices, to local people. Any profits were paid back to those who had originally put up the money or used to improve their lives by providing a library and a school.

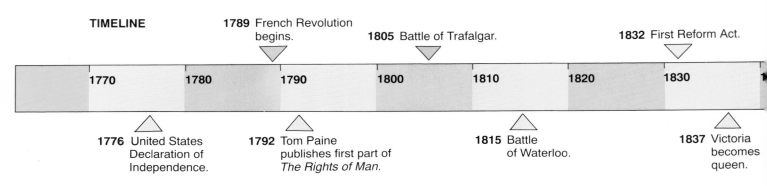

TIMELINE

1789 French Revolution begins.

1805 Battle of Trafalgar.

1832 First Reform Act.

| 1770 | 1780 | 1790 | 1800 | 1810 | 1820 | 1830 |

1776 United States Declaration of Independence.

1792 Tom Paine publishes first part of *The Rights of Man*.

1815 Battle of Waterloo.

1837 Victoria becomes queen.

Chartism, 1838 to 1848

Bitterly disappointed by the limited reform of Parliament carried out by the 1832 Act, reformers draw up a Charter, demanding a vote for all adult males, secret voting, annual Parliaments, no property qualification for MPs, payment of MPs, equal sized constituencies. Chartism was the movement to get Parliament to agree to the Charter. Millions of working people became Chartists, hoping to improve their desperate lives.

The Charter was presented to Parliament in 1839, 1842 and 1848. It was rejected each time. Chartist protests were usually peaceful (see Source 7) but some Chartists threatened violence (see Source 8) and there was a Chartist uprising at Newport, South Wales, in 1839.

SOURCE 7
A very early photograph of a Chartist demonstration in London, 1848.

SOURCE 8
From an article by leading Chartist George Harney, written in 1839.

'Universal suffrage there shall be, or our tyrants will find to their cost that they have universal misery . . . believe me, there is no argument like the sword, and the musket is unanswerable.'

SOURCE 9
'The Last of England', painted by Ford Maddox Brown in 1855.

SOURCE 11
Bloody Sunday Riot, November 1887.

1867 Karl Marx publishes first part of *Das Capital*.
Many working men in towns gain the vote.

1884 Many working men in rural areas gain the vote.

1901 Queen Victoria dies.

| 1850 | 1860 | 1870 | 1880 | 1890 | 1900 | 1910 |

Trade Unions

Trade unions were banned in the 1790s but revived in the 1820s. Robert Owen started the Grand National Consolidated Trade Union (GNCTU) in 1834. Six farm labourers from Tolpuddle, Dorset, joined but were tried and sentenced to be transported; they became known as the 'Tolpuddle Martyrs'. Unions for skilled workers, 'New Model Unions', flourished after the Trade Union Act of 1871. Joseph Arch tried to form a union of farm workers, among the worst paid workers in the country, see Source 10.

Successful strikes of the matchgirls, 1888, and the London dockers, 1889, led to the growth of unions for unskilled workers.

> After the harvest of 1872 had been reaped and the winter had set in the sufferings of the men became cruel. . . . Their poverty had fallen to starvation point and was past all bearing. . . . Oppression and hunger and misery made them desperate and desperation was the mother of the union.

SOURCE 10
An extract from the memoirs of Joseph Arch, published in 1898.

Labour Party

Some SOCIALISTS wanted working people to fight for their rights through Parliament. They organised demonstrations of unemployed workers, see Source 11. In 1893 Keir Hardie and other socialists formed the Independent Labour Party. In 1899 Trade Unions formed the Labour Representation Committee to get more working people elected to Parliament.

ACTIVITY

1 Copy out the timeline and add the events from this page to it. You could use this colour code:
 - red for anything to do with Parliament or voting
 - blue for anything to do with changing people's working conditions
 - green for any other aims of popular movements.

2 Add the letter V to any violent movement and the letter P to any peaceful movement.

3 How can a timeline show a long, gradual process, such as emigration, rather than an event?

The 1832 Reform Act

The following features of the old parliamentary system were criticised:

- 'Rotten boroughs': look again at the picture of Sheffield on page 16 and compare it with Source 12. Before 1832 the great city of Sheffield, along with places like Birmingham, Manchester and Leeds had no MPs at all. Dunwich, Old Sarum and Bramber, on the other hand, had two MPs each.

- 'Pocket boroughs': here the voters did exactly what their landlord told them, they were 'in his pocket'.

- Landowners in power: elections like the one in Westminster shown in Source 13 were rare. Most MPs were landowners from the south of England. In the past, this had reflected where the money and power lay. Now the industrial north and Midlands were becoming increasingly important. Industrialists did not think it was right that Parliament should be dominated by landowners. They objected to laws like the Corn Laws of 1815, which kept up the price of corn to help farmers.

Demands for reform of Parliament had continued since the 1790s. Many working people joined in the campaign, hoping that all adult males would get the right to vote. Huge meetings were held.

SOURCE 12
Three 'rotten boroughs' shown on the cover of a newspaper in 1831.

SOURCE 13
Election scene in Westminster, 1796. The candidates are on a wooden platform (called the hustings), the voters are below. Voting took place in public, over several days. Westminster had an unusually large number of voters.

How much reform?

The Whig Party knew the system had to be changed but were afraid to give everyone the vote. They thought that the working classes were too undisciplined and uneducated to have the vote. They said that any male in a house worth £10 a year or more should have the vote. This would include middle-class male voters in the new industrial towns, but would exclude the working classes. Source 14 outlines the results of the Whig proposals.

Many people were against changing the system. When the House of Lords rejected the Whig proposals there were riots in Bristol, Nottingham and Derby. Eventually the Reform Act was passed, in 1832. The number of voters rose slightly to 700,000 (about 8 per cent of the male population). The Act also gave 40 new towns and cities the right to elect their own MPs (Source 15). Working-class people felt let down by the Act. It gave them nothing and was a main cause of the Chartist movement (pages 52 to 53).

Thirty-five years later, in 1867, the Conservative leader Disraeli gave the right to vote to better-off working men in towns. Voting in secret was introduced in 1872. Only in 1884 was the right to vote extended to some working men in rural areas. All men, and all women, did not have the right to vote until well into the 20th century.

'In the parts occupied by the working classes, not one householder in 50 would have a vote. In the streets occupied by shops, almost every householder would have a vote. In the town of Holbeck, containing 11,000 inhabitants, chiefly of the working classes, but with several respectable dwellings, there would be only 150 voters.'

SOURCE 14
Letter from Edward Baines, newspaper editor in Leeds, to the Whig leader, Lord Russell, 1831. Baines explains how people in Leeds would be affected by giving the vote to those living in houses worth £10 or more per year.

N
0   100 km

▲ lost MPs
■ new with 1 MP
■ new with 2 MPs

SCOTLAND
53 MPs

IRELAND
105 MPs

this area lost 67 MPs

Cornwall lost 18 MPs

ENGLAND and WALES
56 rotten or pocket boroughs lost 2 MPs
30 rotten or pocket boroughs lost 1 MP
21 large towns given 2 MPs
17 large towns given 1 MP
most counties given 1 or 2 extra MPs

SOURCE 15
Changes brought about by the 1832 Reform Act.

attainment target

For each of the statements below, write 'B' if it applies to the situation before 1832. Write 'A' if it applies to the situation straight afterwards.

Theory
Those who own land should rule the country.
Those who have some wealth should rule the country.
Anyone can stand in an election to decide who rules the country.

The vote
The right to vote is an ancient privilege, lying mainly with landowners.
The right to vote should be with any adult.
The right to vote should be with any man in property worth £10 a year or more.

Places represented
There should be roughly equal numbers of voters for any MP anywhere.
The right to have an MP is an ancient privilege, granted to places long ago.
Britain has changed and new places have become important, so needing their own MP.

1 Use your 'B's to write about what the constitution was like before 1832.

2 Use your 'A's to write about the changes made by the 1832 Reform Act.

3 Why were many people disappointed by the Act?

There were many different kinds of working class movement in the 19th century. Some were violent, some were peaceful; some thought their best hope was to change Parliament, others worked to change their working conditions. This depth study looks at some of these movements in more detail.

Violent protest: the Luddites

Today the word 'Luddite' is used to describe someone who is against any new machine. In 1811 to 1812 large groups of workers smashed machines in textile factories in Nottinghamshire, Yorkshire and Lancashire. The punishments for this kind of thing were serious, so the rioters used a made-up name to protect their leaders: 'Ned Ludd'.

Most of them were skilled weavers or other textile workers. New machines such as shearing-frames or power looms did the same work as they did but faster and cheaper. They feared that their wages would be driven down and they would have to become unskilled factory hands. At the same time, the price of bread was very high. The Luddites sent threatening letters to employers with machines (Source 16). If the machines were not removed, gangs of workers would smash them with sledgehammers (see Source 17).

'Great Enoch still shall lead the van,
Stop him who dare, stop him who can'
went one of their songs.

Twelve thousands troops were sent to the areas where Luddites were active to try to keep the peace.

> Sir,
> Information has just been given that you are a holder of those detestable shearing-frames and I was asked by my men to write to you to give you fair warning to pull them down. If they are not taken down by the end of the week I shall send at least 300 men to destroy them.
> Signed, NED LUDD

SOURCE 16
Luddite letter to an owner of shearing-frames.

SOURCE 17
'Great Enoch': a large sledgehammer used by Luddites, made by Enoch Taylor of Marsden, West Yorkshire.

- **1816** riot at protest meeting addressed by radical speaker Henry Hunt, at Spa Fields, London.
- **1817** protest march of 'Blanketeers' from Lancashire: the leaders were arrested.
- **1819** protest meeting at St Peter's Fields, Manchester, charged by soldiers: 13 were killed, many wounded. It was named 'Peterloo' (see pages 50 to 51).
- **1820** six Acts were passed by government banning meetings, demonstrations and the publication of articles.
- **1820** Cato Street Conspiracy: plan to assassinate the entire Cabinet: the leaders were executed.

'Captain Swing'

Farmworkers also suffered from low wages and were often laid off in the winter. One of the few winter jobs which provided them with some paid work was threshing. In the 1820s many farmers were buying threshing machines. These could do several days' threshing in a few hours. In 1830 the price of bread rose and many farmworkers faced desperation.

Radical unrest 1815 to 1820

In June 1815 Wellington and Blucher defeated Napoleon at the battle of Waterloo and the long Napoleonic wars came to an end. The first few years of peace brought terrible distress to working people. There was high unemployment, low wages and high food prices. Radicals called for a more democratic Parliament. Many working people were ready to listen, but the government was not. Many historians think Britain was near to revolution in these years. Here are some key events:

Again the protesters used a made-up name to protect themselves: 'Captain Swing'. Source 18 shows a threatening letter sent to a farmer, demanding higher wages. All over southern England there were outbreaks of rick burning in the summer of 1830 (see Source 19).

The reaction of the government to this kind of violent protest was harsh. Seventeen Luddites were hanged at York in 1812. Following the 'Captain Swing' riots, 19 were executed, 505 transported to Australia and 644 imprisoned.

ACTIVITY

1 Get into groups of four. It is 1821 and you are all skilled hand-weavers with families. The price of bread has doubled in the last month. A local factory-owner has bought a power loom and is making cloth at a much lower price than you can. Think about what you can and what you cannot do. Think about the punishment if you break the law. Think about your starving children. What are you going to do about the situation? Report to the class what you decide. If you decide to send any letters like Source 18, work out what to say.

2 Discuss this problem. It is the present. You all work in an office writing out orders for goods as they come in from customers and sending them to the factory. The boss has plans to introduce a computerised system which will do the job in half the time. Only two of you will be needed. What do you decide to say to the boss?

SOURCE 18
Letter sent by 'Captain Swing' to a farmer, autumn 1830.

this is to inform you what you have to undergo Gentelmen if providing you Dont pull down your mes sheens and rise the poor mens wages the maried men give tow and six pence a day a day the singel tow shilings or we will burn down your barns and you in them this is the last notis from W Sw

SOURCE 19
Hayricks set on fire by rioters.

What happened at Peterloo?

There were angry demonstrations in 1816 in London and protest marches in 1817. Ideas of DEMOCRACY and REFORM from the French Revolution were still alive. Some working people talked of revolution and began to train with weapons. On 16 August 1819 there was to be a big demonstration in St Peter's Fields, Manchester, to be addressed by the great reform speaker Henry Hunt.

Many middle-class people were terrified. They thought working people should accept their position and not complain; they were opposed to any idea of change. They were suspicious of the demonstration and afraid of a revolution.

The local MAGISTRATES who were responsible for law and order called out the local YEOMANRY. These men were mostly opposed to the demonstrators. Soon the yeomanry got out of hand and charged into the crowd, armed with swords. Thirteen people were killed and many wounded. The event became known as 'Peterloo', a sarcastic reference to the victory over the French at the battle of Waterloo, four years earlier. Sources 20 to 25 present various impressions and accounts of these events. They show how each side tried to blame the other. They show how divided Britain was at the time. They provide us with an example of the problems of using sources to find out what really happened in history.

'Before 12 o'clock crowds began to assemble, each village having a banner and some a cap with "Liberty" painted on it. Each party kept in military order, with sticks on their shoulders.'

[French revolutionaries wore 'caps of Liberty'.]

SOURCE 20
Extract from a report in *The Courier* newspaper.

I saw the march proceeding towards St Peter's Fields and never saw a happier sight. The so-called 'marching order' was what we often see in processions of Sunday School children. Our company laughed at the fears of the magistrates, and the remark was made that if the men intended mischief they would not have brought their wives and children with them.

SOURCE 21
Eye-witness account, from one of the demonstrators at Peterloo.

SOURCE 22
Part of a cartoon of events at St Peter's Fields, Manchester, on 16 August 1819.

'The event would have taken place without bloodshed if the mob had not attacked the soldiers with missiles. As a result, the cavalry charged in their own defence.'

SOURCE 23
Another extract from *The Courier*.

'They came in a threatening manner – they came with the banners of death, thereby showing they meant to overthrow the government. I believe you are a downright blackguard reformer. Some of you reformers ought to be hanged.'

SOURCE 24
Magistrate talking to one of the demonstrators.

A club of female reformers, 156 in number, from Oldham, had a white silk banner, inscribed 'Votes for All'.
The cavalry drew their swords and brandished them fiercely. Nothing was thrown at them. Not a pistol was fired during this period.

SOURCE 25
From an article in *The Times* newspaper.

SOURCE 26
Manchester in the 19th century.

attainment target

1 Using only the accounts from *The Courier* (Sources 20 and 23), who do you think was to blame for what happened at Peterloo?

2 Using only Sources 21 and 25, who do you think was to blame?

3 How useful is Source 21 for finding out about the demonstration?

4 Choose the two sources which you think are the most useful and the least useful for finding out about what happened. Explain your choices.

5 The cartoon, Source 22, was drawn afterwards. Whose side do you think the cartoonist was on? How can you tell?

6 Does Source 24 provide reliable evidence about: the demonstration? The attitude of the magistrates to the reformers?

7 Write an account of what you think happened at St Peter's Fields on that day.

8 How accurate do you think your account can be?

What did Chartists want?

Working-class reformers said they had been 'bitterly and basely deceived' by the 1832 Reform Act. Their mass demonstrations had helped to get the Act passed, but they gained nothing from it. Some of the actions of the new Parliament, such as passing the Poor Law Amendment Act, 1834, made life worse for working people. The trial of the Tolpuddle Martyrs (see page 54) led many to lose hope in trade union activity. The further reform of Parliament seemed the best hope for the future. Working-class MPs could then pass laws to solve working people's problems.

A charter was published in 1838, with six basic points:

- A vote for all adult males
- Secret ballots (so that employers could not influence how a worker voted)
- Annual parliaments (to keep MPs in touch with voters)
- No property qualification for MPs (so that working people could stand)
- Payment of MPs (also to allow working people to stand)
- Equal sized constituencies.

Chartism was the first really working-class movement. There were Chartist groups in most towns and cities. They sent delegates to national conventions, entirely organised and paid for by working people's efforts and money. Working-class women took part too and had their own organisations.

'The Charter means meat and drink and clothing, good hours and good beds, and good furniture for every man and woman and child who will do a fair day's work.'

SOURCE 27
From a speech by the Chartist Bronterre O'Brien.

'Let us, Friends, unite together the honest, moral, hard-working and thinking members of society. Let us obtain a library of books. Let us publish our views so that we create a moral, thinking, energetic force in politics.'

SOURCE 28
From a speech by Chartist leader William Lovett, 1838.

The 1840s were difficult times for working people, with factories closing and high food prices. As Source 27 explains, the hopes of millions of people for a decent life were concentrated on Chartism.

The problem Chartist leaders faced was how to get Parliament to accept the Charter. William Lovett (Source 28) wanted to show that working people deserved the vote. Petitions were presented to Parliament in 1839, 1842 (see Source 29) and 1848.

SOURCE 29
The Chartist petition, signed by over 3 million people, being carried to Parliament in 1842.

What if Parliament rejected it?

Many Chartists were so desperate, so angry and so shut out of power that they thought about an armed rebellion (see Source 30). After the 1839 petition was rejected there was a rebellion in Newport, South Wales. Twenty Chartists, mostly miners, were killed (see Source 31). After the 1842 petition was rejected, there were calls for an armed rising and there was a general strike in Lancashire. When the 1848 petition was rejected, Chartism went into decline.

The confusion between peaceful or forceful tactics counted against the Chartists. If they were peaceful, why did some threaten violence? If they were violent the government was ready, with a large army under General Napier. Even armed Chartists knew they did not stand a chance.

Chartism seemed to have failed. However, the movement had inspired many working-class people. They went into other activities: trade unions, cooperatives, newspapers, temperance leagues. Eventually, five of the six demands of the Charter were met.

'A great many people were arming themselves with guns or picks. I bought a gun, although I knew it was a serious thing for a Chartist to have a gun in his possession. It might be said that we were fools, but young people now have no idea what we had to endure. From 1842 to 1848 I did not average 9 shillings (45p) a week.'

SOURCE 30
Benjamin Wilson, an old Chartist, writing in 1887.

attainment target

1 Why did so many people support Chartism?

2 What different attitudes to Chartism are described in Sources 27 and 28?

3 Why did Benjamin Wilson, Source 30, buy a gun?

4 What different attitudes to Chartism might the following people have: a navvy; the wife of a Northumberland miner; a Suffolk landowner and MP; a middle-class woman shopkeeper in Manchester; an engine driver?

SOURCE 31
Chartists attacking the hotel at Newport, South Wales, where their leader was under arrest, 1839.

Trade unions

Some working people did not hope for political change. Instead they worked at improving their working lives. Wage cuts, dangerous work, long hours and sudden lay-offs all threatened their livelihood (look back at pages 12–13). As individuals they were completely at the mercy of their employers and could simply be sacked if they complained. But if all workers combined together, their employer would have to listen to them or lose the entire workforce.

Early trade unions

A trade union is an organisation for all workers in a particular trade. Some kinds of trade union had existed for centuries, but in the panic over French revolutionary ideas coming to Britain (see pages 42 to 43) the government banned them in 1799 and 1800. In 1824 unions were made legal again. Source 32 shows a membership card from one of the first unions for women workers.

In 1834 Robert Owen founded a union for all workers, called the Grand National Consolidated Trade Union (GNCTU). In the village of Tolpuddle, Dorset, George Loveless, his brother James and four other farm labourers formed a branch of the GNCTU. They were fighting a reduction in wages from 9 shillings (45p) a week to 8 shillings (40p).

SOURCE 32
Membership card of the Union of Power Loom Female Weavers, 1833.

The government was worried by the GNCTU as it seemed to interfere with their ideas of 'laissez-faire' (see page 22). Local JPs in Dorset had the six Tolpuddle labourers arrested. The government suggested they could be charged with taking an illegal oath, under a law of 1797. George Loveless, a Methodist lay preacher, gave a dignified speech at his trial. Although they had only committed a minor offence, they were sentenced to transportation to Australia for 7 years. They were pardoned in 1836, but it was 1839 before the last of the six returned. The GNCTU collapsed and many workers turned to Chartism.

Cooperatives

In 1844 seven weavers in Rochdale, Lancashire, got together with 21 others and each put in £1. With this they bought butter, sugar, flour, oatmeal and candles, and set up a little shop (Source 33). They opened the shop in the evenings and sold goods, at fair prices, to local people. Their profits were distributed among the customers. Money was also put aside for a school in the room above the shop, and a library.

Out of this effort to help each other in practical ways by their efforts grew the huge Cooperative movement, with shops and factories all over Britain.

SOURCE 33
Modern reconstruction of the inside of the Cooperative shop, Rochdale, Lancashire, opened in 1844. This became the model for other Cooperative Societies.

New Model Unions

In the 1850s and 1860s unions of skilled workers began to grow (see Source 34). Engineers, carpenters and bricklayers, for example, were well paid, earning up to £1.75 a week. They could afford to pay a high SUBSCRIPTION, say 1 shilling (5p) a week. This paid for a full-time Secretary and a good organisation. They paid all kinds of benefits to their members (see Source 35) and avoided strikes. They seemed a 'model' for others to follow. These 'New Model Unions' joined together to start the Trades Union Congress (TUC) in 1868.

At the same time, hostility between workers and employers sometimes led to violence. If workers went on strike, an employer could hire others to do their jobs. These strike-breakers were called 'blacklegs'. Sometimes blacklegs were threatened (see Source 36), and violence occurred.

The government decided to investigate trade unions and set up an enquiry. They were impressed with people like Robert Applegarth of the Carpenters' Union and William Allen of the Engineers'. They decided it would be better to make unions legal and this was done by the Trade Union Act of 1871. From then on union membership began to increase.

SOURCE 34
Emblem of the Operative Bricklayers' Society.

'The aims of this society are to raise funds to help members in cases of sickness, accident or old age, for the burial of members and their wives, emigration, loss of tools by fire, water or theft and for assistance to members who are out of work.'

SOURCE 35
Robert Applegarth, Secretary to the Carpenters' Union, giving evidence to the Parliamentary Commission on Trade Unions, 1867.

On Saturday last I met the prisoner in Wardour Street, when she said to me 'Well, Mrs Mills, you are doing the dirty work, are you?' I asked her what she meant, and she said 'You are fetching work from the shops that are on strike.' I asked her if that had anything to do with her and she replied 'Yes, it's all to do with me. It's stinking hussies such as you who are keeping the men out of work, you stinking cow. When this strike is over I will do for you.'

SOURCE 36
Mrs Mills speaking about Ellen Meade, who was convicted of attacking a non-union worker during a strike.

1 What evidence is there on these pages of the law being used against trade unionists?

2 Why was Ellen Meade angry with Mrs Mills (see Source 36)?

3 Do you think Ellen Meade's actions, as described by Mrs Mills, were wrong?

4 Why do you think the government were impressed by trade unionists like Robert Applegarth (Source 35)?

5 Why would it be difficult for most workers to set up a New Model Union?

6 Trade unions are still controversial. Is any member of your family a trade union member? Which union? What does the union do for them? Is any member of your family hostile to trade unions? What do they dislike about them?

7 Do you think the story on these pages is one of success or failure for working people?

The voice of the working class

The workers in the New Model Unions were the aristocrats of employees. Industry could not work without their skills and they used this to get what they wanted without having to go on strike. But what about those at the bottom of the heap, the unskilled labourers?

These included the matchgirls who made matches at Bryant and May's factory in the east end of London (see Source 37). Apart from the conditions described in Source 38, they also got a disease called 'phossy jaw' from the phosphorus in the matches. Annie Besant helped organise a strike of the matchgirls and won support for them through her newspaper articles. Within three weeks they had won better wages and conditions.

Then there were the gas-workers, who spent long hours shovelling coal. Will Thorne formed a gas-workers' union in 1889, and won a reduction in hours.

Another large group of unskilled workers were the London dockers, paid by the hour to unload ships. Their harsh treatment and lack of security is described in Source 39. In 1889 they went on strike for a wage of 6d (2½p) an hour, known as the 'dockers' tanner'. They had good leaders, like Ben Tillett and John Burns (Source 40). They managed to hold out for several weeks, helped by money from other unions and from the Australian dockers' union. Ships could not unload at the docks; their cargoes rotted in their holds. The employers gave in and paid them 6d an hour.

SOURCE 37
Annie Besant (sixth from right) and members of the matchgirls' strike committee, 1888.

Born in slums, driven to work while still children, under-sized because under-fed, oppressed because helpless, flung aside as soon as worked out.

The starting time is 6.30 in summer and 8.00 in winter. Work finishes at 6 p.m. The girls have to stand the whole time. A typical girl earns 4 shillings (20p) a week.

SOURCE 38
From a newspaper article by Annie Besant, called 'White Slavery in London', 1888.

'We were driven into a shed, iron-barred from end to end. Outside the foremen walked up and down, like dealers in a cattle market, picking and choosing from a crowd of men who, in their eagerness for work, trampled each other underfoot.'

SOURCE 39
Description of workers on the London Docks by Ben Tillett.

SOURCE 40
John Burns addressing dockers at a strike meeting in 1889.

SOURCE 41
Mineworkers' Union banner showing Keir Hardie.

These 'new unions' of unskilled workers could only collect a small subscription, 1d or 2d a week. They paid only one benefit: strike pay. Their leaders were more aggressive at using strikes to win better pay for their members. Ben Tillett simply said, 'It is the work of the trade unionist to stamp out poverty.'

This is not a simple success story for unions, however. Times were hard in the 1890s. Employers fought back, combining together and using 'blackleg' labour. Will Thorne's gasworkers lost a strike in 1890. The Dockers' Union collapsed in 1891. Even the engineers lost a big strike in 1897–1898. Once again workers turned to Parliament to try to improve their position.

The Labour Party

Annie Besant, Ben Tillett, Will Thorne and John Burns were socialists. That is, they opposed the capitalist system in which trade and industry are controlled by private owners for their own profit. Socialists followed the ideas of Karl Marx, that workers and employers were bound to be in conflict. They believed that industry and banks should be run by the government, for the benefit of all.

After 1884 most men had the vote, but there was no working-class party to belong to. The two political parties were Liberals and Conservatives. Sometimes working-class MPs were elected, but sat with the Liberals. In 1892 James Keir Hardie (see Source 41) was elected MP for West Ham, and in the following year he set up the Independent Labour Party, a working-class party. Socialists from around the country supported him, but their numbers were few and they had little money.

The key to mass support and funds had to come from the trade union movement. In 1899 the TUC set up the Labour Representation Committee (LRC) to get more working-class, socialist MPs elected to Parliament. In the 1906 Election 29 LRC MPs were elected, and called themselves the Labour Party.

attainment target

1 What part did each of the following play in the matchgirls' strike and the dockers' strike?
   Good leaders   Popular support
   Support of other unions   Socialism
   Workers sticking together (solidarity)

2 Why did the strikes of the 1890s fail?

3 Explain how socialist ideas and trade union backing combined to form the Labour Party.

After the Reform Act

The 1832 Reform Act did not give the vote to working people but it did make Parliament pay more attention to industrial problems. In this depth study we look at how people tried to make Parliament pass laws to deal with working conditions in factories and in coalmines and living conditions in industrial towns. In each case there was considerable opposition to be overcome.

Who were the reformers?

EVANGELICALS felt moved by their religion to help the poor and needy. Along with practical help, the needy were given a strong dose of religion (see Source 42). Evangelicals also played a large part in passing Acts of Parliament to improve working conditions in factories and mines.

By 1830 there were 2,500 factories in the textile industry. As we have seen, they employed men, women and children in stuffy and dangerous conditions, for very long hours (see Source 43). Union leaders, like John Doherty of the Lancashire Cotton Spinners, campaigned for a '10-hour day' for all.

The 10 hours campaign

It was not going to be easy to get Parliament to pass a law to restrict the working day to 10 hours. Most middle-class voters knew nothing about factories. Factory-owners had friends in Parliament. They claimed that they only made a profit on the last hour's work done in a 12 hour day. Believers in 'laissez-faire' felt it was wrong to pass laws to interfere between employers and employees (see

Source 44). The 10 Hours Movement worked with Evangelical supporters such as Richard Oastler, Michael Sadler and Lord Shaftesbury. They felt they could win over public opinion by emphasising the effect of long hours on children. If children's hours were cut then adult workers would benefit too.

In 1831 Richard Oastler wrote a powerful letter to the *Leeds Mercury* (Source 45). Michael Sadler asked Parliament to restrict hours of work to 10. Parliament tried to delay things by setting up a committee to investigate and hear witnesses.

The 10 Hours Movement collected witnesses, coached them and arranged for them to get to London. Some impressive evidence was heard, see Sources 46 and 47. This was published and public opinion was shocked, especially at cases of deformity, such as the one described in Source 46.

SOURCE 43
Women and children operating cotton spinning mules.

SOURCE 42
Bible reading at a church hostel for the homeless in London.

'Have those who are in favour of this [the 10 Hours Movement] thought that it would be the first example of the laws of a free country interfering with the freedom of adult labour? Have they considered that if spinners and weavers are protected by Act of Parliament then a thousand others must, in justice, have their claims attended to?'

SOURCE 44
Letter from Richard Cobden, 1836.

Let the truth speak out. Thousands of our fellow creatures, both female and male, the inhabitants of a Yorkshire town are at this moment existing in a state of slavery, compelled by the dread of the strap of the overlooker to hasten half-dressed, but not half-fed, to the worsted mills of Bradford. Thousands of little children, from seven to 14 years, are daily compelled to labour from six in the morning to seven in the evening – Britons blush while you read this.

SOURCE 45
From an article by Richard Oastler in the *Leeds Mercury*, 1830, comparing factory work with colonial slavery.

Questioner: Were you originally a straight and healthy boy?

Joseph Hebergram: Yes I was straight and healthy when I was seven. When I had worked about half a year a weakness fell in my knees and ankles. In the morning I could scarcely walk and my brother and sister used to take me under each arm and run with me to the mill. If we were five minutes late the overlooker would take a strap and beat us until we were black and blue.

Question: At what time in the morning in the brisk time (when they were busy) did those girls go to the mills?
Answer: In the brisk time they have gone about three in the morning and ended at ten at night.
Question: Were the children excessively fatigued by this labour?
Answer: Many times. We have often cried when we have given them the little food we had to give them; we had to shake them and they have fallen asleep with the food still in their mouths.

SOURCE 46
Evidence to Sadler's Committee, 1831 to 1832.

'I really do think it is necessary that children should be protected from excessive labour. That is the first point, and with the hope, I confess, that it will benefit myself and others as well.'

SOURCE 47
Evidence given by David Brook, clothworker, to Sadler's Committee, 1831.

'I never meant to say what you have read to me, of my being so young when I worked at night. I was going 16 and I never worked so more than a month.'

SOURCE 48
Evidence to the Factory Commissioners, 1833.

After the Sadler Report

An election was held: Sadler lost his seat and Antony Ashley, later Lord Shaftesbury, took over leadership in Parliament. Parliament again delayed by setting up a commission. They cast doubt on some of Sadler's evidence, see Source 48.

The 1833 Factory Act

One of the commission, Edwin Chadwick, had an idea to let the government off the hook. An Act was passed, but it only cut the hours of children: no child under nine could work; nine to 13 year olds to work no more than eight hours, plus two hours of school. Middle-class opinion was pleased, but the 10 Hours Movement was bitterly disappointed. Many turned to Chartism. The 10 hour day was not achieved until 1853.

> attainment target

1 Look at Source 45. This article was designed to horrify people. What aspects of factory conditions does Oastler concentrate on to do this?

2 Does the fact that the letter was meant to horrify people mean that it is unreliable evidence of factory conditions?

3 What harmful effects of factory work are emphasised in Source 46?

4 Some witnesses had their stories rehearsed. Does this affect the reliability of Source 46?

5 What does Source 47 tell us about the real aims of the 10 Hours Movement?

6 Use these sources to explain how the 10 Hours Movement hoped to achieve its aims.

Should women and children work in coalmines?

In unit 1 you found out that steam engines provided power for the Industrial Revolution. This meant a huge increase in demand for coal. In 1761, British coal production was 5 million tonnes; by 1801 it was 13 million tonnes, by 1861 it was 90 million tonnes and by 1901 232 million tonnes. But, unlike the cotton industry you looked at in unit 1, all this new production was not achieved by using new machines. Instead, new and deeper pits were sunk. The job of mining remained much the same: hard, physical labour, for long hours, in dangerous conditions. The miner cut the coal in seams which were in some places only a few centimetres thick (see Source 49). The coal was then carried away to the bottom of the shaft to be hauled to the surface. In early years this job was done by women and children, often members of the miner's family.

Another danger was from explosions caused by the build-up of gases in the mine. One solution to this problem was to have a large fire burning at the bottom of one shaft, sucking a draft of fresh air through the mine. Trapdoors ensured that the air circulated properly. Small children, as young as three, had the job of sitting in total blackness, opening and shutting these doors, see Source 50.

SOURCE 49
Miner at work in Wales, about 1900.

SOURCE 50
Hurrier and trapper. A trapper opens the ventilation doors when a tub is pushed through.

Mining reforms

After his success with the Factory Act, Antony Ashley turned his attention to mines reform. Again, a Parliamentary Commission was set up to collect evidence and again a report was published (see Sources 51 and 52). Ashley and his supporters knew how to shock Victorian public opinion. The tiny children left for hours in the dark, the suggestions of immorality (Source 51), were the issues which touched their hearts. Problems of men's working conditions, safety and long hours were not so moving.

Also, we must be careful not to rush to the conclusion that every pit in Britain was like those described here. In fact:

- by the 1840s pit-ponies, pulling coaltubs on rails, had replaced the work done by women like Patience Kershaw (Source 51)
- no women were employed at all in pits in Northumberland, Durham, Cumberland or the Midlands
- only about 5,000 women were employed in mining, out of a total workforce of 150,000
- it was mainly in small, old-fashioned pits that women and children worked.

'I hurry in the clothes I have got on now [trousers and ragged jacket]. The bald place upon my head is made by pushing the corves [tubs of coal – see Source 50]. I hurry [push] the corves a mile and more underground. They weigh three hundredweight. I hurry eleven a day. The getters [men who dig the coal] that I work for are naked except for their caps. The boys take liberties with me sometimes, they pull me about. I am the only girl in the pit. There are about 20 boys and 15 men. I would rather work in mill than coal-pit.'

SOURCE 51
Evidence given by Patience Kershaw, aged 17, to the Mines Commission.

'I have been a trapper [see Source 50] six months. I likes it very much. I get 4 shillings [20p] a week and am quite content. Sometimes I falls asleep; if I'm caught sleeping I gets a hiding with a stick.'

SOURCE 52
Evidence given by Thomas Thew, aged 10, to the Mines Commission.

1. How far does Patience Kershaw (Source 51) push the corves each day?

2. Thomas Thew (Source 52) says he likes the job. Does that mean it is all right for boys of his age to work underground?

3. What does the 1842 Mines Act tell us about Victorian attitudes to: children; women; male miners?

4. Use the sources and information on these pages to write your own report on conditions in coalmines in Britain in the 1840s. What terms would you have put in a Mines Act for that time?

5. Do you think women should be allowed to do any job they want?

The Mines Act, 1842

Nevertheless, as Ashley said: 'The disgust is very great, thank God!' In this mood a Mines Act was passed in 1842. It said that no female and no one under 10 years old could work undergound.

No doubt those who passed the Act expected women now banned from mining to stay at home. But many women did not want – or could not afford – to do this. Mining took place in isolated areas where there were few other jobs to go to. A survey in part of Scotland showed that of 2,400 women miners thrown out of work by the Act, only 200 had found other jobs by 1845. Women in fact continued to work on the surface at coalmines, as Source 53 shows.

SOURCE 53
Pit lasses in Lancashire, late 19th century.

Housing and health: the problem

We saw on pages 16 to 17 that living conditions in the 'walking city' were terribly overcrowded. Whole families lived in just one room or even a shared room. Of 1,462 families surveyed in one parish in London, half only had one bed for the entire family. Houses were built with no toilets. Whole areas of housing had no sewage system.

Typhus, carried by lice, tuberculosis, transmitted from one person's breath to another, and typhoid, spread by drinking polluted water, flourished in these conditions. Source 54 shows the kind of overcrowding still to be found in 1900.

The disease which really made people aware of conditions in cities was cholera. This was a disease new to Britain. It brought sickness, vomiting, diarrhoea and rapid death. In a few months in 1831–1832 32,000 people died. It was followed by further EPIDEMICS in 1848 and 1865–1866. Doctors pointed out the link between bad housing and numerous deaths from cholera (see Source 55).

Ignorance of basic hygiene made matters worse, as Source 56 shows.

> On 26 May the first case of pure cholera occurred in Blue Bell Fold, a small, dirty cul-de-sac containing about 20 houses inhabited by poor families. It lies between the river and an offensive streamlet which carries refuse water from numerous mills and dyehouses.
>
> The first case occurred in a child, two years of age, in perfect health on the preceding day, who became suddenly ill on the morning of the 26th and died at 5 p.m. on the same day.

SOURCE 55
Description of cholera in Leeds in 1833.

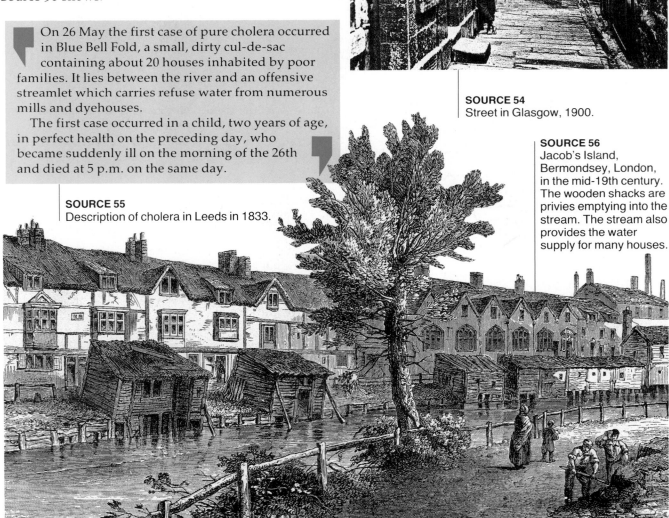

SOURCE 54
Street in Glasgow, 1900.

SOURCE 56
Jacob's Island, Bermondsey, London, in the mid-19th century. The wooden shacks are privies emptying into the stream. The stream also provides the water supply for many houses.

Urban life

Today several museums try to show what 19th century urban life was like. Sources 57, 58 and 59 are photographs from modern museums.

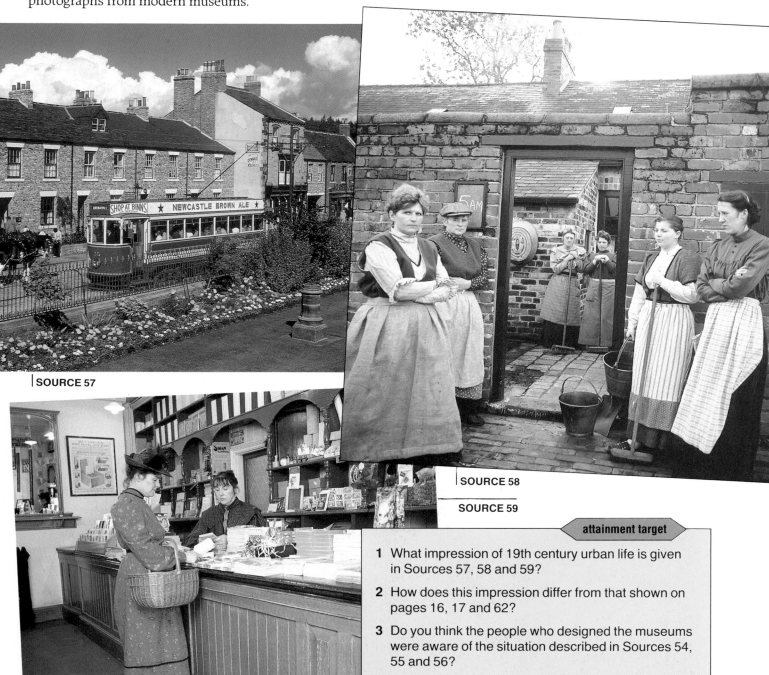

|SOURCE 57

|SOURCE 58

SOURCE 59

attainment target

1 What impression of 19th century urban life is given in Sources 57, 58 and 59?

2 How does this impression differ from that shown on pages 16, 17 and 62?

3 Do you think the people who designed the museums were aware of the situation described in Sources 54, 55 and 56?

4 Do you think the sources on pages 16, 17 and 62 tell the whole story?

5 Which of the two interpretations of city life do you think is:
  a more popular?
  b more truthful?

Why did public health reform take so long?

The late 19th century town shown in Source 54 on page 24 was much healthier than the 'walking city' described on pages 16 to 17. But why did these improvements take so long to achieve?

Opposition to improvement

No one was willing to pay. Better off ratepayers did not live in unhealthy areas of town: why should they pay? People who owned slum houses did not want to pay for improving them. People who sold water (because few houses had their own water supply) did not want to pay to purify it. There were also those who believed, as a matter of principle, that government should not interfere in people's lives. We have met this idea, called 'laissez-faire', before – see Source 44 on page 58.

Local government

Who would do the work? Public health improvement involves water supply, street cleaning and sewage systems. All these things are expensive. They need a proper local government to collect rates and do the work in an organised way. In early 19th century Britain this did not exist: there were lots of separate committees for different things and different parts of town. Their main concern was to keep the rates as low as possible.

Lack of knowledge

What could people do even if they wanted to? The discovery that germs cause disease was not made until 1864. Until then it was generally believed that disease was carried by 'bad air', so getting rid of a bad smell would get rid of the disease.

Cholera

Although there were several common killer diseases, the one which caused British people to pay attention to public health was cholera. The epidemic of 1831 to 1832 killed 32,000, in 1848 53,000 died, in 1854 the epidemic claimed 13,000 lives and in 1865 to 1866 there were 20,000 victims.

After the outbreak of 1831 to 1832 some towns, in a panic, set up a Board of Health to investigate the problem and suggest solutions. However, once the cholera had died away, all the obstacles listed above were raised. By the mid-1830s things were back to normal. It was going to need a more persistent approach.

Edwin Chadwick

Edwin Chadwick (pictured in Source 60) was concerned that the poor were costing the country too much. In the 1830s he had led a complete overhaul of the Poor Law. As a Poor Law Commissioner he became interested in public health. He believed that bad health caused poverty: if people were ill they could not work and so became poor and a burden to others. He began to collect information on public health. His 'Report on the Sanitary Condition of the Labouring Population' was published in 1842. He claimed that 'The annual loss from filth is greater than the loss from death or wounds in any wars in which this country has been engaged'. Over 10,000 copies were given away, 20,000 were sold. Chadwick called on Parliament to act. Parliament, as we have

SOURCE 60
Edwin Chadwick.

attainment target

1 Describe the factors which prevented the country from dealing with its public health problems before 1850.

2 Did these factors disappear after 1850? Did new factors appear which made the country more ready to tackle public health reform?

already seen in this depth study, tried to delay things by setting up a Royal Commission. Chadwick was on it and his diary records their work, see Source 61.

Then, in 1848, cholera returned. The government passed a Public Health Act. It set up a General Board of Health with Chadwick as one of its members. Towns could set up their own local Boards of Health to deal with health issues.

As Source 62 indicates, opposition continued. Chadwick was sacked in 1854 and the General Board of Health wound up in 1858.

The 1875 Public Health Act

However, things were changing from the 1850s:
- public opinion and the press began to show their disgust at the situation, see Source 63
- medical knowledge was increasing, see Source 64
- in 1867 many working men in towns got the vote: politicians now had to pay attention to their needs.

The 1875 Public Health Act, unlike the 1848 Act, made it compulsory, not voluntary, for local government to lay sewers and drains, build reservoirs, parks, swimming baths and public conveniences and appoint a Medical Officer of Health and Sanitary Inspectors.

> I persuaded the Commissioners to go and see conditions for themselves. My annual holiday was taken up in visiting some of the worst parts of the worst towns. Dr Playfair has been knocked up by it and is seriously ill. Mr Smith has had dysentery. At Bristol Sir Henry de la Bèche had to stand at the end of an alley and vomit while Dr Playfair was looking at overflowing privies.

SOURCE 61
An extract from Edwin Chadwick's diary.

'We prefer to take our chance with cholera than be bullied into health. There is nothing a man hates so much as being cleansed against his will or having his floors swept, his hall whitewashed and his thatch forced to give way to slate. It is a fact that many people have died from a good washing.'

SOURCE 62
An extract from *The Times*, 1854.

SOURCE 63
'A drop of London water': a cartoon from *Punch* in the 1850s.

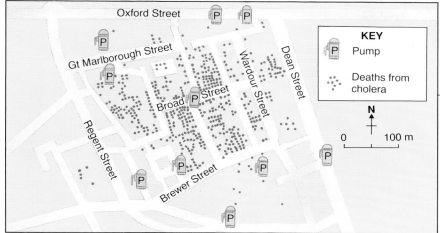

SOURCE 64
Dr John Snow detected a link between cholera and polluted drinking water. When cholera broke out again in 1854 he plotted deaths in one area of London on a map which also showed where the water-pumps were. No new deaths from cholera were reported once Dr Snow had ordered the removal of the handle from the Broad Street pump.

In this depth study, we shall see how the changes you have read about in the rest of this book affected women. It deals first with women's working lives and how far these were changed by industrialisation. It goes on to look at women's roles in the family and at how, over the 19th century, women gradually improved their position.

Women and work

For centuries, women worked at home. As well as childcare, cooking, washing and cleaning, tending vegetable gardens, raising pigs and chickens, milking cows, carrying heavy buckets of drinking water and nursing people who were old or sick, their tasks included all kinds of craft work – anything to help keep their families alive.

Many women worked in the textile industry: carding wool, spinning thread, making lace or knitting stockings. (If you look back to Source 3 on page 5 you can see a picture of all the women in one family busily working at home.) Other women worked alongside their husbands and children in a home-based craft business or, if they lived in the countryside, did seasonal work on farms (Source 65). In towns, there were extra chances to make a living. A woman might take in lodgers, do washing, run a market stall, or, like the woman in Source 66, turn one room of her home into a shop.

Factory work

As we saw on pages 5 to 9, during the 19th century, traditional ways of working were revolutionised by the introduction of machines. Now, instead of working at home, men, women and children went out to work in huge new factories. As Source 67 shows, the textile industry still relied on women's labour, but women also worked in the steel and pottery industries, and in coalmines.

	Numbers of women employed in textile industries	
	1850	1874
Cotton	189,000	292,000
Wool	82,000	135,000
Flax/jute	48,000	120,000
Silk	30,000	32,000

SOURCE 67
Men and women employed in textile industries, mid-19th century.

'[Women's] labour is considered essential for the cultivation of the land. The work of two women is usually required for every 75 acres. . . . Their labour consists in the various operations of cleaning the land, picking up stones, weeds etc; turnip hoeing, hay making and harvest work, rooting and shawing, that is, cleaning turnips; barn work with the threshing and winnowing machines, filling dung carts, turning dung heaps, spreading the dung and sowing artificial manure; turnip cutting in winter for sheep etc and occasionally driving carts or harrowing . . . . The Northumbrian women who do these kinds of labour are physically a splendid race; their strength is such that they can vie [compete] with the men in carrying sacks of corn.'

SOURCE 65
Government report into women's and children's work on farms, 1867 to 1868.

SOURCE 66
Woman shopkeeper in Glasgow, 1790.

Working conditions and pay

What was this new work like? Nineteenth century opinions varied. Source 68 presents a positive image; Source 69 reveals a much grimmer view. Certainly, factory work gave some young, unmarried women, living at home, the chance to earn more than ever before, working alongside loyal colleagues and free from their parents' control. But conditions in many factories and mines were appalling, and, as we can see from Source 70, women were always paid much less than men.

Why were women so badly paid? Partly because women – however skilled – were rarely appointed to better-paid jobs as managers. To 19th century men, it seemed 'natural' that only men should be managers. But there were other reasons, too: traditionally, women's work had never been as highly valued or as highly paid as work done by men. This custom may have originated at a time when male physical strength – useful when clearing land or felling trees – was essential for a community's survival. But now machines were run on steam power, and, anyway, Source 65 reminds us that many women were just as strong as men.

Women's pay was also kept low as a result of the Trades Unions' campaigns for a 'family wage'. Male union leaders believed that every working man should be paid enough to support his wife and children. Their efforts did help to ensure that ordinary men got a decent wage for the work they did but they had disastrous consequences for women. In comparison with men, who were 'family breadwinners', women and their work seemed somehow less important. People were encouraged to think of women, like children, as being 'naturally' dependent on men.

> Not only are women frequently paid half or less than half for doing work as well and as quickly as men, but skilled women whose labour requires delicacy of touch, the result of long training as well as thoughtfulness, receive from 11 shillings to 16 or 17 shillings a week, while the roughest unskilled labour of a man is worth at least 18 shillings.

SOURCE 70
From a campaigning article in a magazine, written by Women's Trade Union leader Emma Paterson in 1874.

Women alone

Not all families had a male breadwinner. Husbands died or were injured in industrial accidents; they became sick and unable to work, or simply deserted their wives. And many men did not manage to earn a full 'family wage'. Few women with young children wanted to go out to work (you can find out about 19th century views of motherhood on page 73). But they had no choice. They had to work to support themselves and their families, or else they would starve. As you can see from Source 71, many (male) factory owners actually preferred to employ women like these; they would put up with the lowest wages and the worst conditions for fear of losing their jobs.

attainment target

Use Sources 65 to 71 and Sources 2 and 3 on pages 4 and 5.

1 Which sources from this book tell you about how industrialisation changed women's working lives?

2 How useful are these sources for this line of enquiry?

3 Choose four sources from this book that tell you about women's work in industry. Write your own captions to each of them. Add a paragraph explaining why you chose these four.

4 What do Sources 67, 68 and 71 tell you about women workers in the textile industry? Write a paragraph, drawing your own conclusions about the good and bad side of their working lives.

> You'd easy know a weaver
> When she goes down to town,
> With her long yellow hair
> And her apron hanging down.
> With her scissors tied before her
> Or her scissors in her hand,
> You'll easy know a weaver
> For she always gets her man.

SOURCE 68
A 19th century folk-song.

> 'I have wrought in the bowels of the earth 33 years. Have been married 23 years, and had nine children; six are alive; three died of typhus a few years since; have had two dead born. [I think] they were so from the oppressive work. . . . I have always been obliged to work below till forced to go home to bear the bairn, and so have all the other women. We return as soon as able, never longer than 10 or 12 days.'

SOURCE 69
Description of her life of work in the mines, given by Jane Peacock Watson, aged 40, in 1842.

> [I prefer to employ] married females, especially those who have families at home dependent on them for support; they are attentive, docile, more so than unmarried females, and are compelled to use their utmost exertions to procure the necessities of life.

SOURCE 71
Comment by a factory owner, 1844.

The choices for working women

The 1851 Census revealed that there were around two million working women – excluding farmworkers and full-time mothers – in England and Wales. One million of them were servants (Source 72). Usually, girls began work aged 12 or 14 and lived in their employers' homes until they married (on average, at around 25). If they did not marry, or manage to find other work (there were not many alternatives), they would remain a servant for life (Source 73).

Class of work	Age	Average annual wage for female servants
Between maid	19	£10.70
Scullerymaid	19	£13.00
Kitchenmaid	20	£15.00
Nurse-housemaid	21 to 25	£16.00
General domestic	21 to 25	£14.60
Housemaid	21 to 25	£16.20
Nurse	25 to 30	£20.10
Parlourmaid	25 to 30	£20.60
Laundrymaid	25 to 30	£23.60
Cook	25 to 30	£20.20
Lady's maid	30 to 35	£24.70
Cook-housekeeper	over 40	£35.60
Housekeeper	over 40	£52.20

SOURCE 73
Servants' wages, 1899. What does this table tell you about the opportunities for 'promotion' open to young women servants?

SOURCE 74
Mother and children assembling matchboxes at home, around 1900.

SOURCE 72
Women domestic servants worked long hours doing heavy, dirty tasks.

Low pay, low status

Women servants' wages were very low. However, their uniforms and board and lodging were provided, and they were given half a day off each week as well as time to attend church on Sundays. Servants had to follow strict rules of conduct. They could not sit down or speak first in their employers' presence; they might even be made to change their name for a plain, simple one (like a dog's) if their employer said so.

Running a home

It was a hard life being a servant; the hours were long, and the work was exhausting. But in fact, all married women worked, all the time, to run their family's home. On page 70 you can see how three very different women spent their days.

The poorest of the poor

Factory workers, domestic servants and working men's wives all endured a standard of living that many people would find unacceptable today. But they were fortunate when compared with women who had no regular income. Some were too old or ill or even too young to work – they became street traders, selling matches or posies of flowers, and begging when no one would buy. They scavenged for rags and collected dog-dung (used to process leather).

Some industries – especially dressmaking – relied on skilled but poorly-paid home-workers (Source 74), who might have to work day and night all one week, then starve, without work, the next.

It is perhaps not surprising that a few women looked for other ways to make money. They turned to crime, perhaps as pickpockets, or became prostitutes. Some women worked in prostitution part-time when they could not earn enough from their usual work. Source 75 shows two glamorous 'ladies' who served men from the upper classes and even the royal family, but, in reality, prostitution was a dangerous, degrading job. It was also illegal. If caught, women (but not their male clients) were punished. They might be attacked or even killed while working, and there was a constant risk of disease.

---

1 What job choices were open to women in the 19th century?

2 How did these differ from those open to men?

3 Make a list of all the jobs described on pages 66 to 69. What were the good and bad points of each? Think about: pay, hours of work, time off, how hard the work was, other plus or minus points.

4 How much choice did women have in their work?

SOURCE 75
Rich, fashionable London prostitutes, 1871.

SOURCE 76
Women's typing class at the Blackheath Road Institute.

New careers

Towards the end of the 19th century, a whole new range of jobs became available to women (Source 76). Shops recruited women assistants, as factories produced an ever-increasing number of goods to be sold. New inventions, such as the typewriter, led to more office jobs for well-educated girls. And, thanks to the tireless efforts of women campaigners (see pages 74 to 75), women could now train for professions like medicine, teaching and the civil service. Women welcomed these new opportunities. But there was a price to be paid. Most employers insisted that women resign as soon as they got married, so women had to choose between having a husband and children, or devoting a single, CELIBATE life to their career.

A servant's day

6.00 am Gets up, washes, dresses neatly.

6.30 am Cleans fireplaces, carries out ashes, carries in coal, lays and lights fires.

7.00 am Empties ashes from kitchen stove and refills with coal. Puts washing

7.30 am water on to boil. Eats breakfast. Prepares breakfasts, lays dining

8.00 am table, sets out clean clothes, cleans shoes. Carries up hot water for

8.30 am washing to bedrooms; removes and empties chamber pots. Carries down

9.00 am used washing water.

9.30 am Clears away breakfasts, washes up, tidies dining room. Cleans kitchen.

10.00 am Makes beds, sweeps bedrooms. Dusts furniture and tidies rooms.

10.30 am Answers front door to callers; takes in deliveries. Serves morning coffee.

11.00 am Cooks lunch; lays dining table.

11.30 am

12.00 pm

12.30 pm

1.00 pm Serves lunch. Eats own lunch in kitchen. Clears away lunch, washes

1.30 pm up, tidies kitchen.

2.00 pm Weekly tasks like cleaning windows, tidying cupboards.

2.30 pm

3.00 pm

3.30 pm

4.00 pm Makes and serves afternoon tea. Washes up afterwards.

4.30 pm

5.00 pm Stokes kitchen range. Starts to make dinner. Lights fires in dining room and

5.30 pm sitting room. Lays dining table.

6.00 pm

6.30 pm

7.00 pm Serves dinner. Has own dinner in kitchen. Clears away dinner, washes

7.30 pm up, tidies kitchen. Locks up.

8.00 pm

8.30 pm

9.00 pm Sits in kitchen to read newspaper, write letters home, or knit and sew.

9.30 pm

10.00 pm Goes to bed.

10.30 pm

11.00 pm

11.30 pm

12.00 am

A working-class wife's day

Gets up, feeds baby.

Wakes up five other children, washes and dresses them.

Makes and serves husband's breakfast – cooked fish and tea. Feeds baby.

Husband goes to work. Gives children breakfast of bread and dripping. Sends children to school; eats own breakfast. Washes up.

Brings chamber pots downstairs; empties them outside. Fills buckets with fresh water from outside tap and takes them upstairs. Makes beds. Washes baby; dresses him in clean clothes. Feeds him; puts him to bed. Sweeps bedroom; scrubs stairs and passage. Goes to shops to buy food.

Children come home from school. Cooks and gives them lunch; feeds baby. Sends children back to school.

Eats leftovers from lunch. Washes up; scrubs kitchen. Empties ashes from fireplace, carries dirty washing-up water downstairs. Takes buckets of fresh water upstairs. Feeds baby.

Washes herself; sits down to mend clothes. Children come home from school, gives them their tea. Eats bread and butter.

Washes up tea things. Feeds baby. Continues mending clothes.

Husband comes home from work. Cooks and serves his tea.

Puts younger children to bed.

Tidies up, washes husband's tea things, cleans kitchen. Puts older children to bed. Feeds baby.

Gets supper for husband. Mends clothes.

Feeds baby; settles him to sleep.

Goes to bed.

An upper-middle-class woman's day

Gets up, has warm bath, dresses.

Goes to nursery to check that maid is getting children up and dressed. Has breakfast. Chats with husband, children and any guests.

Goes to kitchen to give daily orders for housework and gardening tasks. Inspects kitchen; discusses menus.

Inspects bedrooms. Visits children in schoolroom; discusses them with nanny and governess.

Writes letters to friends and contacts. Drinks coffee in drawing room. Walks in garden, reads or plays the piano.

Plans seating and table decorations for dinner party.

Eats lunch with husband.

Changes into best day-dress.

Driven off by coachman for short visits or 'morning calls' to friends and neighbours. Such visits are very important for making useful social contacts and furthering her husband's or children's careers.

Back home. Checks up on kitchen. Watches children having tea in nursery; reads them a story.

Inspects dining and drawing rooms.

Changes into evening wear. Says goodnight to youngest children.

Greets dinner guests.

Dinner is served. As hostess, she will be judged on the success of the evening.

After dinner, the women go to the drawing room.

Men join the women. Everyone drinks coffee, talks and listens to piano and singing.

Guests leave. Undresses (with help of maid).

Looks at children asleep in nursery. Goes to bed.

Women and families

Source 77 shows an illustration from a 19th century woman's magazine of a sweet, shy bride, surrounded by family and friends at a lavish wedding 'breakfast'. It reflects one – very romantic – 19th century view of marriage. Stories in magazines taught young girls to believe that their wedding would be 'the happiest day of their life'. For some women, this may have been true; all girls hoped to marry for love, and many did find a partner they were happy to live with for the rest of their life. But there was another 19th century view of marriage: girls were also taught – by their mothers and grandmothers, as well as by novels and newspapers – that 'any man was better than none'.

Was this really true? In some ways, yes. As we have seen, women's wages were low; a woman could not earn enough to pay for rent, food and clothes for herself. She needed a husband to survive.

SOURCE 77
From *Cassells Family Magazine*, 1867.

Alternatives to marriage

The alternatives were working as a servant (or, if a middle-class woman, as a governess – Source 78), or living at home with her parents as an 'old maid'. This might be miserable and was always shameful (Source 79). It was also very restricting. Unlike today, there were many things that a single woman could not do alone. She could not go to a dance, concert, café, restaurant, pub, theatre or even a museum or art gallery by herself. It was unsafe to go out alone at night. Even in daytime, she could not wander round the streets or go to the shops – although working-class women could go out to buy food – without a man or another 'respectable' woman, preferably older, to accompany her.

SOURCE 78
Being a governess was exhausting and often very lonely work.

'It was the aim of every girl to get married, and those who did not were looked on with pity.'

SOURCE 79
Recollection by Grace Foakes (born 1901).

ACTIVITY

1 Suppose you visited the three women (in the table opposite) at about 10.00 am one morning and 7.30 pm one evening. What would be going on?

2 Which would you prefer to be: the servant or the working-class housewife? Which of these two worked hardest? Which one was better fed? Which one was more independent?

3 Do you envy the life of the upper-middle-class woman? Do you think it was easy? What is there about her life you would not like?

Love or duty?

Many people also believed that it was a woman's duty to get married. She was designed (by God) to look after the needs of others: that is, men and children. She was too delicate to face the rough, dirty, working world. Her place was in the home. Conveniently, this rule could be ignored for working-class women and servants, but, as Sources 80 and 81 reveal, it was held by men from all social groups.

Many 19th century women questioned this view, but they had little power to change it. So they made the best of things. For upper-class women, this meant taking a pride in supporting their husband's careers, by advising and encouraging them and by playing a leading role in 'polite society' (Source 82). For working-class women, it meant being uncomplainingly loyal (Source 83), even if they were treated badly by their husbands.

> This is the true nature of home – it is a place of peace, the shelter, not only from all injury, but from all terror, doubt and division. . . .
> And wherever a true wife is, this home is always round her.

SOURCE 80
Women and home in the words of John Ruskin, a 19th century writer.

'Wives should be in their proper sphere at home, instead of being dragged into the competition of livelihood with the great strong men of the world.'

SOURCE 81
Resolution at the Trades Union Congress, 1877.

SOURCE 82
A grand party arranged by a leading 'political hostess' to further her husband's career.

SOURCE 83
A working-class couple with their children, photographed in 1912.

The 'perfect mother'

As well as being an 'angel in the house' a 19th century woman was also expected to be 'a perfect mother', devoting her life to her children. Queen Victoria, who had nine children, provided the nation's model for the ideal mother. For most of the 19th century family size increased as a result of higher birth-rates and falling rates of INFANT MORTALITY (Source 84). Upper-class women could afford to pay for nursemaids and nannies to help care for their children. They could also afford big houses and gardens with space for children to play, children's clothes and laundry, toys, books and plenty of food.

Working-class women were not so lucky (see Source 85). For them, a large family was often not a matter of choice; contraceptives were available, but were too expensive for ordinary people to buy. More children meant more work, and every new baby – however loved and welcome – was an extra mouth to feed. Working-class mothers often went hungry so that their husbands and children would have enough to eat.

Year	Percentage of children born in that year dying by the age of 5
1801	32%
1831	27%
1861	26%
1891	24%

SOURCE 84
Falling death rates among children in the 19th century.

SOURCE 86
A girl pupil being taught housework at a state school, 1907.

Dissatisfaction

Sources 86 and 87 show us how girls were taught to perform the duties of wife, mother, and family provider. Many working-class girls stayed away from school altogether when they were needed to help their mothers with domestic work and childcare at home. Others abandoned school to supplement family incomes by selling firewood, sewing or doing seasonal farm work. However, as you will see on pages 74 to 75, a growing number of 19th century women felt dissatisfied with the self-sacrificing roles they were expected to play.

SOURCE 85
Working-class mothers struggled to rear their children in conditions like this.

'My education, and that of my sister, were scarcely discussed at all. . . . A girl's education at that time seemed to have for its prime object the art of 'making home attractive' – presumably to male relatives.'

SOURCE 87
From *My Own Story*, by the campaigner Emmeline Pankhurst, published in 1914.

1 What were the lives of married women supposed to be like?

2 Why was it difficult for working-class women to live up to this ideal?

Legal rights?

Marriage was for life. Until 1870 and 1882, a married woman could not own property (houses, clothes, books etc), even if this was inherited from her parents. It all belonged to her husband. Until 1839, she had no custody of her children. Until 1891, she had no right to live apart from her husband, and, until 1878, no right to claim maintenance for her children or herself. Divorce was almost impossible before 1857; it required a vastly expensive and humiliating court case, and divorced women – like criminals and prostitutes – became social outcasts. And, until 1891, a wife could not leave her husband because of adultery, though he could divorce her if she was unfaithful to him.

Changing the world

Many women were unhappy about their unequal status. But most were too busy working, earning a living and raising a family, to be able to campaign for change. However, a growing group of mostly middle-class women, who did have spare time and money, devoted their lives to working for women's rights. You can read about just some of them, and their achievements, in the sources and timechart on these pages. The results of their campaigns still influence women's lives today.

SOURCE 88
Contraception: Marie Stopes (1880-1958) and Annie Besant (1847-1933, above) campaigned for contraception information to be available, at low cost, to all women, not just to the rich.

SOURCE 89
Sex discrimination: Josephine Butler (1828-1906) campaigned against laws which treated prostitutes as criminals but let their male clients go free.

SOURCE 90
Equal rights: Mary Wollstonecraft (1759-1797, above) and Harriet Taylor Mill (1807-1858) wrote influential books demanding equal rights for women.

SOURCE 91
Literature: novelists like Mrs (Elizabeth) Gaskell (1810-1865), 'George Eliot' (Mary Anne Evans, 1819-1880, above), and editors like Bessie Parkes (1828-1925), raised issues about women's rights and women's roles in many of their publications.

SOURCE 92
Professional women: the 'Langham Place Group' of women, led by Barbara Leigh Smith Bodichon (1827-1891), campaigned for women's right to work in male-dominated professions, and for equal property rights.

SOURCE 93
Trade Unions: women like Emma Paterson (1848-1886) demanded the right to join male-dominated Trade Unions, and campaigned for women workers' welfare and rights.

SOURCE 94
Education: pioneers like Frances Mary Buss (1827-1894) and Dorothea Beale (1831-1906, above) founded schools for girls where they could get the same academic education as boys and have the chance to go to university and into professional careers. Emily Davis (1830-1921) founded the first women's university college.

SOURCE 95
Medicine: Florence Nightingale (1820-1910) and Mary Seacole (1805-1881, above) reformed nursing practice during the Crimean War (1853-1856). Later, Nightingale worked to improve nurse training. Elizabeth Garrett Anderson (1836-1917), campaigned for the right for women to train as doctors.

SOURCE 96
The vote: peaceful 'suffragist' campaigners, like Millicent Garrett Fawcett (1847-1929) and militant 'suffragette' activists, like Emmeline Pankhurst (1858-1928, above), campaigned for women's right to vote on equal terms with men.

1830s
First women's Trade Unions founded; women mostly kept out of men's Unions.

1842-1847
Laws protect women working in factories and mines, but ignore poorly-paid homeworkers and street traders.

1848-1849
First training colleges for women governesses, Queen's and Bedford, later joined with London University.

1857
Ordinary women can now get a divorce, although not on equal terms with men. Previously, only the rich could afford divorce.

1860-1870
Women begin to be accepted for office work. They campaign for the right to train for other professions as well.

1869
Single women ratepayers (that is, property-owners) can vote in Town Council elections.

1870s
First women teachers in state primary schools.

1873
Girton College, Cambridge, founded, the first college for women at Britain's ancient universities, but women can't take degrees until 1948.

1880s
Most male Trade Unions now accept women members.

1888
Women can now vote in County Council elections.

1897
National Union of Women's Suffrage Societies ('Suffragists') founded by Millicent Fawcett, to run large-scale but peaceful campaign for votes for women.

TIMELINE

1830

1840

1850

1860

1870

1880

1890

1839
Women gain rights of custody over their children under 7, and rights of access to older children. Previously, they had none.

1847
English Female Political Association begins to campaign for votes for women.

1850
First academic school for girls opens in London.

1860
First training school for nurses opens in London, run by Florence Nightingale.

1867
Elizabeth Garrett Anderson becomes first woman doctor, through a legal loophole, soon closed.

1870
Married women can now keep everything they owned before they got married. Previously, a married woman's possessions legally belonged to her husband.

1876
Women can now legally train as doctors.

1878
London University is the first to allow women to take degrees.

1878-1882
Deserted and separated wives can now claim maintenance from their husbands for themselves and their children.

1890s
Radical campaigns for votes for women in big industrial cities led by Eva Gore-Booth, Cissie Foley.

1894
First women Parish Councillors and District Councillors elected.

Growing up in modern Britain

Before we turn to any history, think about what is it like growing up as a young person in modern Britain. You probably feel that some things are good, others not so good. Does where you live affect your answer? Or who you mix with? Or how much money you have? Or how much there is to do? Do other factors come into play – like news about the wider environment? Or the chances of you achieving your ambitions?

How do you view Britain's position in the world today? Do you think of Britain as a powerful nation? In pairs consider: its industrial strength; its military strength; how it is viewed by other countries.

SOURCE 1
Young people today.

The new century: 2000 and 1900

Are you looking forward to living as an adult in the 21st century? The turn of the century celebrations should be something special. One hundred years ago young people also looked forward to the start of a new century. Source 2 describes how some people greeted this century in 1900.

> The first stroke of midnight crashes through the frosty air and is hailed by . . . a roar of jubilation. The . . . other strokes are all lost in the . . . cheering . . . Hurrah! The twentieth century has dawned.

SOURCE 2
From the *Daily Mail*, 1 January 1900.

SOURCE 3
Map showing the British Empire in 1886.

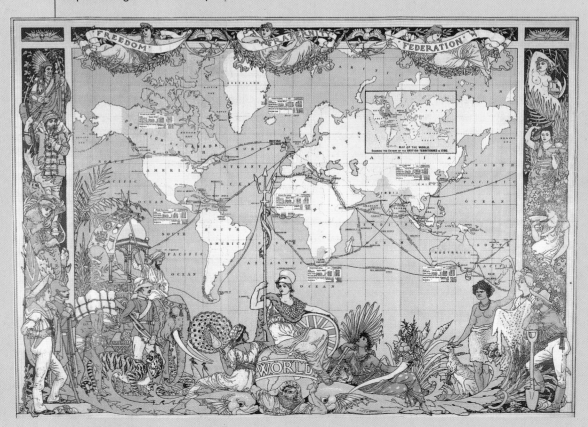

What were young people in 1900 taught about in school?

From 1880 onwards all children aged 5 to 10 had to attend school. Learning the 3Rs (reading, writing and arithmetic) took up most of their time. Young people were also taught a range of attitudes:

- to respect the monarch. By 1900 Queen Victoria had reigned for 63 years;
- to respect the British constitution and its system of elections;
- that Britain was the 'Workshop of the World';
- that Britain's greatest asset was an empire 'upon which the sun never sets' covering one quarter of the earth's surface;
- that the 372 million people in the empire were 'lucky' to live under Britain's 'civilising' influence;
- that Britain was the most powerful nation on earth.

How did all this affect classroom routines?

Most classrooms would have a large world map such as Source 3, showing the extent of the empire. Some other clues may be seen from the headteacher's comments seen in Source 4. Source 5 might have found itself in a playground swop among children keen to collect such postcards.

Children were taught that Britain's position as 'top nation' was the natural result of its recent past. The phrase 'Workshop of the World' had been used back in the 19th century, as you saw in the first part of this book.

Source 6 provides a link between *Britain 1750–1900* and *The 20th Century World* by showing how people at the time thought about the history of Britain. It tells us a good deal about the attitudes of the time, many of which were still held in 1900.

---

1 Use the Copy sheet in the Teacher's Notes to record your ideas about growing up in modern Britain.

2 Find out what is meant by a 'millenium'.

3 What did you learn in the first part of this book (Britain 1750-1900) about why Britain was known as the 'Workshop of the World'.

4 Study Source 3 and compare it with a map of the world today. What has happened?

5 Find some examples of the British attitudes to colonial peoples shown in Source 6.

'1914

May 15   Practice of Empire Music will be taken each day, 3.30 to 4.00 with IVA, V, VI

May 22   Empire Celebration this morning and half term holiday this afternoon.'

SOURCE 4
From the Priory Street School, Gateshead, daily book.

READY !

SOURCE 5
Postcard of 1900.

'Once the power of steam had been discovered, there seemed no end to all its uses. It could move engines, it could turn machines. The English were among the first people to discover the power of steam and they went on inventing new machines to help their increasing work. I want you to understand the great importance of these machines and the great increase of commerce and wealth they brought to England.

Australia . . . is largely a sheep farming colony and meat is sent frozen all the way home for us to eat. The Australians like to feel they are still part of their beloved homeland. They could become independent nations like France and Germany, but I am glad to say that our colonies are not like that. They would rather be part of our great British Empire, and are ready, in case of danger, to take their places by our side.'

SOURCE 6
An extract from *Little Arthur's History of England* by Lady Maria Calcutt, 1835.

Evidence of empire

This section is designed so you can follow up any one of the three lines of enquiry in the activities with your own investigation.

Can you name any colonies which Britain still owns? As we approach the 21st century there are only a few left. Nevertheless, even in the 1980s and 1990s British overseas territories have 'hit the headlines' for very different reasons.

Seeking out the legacy of empire

The Boer War, 1899–1902

This is a case study to give you some ideas as to how to proceed with the activity on page 79. It takes the topic of the Boer War, which broke out in 1899 between Britain and the Boer farmers of South Africa. Sources 8 and 9 show some evidence of this conflict which still exists in the built environment of Tyneside.

Source 8 is a street sign that commemorates a major event in the Boer War. The town of Mafeking and its British troops led by Colonel Baden-Powell (see Source 9), was surrounded by Boer forces for seven months. Eventually in May 1900 the siege was broken. The 'Relief of Mafeking' was greeted with two days and nights of wild rejoicing throughout Britain. It was seen as a symbol that the war, which had started badly for Britain, was going better. In celebration, many newly built streets in towns and cities were named after the event and key British commanders such as the Commander-in-Chief, Lord Kitchener.

SOURCE 7
Chris Patten, Governor of Hong Kong, 1994.

the activity on page 79

ACTIVITY

The Falklands War, 1982

The Falkland Islands are in the remote South Atlantic. The war in the Falklands in 1982 is a good example of how Britain is still willing to protect its colonies from aggression. When Argentine forces invaded the islands in 1982, a military Task Force was despatched. After a short war, the islands and its people were returned to British control. Such actions had been repeated countless times in Britain's colonial past.

Interview your teacher (or another adult) about their memories of the Falklands War. Note down the main point of what he or she says. How did your interviewee react when:

a the Argentinians invaded the Falklands

b a British task force set sail

c British submarines and aircraft attacked Argentinian positions

d British ships were sunk

e British troops forced the Argentinians to surrender

f the Falklands became British territory again.

Study your interview notes. Try to decide what the overall attitude of your interviewee was to the British recapture of the Falkland Islands. Were they for or against the use of military force? Did they think a peaceful solution might have been found?

ACTIVITY

Hong Kong, 1997

More recently, Hong Kong in South-East Asia has been much in the news. British since 1842, part of this wealthy trading territory has been leased by Britain since 1898 and is due to be handed back to neighbouring China in 1997. Source 7 shows the last British Governor of Hong Kong on official duties.

Compile a file of newspaper items, magazine articles relating to the Chinese take-over of Hong Kong in 1997.

As Source 10 reveals, the Boer War did not end without casualties. This is a memorial to men of the Northumberland Regiments who died in the Boer War. Total British casualties were 21,000, though two-thirds of the deaths were the result of illness and disease. Stubborn Boer fighters, such as those seen in Source 11, mostly avoided pitched battles. They fought a GUERRILLA war of raids and ambushes in their familiar terrain. Against such tactics, the British troops struggled despite their superior numbers. Eventually after two years and seven months, Boer leaders were forced to surrender and accept British colonial rule.

The poor showing by the British army early in the war caused concern. The army's organisation, strategies and tactics, and the men's levels of fitness were all criticised. As a result, measures to improve the army's efficiency were put in place after the Boer War. By 1914, events were to prove that this programme of military improvements was well timed.

SOURCE 8
Mafeking Street, Gateshead.

SOURCE 9
Baden-Powell Street, Gateshead.

SOURCE 10
War memorial to those in the Northumberland Regiments who died in the Boer War.

SOURCE 11
Three generations of Boer fighters, from a 15-year old to his 65-year old grandfather.

ACTIVITY

As you saw in Source 3 on page 76, the British Empire was at its grandest at the end of the 19th century. Its legacy is likely to exist in various forms around where you live. The case study on page 79 gives some examples from Tyneside. You could undertake an enquiry into the evidence for the British Empire in your local community.

Contents

The 20th Century World

attainment target

This symbol appears with questions which are targeted at the attainment target for history. At the end of Year 9 you will be given a level in history on the basis of how well you have answered these questions.

Some questions are about how much you know about different periods in the past: how people lived and what they believed. Others are about how things change through history and why these changes happen.

People are always trying to describe the past and sometimes they say different things. You will be asked about these differences and why they occur.

We find out about the past from historical sources. You will be asked about how we can use these sources to reach conclusions about the past.

Introduction

The picture below was taken in September 1939 and shows one of the first activities of the Second World War. In the First World War bombing raids killed 1,413 people. By the 1930s bombers were much bigger. The government feared that the bombing of British cities would be so heavy that thousands of people would be killed. They therefore arranged for children like those in the picture, pregnant women, mothers with children and disabled people to be evacuated from target areas, like cities, to safe, rural areas. Over four days one and a half million people were evacuated.

This was obviously a tremendous upheaval in these people's lives. Some returned home fairly quickly, but others stayed in the country throughout the war. Their lives were never the same again.

This book is about the two world wars and the changes they brought to people's lives. It often has to focus on politicians and great international events, but do not forget that these events affected the lives of ordinary people, whether they wanted to be involved or not. In previous centuries wars only affected a small number of people. In the 20th century, wars and other great events cannot be avoided so easily. You will find out why in this book.

AIMS

The aim of the first part of this unit is to give an overview of the First World War, or the Great War as it was called. We will look at which countries were involved, why it started in 1914 and where it was fought. We will also look at the nature of the fighting and what the effects of the war were at home. The unit then goes on to a depth study of the Western Front in the First World War, based on the real life experiences of one British soldier.

The First World War

The causes of the Great War

On 10 February 1906 King Edward VII of Great Britain launched the most powerful warship the world had ever seen, HMS *Dreadnought* (Source 1). Naval experts believed that *Dreadnought* would make all other ships out of date, but many others feared that it only served to fuel the naval building race between Britain and Germany.

With its vast overseas empire to protect, Britain's Royal Navy was the key to its control of the world's oceans. Yet, since the turn of the century the German Kaiser's intention to develop the strength of the German fleet was seen as an increasing threat. By 1908, Germany had launched its own dreadnought battleship, SMS *Westfalen*. As the two powers built up their fleets, the naval arms race and tension gathered speed (Source 2).

The naval race was only one example of pre-war rivalry between the great powers of Europe. It can be seen as one long-term cause for the outbreak of the Great War. But this, alone, cannot explain why the war began. The outbreak was based on a combination of causes. Some, like the naval race, were long term, others were more short-term ones.

There were many rivalries between nations in the pre-war years. France had lost valuable land to Germany in 1871 and wanted revenge. Austria-Hungary and Russia were competing for power, especially over the Balkan area of south-eastern Europe.

Germany and Italy had only emerged as new nations in 1871. Germany in particular was anxious to assert its power and build up an overseas empire to match older-established colonial nations. Other peoples in central and eastern Europe wanted independence for themselves. Nationalism was feared by the leaders of old sprawling empires like Austria-Hungary and Turkey.

SOURCE 1
HMS *Dreadnought*. It was the largest, fastest battleship afloat at the time.

Naval Race	Numbers of Battleships/ Battle cruisers built yearly	
	Germany	Britain
1906	0	1
1909	3	3
1913	5	8
Total by 1914	24	38

SOURCE 2
Resources of the British and German navies.

Alliances

Countries tried to protect themselves against possible enemies by promising military assistance to each other if they were attacked. A system of agreements, creating two 'armed camps' in Europe had been set up well before 1914 as Source 3 shows. This structure of alliances, together with the arms race, meant that a single event could escalate into war. Friends would 'fall in' against foes in an automatic way.

Ferdinand and Sarajevo

Nationalist rivalries between ethnic groups in the Balkans – the Serbs, Croats and Bosnians – erupted into a long civil war in 1991. Nationalist feelings were equally strong in 1914, when the people of Bosnia, mainly Serbs, were ruled as part of the vast Austro-Hungarian empire.

On 28 June 1914, the Bosnian capital, Sarajevo, played host to a royal visit from Archduke Franz Ferdinand and his wife Countess Sophie. The Archduke was heir to the throne of the Austro-Hungarian empire. Crowds of people thronged the streets of Sarajevo to cheer the royal couple, but among them were Bosnians who fiercely resented imperial rule from Austria-Hungary. A group of students had plotted to ASSASSINATE the Archduke. One of them, Gavrilo Princip, fired the fatal shots and was immediately arrested by the police.

The leaders of the Austro-Hungarian empire blamed Serbia. Austria-Hungary consulted its ally, Germany, and issued Serbia with an ULTIMATUM: Austria-Hungary threatened to go to war unless Serbia admitted involvement in the Sarajevo episode.

Serbia called upon Russia for protection. This was not the first crisis in the Balkans, but earlier ones had often been solved by diplomacy (international talks). This time, to add pressure, orders for troops to MOBILISE went out. Long-prepared plans to move vast armies into position by rail were put into action.

The Schlieffen Plan

The German war plan had been drawn up by Alfred von Schlieffen in 1905. Although the plan was updated, it made two assumptions which turned out to be wrong:

- Germany had always planned to attack France first, whatever the circumstances. They expected to defeat France before the Russians were ready to mobilise their army;
- The Plan involved German troops marching through neutral Belgium. In 1839, Britain had agreed to protect Belgium's right to be neutral, but Germany thought that this old agreement would not be enough to pull Britain into war.

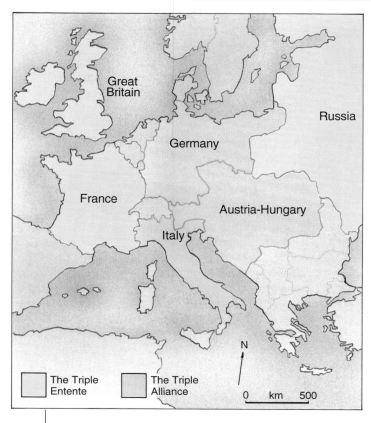

SOURCE 3
Two armed camps in Europe: the alliance system.

The Schlieffen Plan left no time for diplomacy to avoid war. On 1 August Germany declared war on Russia. On 3 August Germany declared war on France. On 4 August German troops crossed neutral Belgium, Britain declared war on Germany and the Alliance System was called into play. Europe was at war.

attainment target

Look at pages 82 to 83 before you answer these questions.

1 List as many reasons as you can why the great powers of Europe were close to war with each other for some time before 1914.

2 What new reasons for war developed in 1914?

3 Which of the following do you think was the most important reason for war: the Schlieffen Plan; nationalism; the alliances? Choose one reason and explain your choice. Compare your choices with each other.

4 Who do you think was to blame for the outbreak of the Great War?

The scope of the war

The First World War probably seems a remote, distant event to you. Few of its survivors are still alive today. Yet its impact was very great, both at the time and since.

Why was it called 'The Great War'?

Warfare as a human activity has a long history. Why, among all of these wars in history, is the conflict between 1914 and 1918 called the Great War? This was because of a number of linked factors:

- there was fighting in several areas;
- many countries and peoples were at war, on one side or another;
- the conflict lasted a long time;
- fighting spread to war at sea and in the air;
- the war affected millions of households by creating shortages and altering patterns of work;
- for the first time ever people at home, as well as soldiers, faced death or injury from air attacks;
- the weapons used caused a high casualty rate (5,509 deaths per day on average)
- fighting on land was based on heavily defended positions (both sides dug trenches to create fronts), see Source 4.
- the degree of fighting, in a small area, caused mass casualties (over 8,200,000 deaths alone on the Main Front).
- most battle tactics led to heavy casualties (both sides mounted OFFENSIVES; many of these failed with heavy loss of life);
- most families and communities were permanently changed by the effects of the conflict (the annual Poppy Day appeal and war memorials are visible signs that people in Britain still remember the war). The timeline (Source 6) offers an outline of the key events in the War.

SOURCE 4
German troops preparing trenches.

'Space voyagers would have been able to spot the Western Front, though they might also have been surprised by its narrowness. Soldiers withdrawing a mere matter of ten miles from it would find themselves in a world where the war had never been.'

SOURCE 5
An extract from a modern writer about the Great War.

Was the conflict a World War?

The Western Front battles or 'offensives' of the Great War were fought in north-west Europe. The main zone of fighting was the Western Front which snaked across Belgium and France for a distance of 700 km. Source 5 describes its two unique features – its narrowness and its length. Both sides remained deadlocked on the Western Front for over three years: there the full horror of trench warfare developed (see the depth study, pages 90 to 101).

Europe's other main front, the Eastern Front, was on the borders of Germany, Austria-Hungary and Russia. The Eastern Front had its own problems: harsh winter weather and the vast distances involved. Germany was more willing to launch major offensives along the Eastern Front than in the West. At the beginning of the war the vast Russian army was mobilised with great speed. This surprised Germany's leaders. German troops had to be moved from the Western Front to force the poorly equipped Russian armies out of German territory. So, against all their pre-war plans, Germany was forced to split its forces between its western and eastern borders.

The Eastern Front also became deadlocked by the end of 1914, although it was never as static as in the West and with fewer troops 'holding the line' limited movements of the front line were possible.

TIMELINE

Periods of intense fighting

1914

June
Franz Ferdinand assassinated

November
Trench warfare begins on Western Front

1915

April
Allied landings at Gallipoli

July
Germans first use Fokker fighter aircraft to shoot down Allied planes

December
Allies evacuated from Gallipoli

1916

February
Verdun offensive begins

July
Somme offensive begins

1917

April
French offensive

July
Flanders offensive 'Passchendaele' begins

November
British victory at Cambrai using tanks

December
Russia pulls out of the war

1918

March
German spring offensive begins

July
Allied counter-offensive begins

11 November
Armistice with Germany signed by Allies

SOURCE 6
The progress and scope of the war.

SOURCE 7
Indian troops during a training exercise.

Side-shows

With deadlock on the Western Front, the Allies opened up several new fronts, mostly against Germany's allies, Austria and Turkey. These brought only limited success. An Allied invasion of Gallipoli against Turkish forces in 1915 ended in disaster. From early in 1916 onwards it was clear that the Great War could only be won or lost on the Western Front.

An empire at war

The Great War was the first total war of modern times. For each country at war all its key elements – its resources, people and means of production were stretched to breaking point. Countries with large overseas empires, like Britain and France, expected their colonies to provide men and resources. As Source 7 shows, many colonies sent volunteers to fight in the alien world of the Western Front. In Africa, the Middle East and Far East fighting developed over the control of European colonies.

The war at sea

Before 1914 the German navy had grown rapidly until it challenged the Royal Navy's control of the seas. Yet both fleets tried to avoid direct conflict. The only major battle, at Jutland in June 1916, was indecisive. The events at sea from 1917 onward show the global scale of the War. With deadlock on land, both sides turned to the seas to put more pressure on the enemy. Each side wanted to weaken the war effort of the other side; in the winter of 1917 food stocks in Britain were down to just six weeks' supplies. The Germans mobilised their fleet of U-boat submarines to sink allied merchant ships with torpedoes. The British STRATEGY was to impose a BLOCKADE on German ports to prevent the entry of supplies.

The nature of the fighting

Source 8 is a classic image of the Western Front. What key features of trench warfare can you see in the painting?

Soldiers who experienced such carnage reacted differently, as Sources 9 to 12 show. Use these sources to identify the key weapons used in the Great War. What can you learn about the tactics used by army leaders?

The courage of the troops on the Western Front was rarely in doubt (Source 11). It is easy to blame the army leaders for their short-sighted tactics as the prime cause for the long casualty lists. Many soldiers have bitter memories of their generals. Later historians have also been critical. However, the Great War posed a unique combination of problems for both sides. They could not find an answer to the success of defensive weapons (see page 84). Mass attacks against well-defended positions led to mass casualties.

SOURCE 8
'Hell' by the French artist, Georges Leroux.

As soon as the signal for the advance was given . . . machine-gun fire opened up on us.
Heaviest casualties occurred on passing through the gaps in our own wire where the men were mown down in heaps.

SOURCE 9
Extract from an entry from the war diary of the Newfoundland Regiment, 1 July 1916.

'We are now at Carskerke and the shrapnel (the splinters from shells) is screaming over our heads and the big guns are booming all at once. The German shells are falling quite close and it is just like hell itself – one's head is absolutely splitting with the din.'

SOURCE 10
An extract from Mairi Chisholm's diary, 25 October, 1914.

Over and over again it is the duty of men to charge against barbed wire into almost certain death. Often no-one comes back. Yet there is never any hesitation or questioning.

SOURCE 11
Extract from letter written by Rowland Fielding to his wife.

'I am making this statement as an act of defiance because I believe that the War is being deliberately prolonged by those who have the power to end it. I am a soldier, I believe that this War has now become a war of aggression and conquest . . . I have seen and endured the sufferings of the troops, and I can no longer be a party to ends which I believe to be evil and unjust.'

SOURCE 12
Extracts from the statement which the soldier-poet Siegfried Sassoon made to the army authorities in June 1917.

SOURCE 13
New technology in warfare.

Weapon	First used by	Where	When	Effect
Flame throwers	Germany	Ypres	1915	
True fighter aircraft	Germany		1915	Start of air warfare
Chlorine poison gas	Germany	Ypres	April 1915	Initial breakthrough
Phostrogene poison gas	Germany	Ypres	Dec 1915	
Tanks	Britain	Somme	Sept 1916	
		Cambrai	Nov 1917	Initial 6 km advance
Linked high explosions	Britain	Ypres	1917	Capture of ridge

SOURCE 14
'Gassed' by John Singer Sargent, an official war artist. Sargent was at the Front and produced his painting after seeing columns of gas attack victims. The painting was finished a year after the war ended.

New weapons

Throughout the war, both sides tried to restore movement to the battlefield by inventing new weapons. These were usually based on the application of science to new technologies. Some of these are shown in Source 13.

Source 14 shows the effects of a poison gas attack. The German chemical industry was usually first to develop new types of gas but both sides used it to support their INFANTRY attacks. Gas attacks failed to achieve a major breakthrough on the Western Front because both sides took careful precautions against their deadly effects. However, many soldiers exposed to it either died, as in Wilfred Owen's poem (Source 15), or suffered from its effects for the rest of their lives. Despite these various weapons, movement was not restored to the Western Front until the spring of 1918. Whatever the weapons, flesh and blood were no match for the bullet and bomb. The Great War retains its image as the bloodiest war in human history.

Look at Source 14. Photographers also took official photos of similar scenes to the one in Source 14. What extra things can artists show in paintings?

Study the image carefully. Why is it long and thin? Why does it have a yellow background? What seem to be the main injuries? Why are the men lying down? Would an eye-witness show such an event with accuracy?

After the Great War, governments banned the use of chemical weapons in future wars. Should poison gas have been used in the Great War? Did poison gas, or any other new weapons, offer turning points in the Great War?

SOURCE 15
Extract from Wilfred Owen's 'Dulce et Decorum est'. (It is sweet and proper to die for one's country.)

'Gas! Gas! Quick boys. An ecstasy of fumbling,
Fitting the clumsy helmets just in time:
But someone still was yelling out and stumbling,
And floundering like a man in fire or lime.'

The impact of war

The Home Front

The armies of the Great War needed vast and constant supplies of weapons and ammunition. Trench warfare placed massive demands upon civilian populations. Huge resources of land, labour, money and enterprise were needed. In Britain, maintaining the war effort involved more people, for longer periods and in more direct ways, than ever before (see Source 17).

Under fire: From the sea

On 16 December 1914, Bertie Young from Hartlepool arrived at school as normal. Like all his school friends, Bertie had been told that the war would be over by Christmas. He never found out. That morning he was fatally wounded by a splinter from a shell fired 6 kilometres away by a German battle cruiser, SMS *Seydlitz*. He died the same day. Altogether, 121 civilians were killed on that day in Hartlepool. Was this the start of the long feared invasion? Where was the Royal Navy? Why was it anchored 800 kilometres away at Scapa Flow?

Under fire: From the air

15 December 1915. On a sub-zero night, the people of Yarmouth awoke to the drone of three German Zeppelin air ships. Samuel Smith and Martha Taylor made history by becoming the first fatal casualties of an air raid on Britain. Living on an island could no longer protect the British people from the dangers of the Great War. By April 1915, London was regularly being attacked. In all, 57 Zeppelin raids killed 564 people and caused injury to 1,370 people. From 1917, Germany launched air raids using bomber aircraft which caused even greater loss of life and damage.

Government control and propaganda

The war gave the government the opportunity to involve itself in people's private actions as never before. The Defence of the Realm Act, passed in 1914, gave the government wide powers. Civilians relied on the media for most of their knowledge about the Great War. As a result it was hard for them to build up a reliable picture of what trench warfare was really like. The same thing happened in Germany and in other countries: note the impression of the trenches suggested by Source 16. In addition, the soldiers themselves often found it hard to describe their experiences to relatives while on leave.

SOURCE 16
Civilians from Berlin being given guided tours of replica trenches.

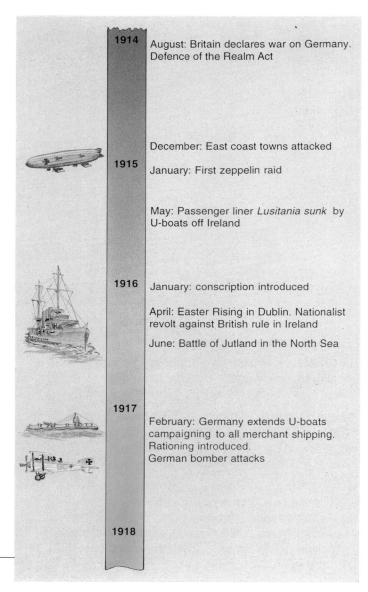

1914	August: Britain declares war on Germany. Defence of the Realm Act
	December: East coast towns attacked
1915	January: First zeppelin raid
	May: Passenger liner *Lusitania sunk* by U-boats off Ireland
1916	January: conscription introduced
	April: Easter Rising in Dublin. Nationalist revolt against British rule in Ireland
	June: Battle of Jutland in the North Sea
1917	February: Germany extends U-boats campaigning to all merchant shipping. Rationing introduced. German bomber attacks
1918	

SOURCE 17
The impact of the war on Britain.

Press reports always presented a positive image of the fighting. Once deadlock developed, the media was used to influence public opinion. The authorities censored the press so it became a channel for their PROPAGANDA. So did the army which censored soldiers' letters home. At the same time, every possible opportunity was taken to fuel public hostility against the enemy.

'Home fires'

Families in Britain had to 'keep the home fires burning' and as Source 18 reveals, it was a difficult task. Because of the U-boat campaign from 1917, many families had to cope with hardships and shortages. The government tried to encourage people to economise in the kitchen. In 1917, the Ministry of Food introduced a system of rationing to make sure that food supplies were shared out equally.

'Missing – Presumed Dead'

Casualties were so high that few families were spared the grief of bereavement, especially after the mass offensives of 1916 to 1918. Source 19 reveals something of this pain.

One in nine British soldiers never came home. Lowered window blinds and black clothing were common everywhere, signs of families in mourning. Even government press censorship could not conceal the true extent of the casualties, nor as Source 20 emphasises, their long-term results.

> The average wife and mother . . . had to clothe and feed the children, managing in spite of shortages to make sure that there was enough, or nearly enough, to eat. She had to see that adult members of the family on heavy manual work – which might include herself – had suitable diet for their jobs.
>
> In many parts of the country, she had also to endure air raids, and the drab, colourless life of a nation that had been at war for several years. Yet somehow she had to keep going, binding the family together in the face of general worries and anxieties about the safety of a husband, father or brother away fighting.

SOURCE 18
This extract, written by historian Stuart Sillars in 1987, describes some of the pressures of life on the home front.

'I sat and stared at that slip of paper. I had looked upon my boy for the last time. I was quite numb. Then came a great pain . . . I whispered . . . the one terrible word "dead".

For me . . . there would be no future. Everything had been swept away by . . . the hand of fate. I was beyond the power of human words to comfort.'

SOURCE 19
The music hall comedian, Harry Lauder's reactions to his son's death. Written 1 January 1917.

1 Why did attack from the sea and air come as a shock to the British people?

2 Work in pairs. Why did governments use propaganda and censorship? Find a good example of propaganda in this book. What is its appeal and why is it effective?

3 Are poppies sold in your school for Remembrance Day? Which charity organises the selling of poppies and how do they use the money which is collected?

4 Try to find out how your local community was affected by the Great War. You may be able to obtain some information by talking to elderly relatives or making a study of a nearby memorial or cemetery. You could also try to find out if any local buildings – factories, hospitals, schools – were used during the Great War.

'I can remember my mother getting that telegram that evening as she was bathing us for bed. She collapsed on the floor. We helped her into a chair and she told us Daddy was missing . . . It ruined us for the rest of our lives, because my father had a good job and we were just left with mother having to struggle, we had to do without lots of things other children had.'

SOURCE 20
A woman remembers hearing the news that her father was missing . . .

The call to arms

When war broke out in 1914 the young men of Britain were eager to volunteer in a way that seems incredible to modern minds. This response to a call to arms is usually seen as simple PATRIOTISM. In reality the reasons for enlistment varied according to status, social class and jobs as the recollections in Source 21 show.

Many people expected that the war would be short and certainly over by Christmas 1914, something that made men keen to volunteer. One man who was aware that the conflict might be longer and bloodier was Lord Kitchener, the British Secretary of State for War. He launched a poster campaign which appealed to national feelings of patriotism. Other posters used emotional blackmail and tapped men's feelings of guilt or embarrassment in different ways to persuade men to join up. The eventual result of Kitchener's appeal for 100,000 men was staggering: 2½ million men volunteered in 1914 and 1915.

SOURCE 22
Oliver Hopkin in his army uniform.

> "Because I got fed up with the Foreman on the farm"
> "King and Parliament had decided upon it. That was all we needed"
> "I was bored to tears with shop life"
> "The chaps round about started to go so I said I'm going"
> "Well it was gonna be a change. Those volunteers went to get away from their environment"

SOURCE 21
Recollections of enlistment from veterans.

> Dear mother, father and all of you, I now have the pleasure in riteing you a few lines . . . We started on Saturday January 9th at 3 o'clock in the morning and had a long ride in the train to a place named Folkstone. We got up on Sunday morning, got on the boat and had a nice ride. Took us an hour and a half on the water, we landed at a big place named Buloung. We marched four miles to the camp and layed under canvas. On Monday we marched to the station and they put us in some old box wagons 30 in a truck and we had 5 hours ride we got out, got formed up and ready and then we got 6 miles to march. We got to an old barn like our old farm that is where we are now and I don't know when we are goneing to move.

SOURCE 23
From a letter home by Private Oliver Hopkin.

Oliver's story

One of these volunteers was Oliver Hopkin (Source 22). Oliver worked on a farm in a small Fenland village in Cambridgeshire where he had spent all his life. Oliver wrote many letters home to his family to try to explain his experiences of the war. By using these letters we can get an idea of one person's experience of war on the Western Front. It is an experience which was common to millions.

Recruitment

In November 1914, Oliver, aged 17, volunteered to join up and was placed into the 11th Suffolk Regiment. After a period of basic training, recruiting duties and specialist courses, the new volunteers awaited the order to mobilise. All over Europe troops were being mobilised and deployed to the areas of assembly. Source 23 recalls Oliver's impressions of his own move to the battle front.

By the time Oliver arrived in France the ambitious pre-war plans of Germany and France for a brief war of movement had ground to a standstill. The Western Front was the result. Once they arrived at the front new troops such as Oliver gradually realised the dangers and the horrors they were about to face. Oliver's first experience of war was in holding the relatively quiet frontline in the British sector around Armentières in north-east France in late 1915. Yet even here the dangers of night-time patrols into NO-MAN'S LAND and the uncomfortable nature of trench conditions are clear in his letters home.

Verdun 1916

Further south along the Western Front a major offensive was beginning around the French city of Verdun. This 11-month battle, which began in February 1916, has been called the worst in history. The German plan was simple. They wanted to bleed France white by sucking France's best troops into defending the fortress city of Verdun. The German artillery would then inflict heavy casualties by mass attacks along a narrow front.

Verdun was protected by a ring of forts, but by 1916 French firepower and troops had been badly run down. The French knew that if Verdun, a symbol of their military power, fell to the Germans then the road to Paris would be open.

The battle grew into a trial of strength with both sides throwing ever more troops into the combat. The French led by General Philippe Pétain were determined to hold on to Verdun. The stirring order *'Ils ne passeront pas* (they shall not pass)' was issued to the troops.

Endurance

The French forts around Verdun withstood colossal bombardment from the German guns yet they proved very difficult to capture. In the 11 months of fighting only two major forts fell into German hands.

As the battle wore on both sides grew weary. The German strategy of ATTRITION had not succeeded, see Source 24. German troops had suffered heavy losses and their leaders knew that they themselves had been bled white by Verdun. By the time the French counter attack was mounted the Germans had given up hope. It is estimated that in total there were 377,000 French losses and 337,000 German losses.

The French claim Verdun as an epic victory. In the short term it was a victory but its memory scarred the minds of the French. Verdun exhausted the French army. Their leaders looked to the British to attack the Germans elsewhere on the Western Front. The result was that a joint attack planned for the summer of 1916 became much more of a British offensive.

Oliver's story

One British soldier caught up in the transfer of troops along the line was Oliver Hopkin. Having gained experience of trench warfare, Private Hopkin had a specialist job which he describes in Source 25. From a letter of the 14 May 1916 it is obvious that Oliver is aware of the army rules of censorship (Source 26), but also that something big was about to happen.

SOURCE 24
This cartoon by Louis Raemakers shows Crown Prince Wilhelm, who led German forces at Verdun, standing on a pile of dead German soldiers and saying 'We must have a higher pile to see Verdun'.

'I will tell you what I am on it is a small gun they call it a trench mortar. I am one of the lucky ones to get on it. It fires a four and half pound bomb and it will fire 300 yards. It is a fine thing there is 5 of us to a gun. We carry it about where we go. The gun is not very heavy it is 50 pounds.'

SOURCE 25
Letter home by Oliver Hopkin describing his job with a trench mortar.

'We are having a lot of moving about lately from one place to another. We are moved along way down the line, but I must not say where we are but there is a lot of trouble about this letter writing to England, so it don't do to say much.'

SOURCE 26
From a letter home by Oliver Hopkin.

---

1 Use Source 21 to list the reasons why men joined up in 1914.

2 Source 23 is printed exactly as Oliver Hopkin wrote his letter. What can you learn from it about Oliver? If the same source had been re-written would it have been as useful?

Life in the line

Trench warfare created its own routines. In one month a soldier might spend four days in the front line, four days in the support line, eight days in reserve and 14 days 'resting'. These periods of 'rest' were often taken up with army tasks (FATIGUES) such as fetching and carrying wood, wire and water to keep the trenches in good order.

The front line routine

Troops holding front-line positions had to be continually alert to the possibility of enemy attack, see Source 27. However, the long periods of inactivity in the appalling trench conditions were also hard to endure as Source 28 explains. Each day started with 'stand to', half an hour before dawn, when all men waited with rifles at the ready. After dawn, one SENTRY per PLATOON remained on the FIRE STEP. The others would go to the DUGOUT to receive their daily rations.

SOURCE 27
A sentry using a PERISCOPE

The rota of duties

After breakfast, the sergeant in charge of each platoon would organise a rota of duties. For those on sentry duty, the tension of standing still for several hours at a time without losing concentration for a moment was exhausting. Of those who were not on sentry duty, some were sent to the support and reserve trenches to pick up more rations. The others were entitled to 'rest'. However, there were still more jobs to be done: digging, filling sandbags, replacing DUCKBOARDS, strengthening the barbed wire defences and carrying ammunition. The day ended with another stand to at dusk. The ration parties returned under the cover of darkness with fresh supplies from the reserve trenches.

Activity by night and day

Trench activity increased at night. Small patrols were sent out into no-man's-land under the cover of darkness. They attempted to discover details about enemy resources and strength. Sometimes, full-scale trench raids were mounted to capture prisoners and gather information about enemy plans and positions. To guard against such night-time activities, both sides kept men on sentry duty at night and regularly lit up the night sky with star shells to reveal any trace of troop movements in no-man's-land.

By day this task was often done by the newly formed air forces. They acted as the eyes of the army and flew observation patrols over enemy lines taking thousands of aerial photographs showing enemy positions, such as the one in Source 29. From all these sources detailed maps of the enemy's positions were created.

You stand in a trench of vile stinking mud
And the bitter cold wind freezes your blood
Then the guns open up and flames light the sky
And, as you watch, rats go scuttling by.

The men in the dugouts are quiet for a time
Trying to sleep midst the stench and the slime
The moon is just showing from over the hill
And the dead on the wire hang silent and still.

A sniper's bullet wings close to your head
As you wistfully think of a comfortable bed
But now a dirty blanket has to suffice
And more often than not it is crawling with lice.

SOURCE 28
A poem written by Sidney Champlin who served in the Gloucestershire regiment.

SOURCE 29
An aerial photo showing the Somme area prior to the main offensive in 1916.

Trench conditions

Conditions in the trenches were often made worse by bad weather. Heavy shelling coupled with rain or snow made the trenches muddy and waterlogged. The trenches quickly became infested with lice and rats and disease spread rapidly among the troops.

In the face of all these problems the men serving on the frontline felt a strong sense of togetherness. Yet despite the shared squalor and dangers of trench life, there were different living quarters and rations according to rank. Rank, in turn, reflected pre-war social divisions based upon birth, education, occupation and wealth.

'Out here dear we're all pals. What one hasn't got the other has we share each others troubles get each other out of danger. You wouldn't believe the humanity between men out here. It's a lovely thing is friendship out here.'

SOURCE 30
A letter home written by Private Mudd. Four days later he was killed.

The group helped each carry the guilt of killing, ease the fear and gave such security as was possible, gave mutual support united by a common jargon, by shared secrets, experiences, discomforts, deep fears, sudden violences and long stillnesses men belonged to platoon or section as to no other aspect of their war life.

SOURCE 31
An account of the shared experiences of soldiers written in 1978.

Why stay?

Why did so many men suffer in the trenches to live and perhaps die in such conditions? Would you have been willing to?

- Once enlisted all men were subject to the strict codes of army discipline and punishments, including being shot for cowardice or mutiny. Some men did run these risks. In recent years reports of mutinies among British troops have been made public, such as one at a top training base in September 1917. Army records about the 307 British troops who were executed by firing squads for cowardice or desertion have also been made public. More serious for the allied war effort were the French mutinies of 1917, and the mass Russian desertions on the Eastern Front.
- The strong feeling of being all in it together created deep bonds of fellowship, mutual support and loyalty (Source 30). Old soldiers often speak of the feeling of not wanting to let their mates down. Source 31 reveals other feelings.
- Although men on both sides had orders to kill the enemy, this did not mean that the two sides hated each other. The mutual suffering meant that both sides shared a kind of brotherhood and at times an unofficial system of 'live and let live' existed whereby troops were able to undertake their routines mostly ignored and undisturbed by the enemy. This came mostly from the men in the trenches and was frowned upon by higher ranking officers who believed that the troops should regularly engage the enemy in set piece battles.

ACTIVITY

Use the information on these pages to design a 24-hour diagram for the trench routine.

How do you think a 'live and let live' system of trench warfare might work? How might the army authorities react to such a system?

The Somme, 1 July 1916

Before the summer of 1916 the Somme, an area of gently rolling chalklands around the River Somme, was seen as a quiet sector of the Western Front. But the Germans had fortified all the high ground which they occupied. Capturing it would always be difficult.

The Allied plan

Many of the allied troops had high hopes of success. Surely German positions could not withstand the week-long bombardment by 1,500 allied guns firing 2 million shells? But as the details of the allied plan (Source 32) were explained, doubts began to arise. What if the German barbed wire wasn't cut? What if the mines alerted the Germans? Why did they have to walk across in waves of troops, sometimes for a distance of over 2 kilometres, sometimes across no-man's land and uphill?

Zero hour

As the 1 July 1916 dawned in northern France an early mist gave way to a hot and cloudless midsummer's day. Moments before zero hour at 7.30 a.m. the guns fell silent along a 29 km front as allied troops waited to attack.

The allies were confident that nothing could have survived the bombardment. As Oliver Hopkin, along with thousands of others, waited to go over the top, a huge mine of 24 tons of high explosive was blown up. As the seconds ticked away, the tension mounted. Oliver's big push up the exposed slopes shown in Source 33 lasted just half an hour. He became another statistic and joined a total of 68,000 first day casualties with over 21,000 troops being killed. This was the worst single day's disaster in British military history. Back in Cambridgeshire Oliver's parents would doubtless receive his letter (Source 34) with mixed feelings.

Flawed tactics

In another letter home (Source 35), Oliver himself touches upon several reasons for the attack's failure. All along the British sector it was a similar story of carnage.

The Somme offensive went on until November 1916 at a cost of 1,250,000 lives for little ground gained. It was only later that the grim realities of the Somme really struck home. Every local newspaper across Britain began to list its fallen heroes.

SOURCE 32
The Allied plan for the Somme offensive, 1916.

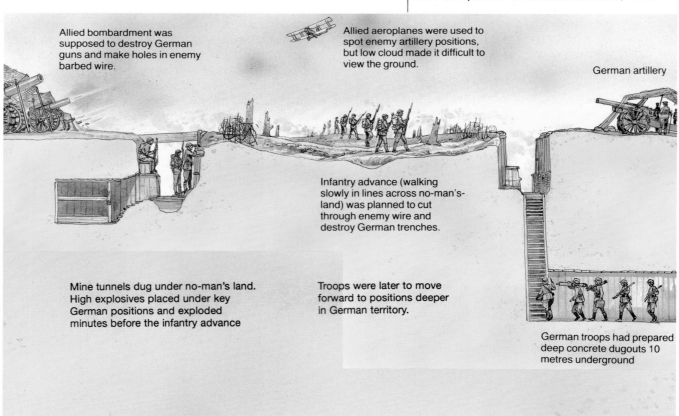

Allied bombardment was supposed to destroy German guns and make holes in enemy barbed wire.

Allied aeroplanes were used to spot enemy artillery positions, but low cloud made it difficult to view the ground.

German artillery

Infantry advance (walking slowly in lines across no-man's-land) was planned to cut through enemy wire and destroy German trenches.

Mine tunnels dug under no-man's land. High explosives placed under key German positions and exploded minutes before the infantry advance

Troops were later to move forward to positions deeper in German territory.

German troops had prepared deep concrete dugouts 10 metres underground

SOURCE 33
Men including Oliver advance across no-man's land at the start of the infantry attack on 1 July 1916.

Dear mother and father and all I now take pleasure in riteing you a few lines. I have got two very nice wounds to be getting on with for a week or two but I am very glad I have got to England.

They gave us plenty of rum that morning so we were well fit for the Germans. It was a nice morning, the sun was just getting up well we got out of our trenches at 7.30 on the 1st July. Everybody went over like brave lads and as soon as the Germans saw us they had their machine guns on us and mowed us down like mowing down corn.

We could see our mates falling down, some died and some wounded. And then the next man to me fell. I thought it was my turn, but I kept on till I got a wound in my left arm and then another in my body, I fell in a shell hole and kept there till 3 in the afternoon. Then I got up and got back in our trenches and walked to Albert, that was 2 miles, and I had my wound dressed there and then they took us by moter to a hospital.

SOURCE 34
Extract from a letter home from Private Oliver Hopkin.

The begers have got some very deep dug-outs to get in or they wouldn't have stood an earthly charnce in the bombardments. Their dug-outs was 100 feet deep and would hold 70 men. They're far better than us in that line. They all got down there out of the way till we was ready to go over they nowd the very hour we was coming over and they waited for us there with their machine guns. It was them that mowed us down. . . . Each man had a good drink of rum, in fact some chaps had more than they wanted. At 5 o'clock the officer fell us in with our guns and shells. Those carrying shells had 66 pounds and other things as well. We were all loaded down well.

SOURCE 35
Extract from a letter home from Private Oliver Hopkin.

Oliver's story

Separated from home as he recovered from his wounds in Leicester, Oliver's letter of 13 July seeks news of his village pals (Source 36). As with Oliver's village, as in other parts of the country, those who fought on the Somme often joined up in groups from close-knit rural communities or from the same firms, trades or clubs in urban areas. Volunteers in these so called 'pals' battalions' were promised that they would be able to serve together. In reality they often died together too.

Whole communities went in to mourning. The survivors of the Somme on both sides now prepared for 1917 with no great enthusiasm but with the determination to see things through.

'They do say there is not many of our battalion. Will you get to know about Fred Sulliman, Sharpe and Alott? Corporal Day got hit in the heart by a piece of shell. There was more killed than there was wounded, so I think some of the Willburton boys is gone.'

SOURCE 36
Extract from a letter home from Private Oliver Hopkin.

1 Discuss Source 32 in pairs. Decide upon the vital things needed for success on the Somme.

2 Now look at Source 33. What problems can you see for the troops? Using your answers for question 1, what things would you think the troops would expect ahead? What would be the unexpected things they would have to face?

3 Use Source 35 to pick out key reasons why the attack failed.

4 Use your answers to Questions 1, 2 and 3 to write a brief explanation of why the attack on the Somme failed.

Slaughter on the Somme

The battle of the Somme was fought around 80 years ago. Today only a dwindling number of veterans survive in their 90s who were eyewitnesses to the events. The oral TESTIMONIES of such veterans have been often recorded for various TV or radio documentaries.

Field evidence

How can the detailed study of field evidence help us understand the nature of events on the Somme? Today most of the Somme battlefields have returned to farmland, but sometimes live shells are still ploughed up. Elsewhere zigzag markings across ploughed fields and rough circles in the soil provide clues to the old trench lines and mine craters of 80 years ago.

Newfoundland Memorial Park

Of the thousands of kilometres of trenches along the Western Front, only a few survive today and even fewer are in their original condition. The most complete section of original battlefield is at the Newfoundland Memorial Park near Beaumont Hamel on the Somme (Source 38). It was the site of a British and Canadian attack on German positions on the 1 July 1916.

The trench lines are so well preserved because the site was bought by the Newfoundland government in memory of its 684 casualties (Source 39). Field evidence from Beaumont Hamel together with primary sources (such as trench maps, oral testimonies and written accounts) can help explain the events of the battles which were fought there.

SOURCE 37
The original German front line trenches at Newfoundland Memorial Park.

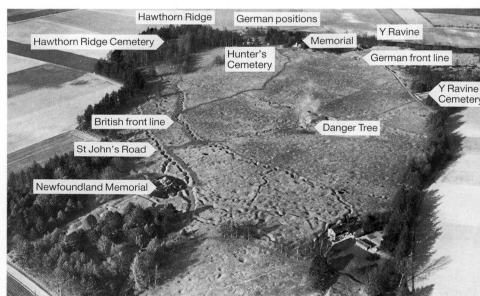

Hawthorn Ridge · German positions · Y Ravine · Hawthorn Ridge Cemetery · Memorial · Hunter's Cemetery · German front line · Y Ravine Cemetery · British front line · Danger Tree · St John's Road · Newfoundland Memorial

SOURCE 38
An aerial view of the preserved battlefield at Newfoundland Memorial Park.

> As soon as the signal for the advance was given machine gunfire opened up on us. Heaviest casualties occurred on passing through the gaps in our own wire where the men were mown down in heaps.

SOURCE 39
Part of an entry for 1 July 1916 from the war diary of the Newfoundland Regiment.

Beaumont Hamel

Beaumont Hamel was one of a number of small French villages which the allied attack was intended to capture from the enemy. Source 40 is a German account of the attack on Beaumont Hamel in which 5,240 allied troops were killed from positions such as those shown in Source 37.

The allies gained no ground on the first day of the Somme offensive, and lost 21,000 troops. Despite this disastrous beginning the offensive was kept up.

Elsewhere some ground was gained but no breakthrough was achieved. Beaumont Hamel was finally captured by the allies 3½ months later when a mixture of November fog and poison gas helped a second attack. Even this success involved the loss of 2,200 troops. It was only then that the dead from both attacks could be properly buried.

Cemeteries and memorials

The Battle of the Somme changed the landscape of these French fields. Dotted everywhere are hundreds of British cemeteries such as Y Ravine near Beaumont Hamel (Source 41). They bear witness to the futile offensives carried out by British troops.

In memory of the dead a huge memorial to the missing was erected in the 1920s at Thiepval. It dominates the landscape for miles around and contains the names of over 73,000 men who are soldiers with no known graves.

Today the Newfoundland Memorial Park is well managed for visitors. Neat pathways cut across the grass-covered shell holes and the zig-zagging trench lines. But thinking back to the grim events of 1916 it can still release a powerful emotional response. For example, this is one person's impression of the site, written in 1976: 'It was late July and as I wandered across the shell-torn slopes towards the German lines the sound of thunder was heard in the distance getting gradually nearer . . . the light grew dim and black clouds gathered overhead, lightning streaked across the sky in a veritable reincarnation of what a barrage must have been.'

---

1 The trenches in Source 37 are in their original positions but not in their original state, what features are missing? Use your previous knowledge to help you.

2 Use Source 38 to mark the following features on to the simplified trench map which is on a copy sheet in the Teacher's Notes: the British frontline, the German frontline, No-man's land.

3 The sites shown on these pages are all original ones. Elsewhere on the Western Front there are sections of trenches that are reconstructions or replicas of the originals. Do you think it is better to use original pieces of evidence, or copies, or both to understand the Great War? Give reasons for your answers.

4 What is the value of studying surviving sites from the Great War? Is it in using them as sources? Is it in using the sites as a stimulus to our emotions?

'By degrees the bombardment began once more . . . it became intense. The moment for the assault had come.

In thick waves the British left their trenches and moved at a walk down into the valley and up the further slope. In a few seconds the firing trenches were occupied and fire opened. Artillery support was asked for by telephone.

The storming troops, mown down by the rifle and machine-gun fire, suffered so heavily that they were forced to halt and take cover.

No-man's land was horrible sight. Khaki dead and wounded lay in hundreds among the barbed wire . . . the British lay in thick heaps.'

SOURCE 40
A German account of the British and Canadian attack on 1 July 1916 from the History of the Württemburg Reserve Infantry Regiment No. 119.

SOURCE 41
Y Ravine cemetery at Beaumont Hamel, with the graves of some of the soldiers who died.

1917: failures and fatigue

After convalescing in Leicester from his wounds on the Somme, Oliver Hopkin, now decorated with a military medal, returned to the front in October 1916. Oliver and the 11th Suffolks returned to the Armentières sector.

From his letters home (Source 42), Oliver's mood, like that of millions of war-weary troops, can be seen to have changed. He was now a Lance Corporal, but Oliver explained some of the disadvantages of promotion (see Source 43). As the third Christmas of the war approached, Oliver's letter of the 20 December (Source 44) looked forward with no great joy to the spring.

The allies believed that 1917 would be the year in which Germany would finally be defeated. More offensives were planned for the spring and summer of 1917. For a brief moment in March it seemed that the allies might have been right. Suddenly the allies found themselves able to advance with little resistance into German-held territory.

But it was not to be. The Germans had found out about French and British attacks to come and withdrew to their long prepared, strongly fortified defensive zone called the Hindenburg Line. The deadlock became harder than ever to break. All the troops were battle-weary and because of this the various allied offensives ended in unexpected ways.

SOURCE 45
The memorial to the missing at Arras.

> While you will be in a nice home enjoying yourselfes, I shall be dodging the bullets and shells. It is sometime since I had a letter. I don't know if they will think about me this Christmas. If thay don't dam soon rite to me I will stop riteing to them. It is wasting my time and you know I'm not a lover of riteing letters.

SOURCE 42
Letter from Oliver Hopkin.

> I expect we shall have to try and make another move this spring. The people in England do not know the half what goes on out here. I'm sorry to say if they did know this war would have been over long ago I am sure.

SOURCE 44
Letter from Oliver Hopkin.

> 'We sleep in a room to ourselves and the men sleep by theirselfes. For it dose not do for us to sleep with them. For we are like masters on a farm and the men under us so you see how the thing works.'

SOURCE 43
Letter from Oliver Hopkin.

The French mutiny

The failure of the French offensive was just too much for some of the French troops. About 30,000 men deserted from duty, and some even mutinied. Strikes and riots spread across France. The French government turned to General Pétain, the 'Saviour of Verdun', to restore order. The ring-leaders of the mutiny were shot, but the morale of the French army had been badly shaken. In the meantime, any other major attacks on the Western Front would have to be mounted by British and Empire troops.

Oliver at Arras

Oliver's 11th Suffolks were moved to another sector and were set to work on battle preparations for a forthcoming offensive. The Battle of Arras began on 9 April and the 11th Suffolks achieved their first day's objectives by capturing sections of the German first and second line trenches.

Among those killed on that first day was Oliver Hopkin. His body was never identified. His name is listed along with others with no known graves on the memorial to the missing at Arras (Source 45). Source 46 is part of his last letter home.

Flanders fields

The area chosen for the main British offensive of 1917 was Flanders, in Belgium. Despite its low-lying land, the wet autumn weather and the strongly defended German positions, General Haig thought that it would be possible to break through the German lines. Today it is an area of peaceful farms, villages and small towns. One of them was called Passchendaele. It was here that the exhausted allies stopped, having gained only 11 kilometres of mud and shell holes at a cost of over 500,000 lives from both sides. Haig justified his tactics as a war of attrition, wearing down the enemy to breaking point, but the horrors were shared equally by all who fought in Flanders.

In people's memories the battle of Passchendaele is no longer just part of an historic event: it has come to symbolise the whole of the Great War in being the blindest slaughter of a blind conflict (see Source 47).

Fatalism

Troops facing each other felt more in sympathy than ever. They had other enemies in common. Their own leaders, profiteers back home who were doing well out of the war, politicians, in short, all who were keen to continue the war.

Heavy losses forced the British government to introduce conscription after 1916. At first only single able-bodied men were called up. Later this was extended to married men.

In spite of the massive losses, the endurance of all troops was remarkable and civilian support held firm. All concerned at the front wanted an end to the war as quickly as possible.

After the slaughter of 1916 and 1917 many soldiers lost the optimism and enthusiasm which had been so strong among them when the war started. They were now only concerned with survival. Every soldier knew that the attrition meant being wounded or killed sooner or later.

'Well I must tell you that we shall be up in the thick of it again before you get this letter. But I don't think we shall get such a cutting up like we did at Albert last year. I hope, please God, I come through alright this time. I will let you know as soon as I can if I come though.'

SOURCE 46
Oliver Hopkin's last letter home to his parents.

SOURCE 47
This painting which recalls the horrors of the Great War was painted by a German artist, Otto Dix, who served with the German army in the trenches.

attainment target

1 What aspect of the soldier's life in the First World War would you like to find out more about?

2 Which sources in this depth study help you begin to find out about your chosen topic? What do they tell you?

3 Draw up a list of five questions you would like to find the answers to. What kind of sources would help you find the answer to your questions?

SOURCE 48
A German poster appealing for metal goods to help continue the war effort, 1918.

SOURCE 49
A French poster from 1918 declares 'They shall not pass'.

Why did the Great War end in 1918?

At the start of 1918, there was still no end in sight to the deadlock. Yet by the end of the year the Great War was over. What caused such a dramatic turnaround of events? Opinions among historians have varied on the key reasons for the Allied victory. How were these victories achieved? Why were German forces exhausted by the summer of 1918?

Germany tried to win the war first. Once Russia had been forced to sign a separate peace treaty, the spare troops were moved from fighting the Russians on the Eastern Front to support a final attack on the Western Front.

Germany's 'Spring Offensive' began on 21 March 1918. The surprise attack, launched by chance in dense fog, caught the Allies unaware. At first the German attacks were successful. Old trench lines were broken through and a degree of mobility not seen since 1914 returned to the war. German troops quickly pushed forward over hard-won Allied positions, such as the Somme and Passchendaele.

The Allies were forced to retreat and defend (see Source 49). At one point Paris itself seemed in danger, with German troops less than 80 kilometres away. Allied casualties grew, and the Army leaders issued desperate orders like the one in Source 50.

The Germans seemed poised for victory, but the pace had been too quick and created exposed bulges vulnerable to Allied counter-attacks. Soon their own supply lines were under threat. German losses mounted, and the troops became tired and demoralised. Meanwhile, despite heavy losses, especially among the Australian and New Zealand soldiers, Allied troops held their positions and kept their morale.

DEPTH STUDY

The Western Front

> Three weeks ago the enemy began terrific attacks against us. . . . Victory will belong to the side which holds out the longest. . . . Every position must be held to the last man: there must be no retirement. With our backs to the wall, and believing in the justice of our cause, each one of us must fight on to the end.

SOURCE 50
The day's order issued by Haig to all ranks, 11 April 1918.

SOURCE 51
A sea of German prisoners, 1918.

'Never at any time in history has the British army achieved greater results in attack. The victory was indeed complete, thanks to the commanders of armies, corps and divisions, thanks above all to the wise, loyal and energetic policy of their Commander-in-Chief.'

SOURCE 52
The Allies' Supreme Commander, Marshal Foch, pays tribute to the British army, 1918.

Allied victory or German defeat?

By mid-July, the Allies were reinforced with fresh American troops. They halted the German advance and mounted a series of counter-attacks. The German army was exhausted and its short-supplied troops surrendered in vast numbers, see Source 51. By the autumn, the German forces were in retreat along the Western Front. The battlefields of 1915 to 1917 were re-captured by the Allies for the last time.

The Great War, known for its stubborn deadlock, was ending as it began: with a flurry of rapid movement of men and machines. The Allies learned from the experience of various successful opening attacks in 1917, using a combination of improved infantry tactics and new weapons. The British armies bore the brunt of the fighting in the autumn of 1918. They achieved a series of nine victories from August to November which forced Germany to seek an ARMISTICE. Source 52 acknowledges these achievements.

'Runner in at 10.30 am with order to cease firing at 11.00 am. . . . Firing continued. Machine gun company on my right lost 12 men at 10.55, when a high explosive landed in their position. . . . At 11.00 sharp the shelling ceased on both sides. . . . Captain came up and told us that the war was over.'

SOURCE 53
Part of the entry from Sergeant Grady's diary, 11 November 1918.

1 Which argument do you generally support?
  • The Allies defeated the German army on the Western Front.
  • The German army lost the war as a result of its own actions.
  • The German army lost the war as a result of forces beyond its control.

2 Why have the Allied victories of 1918 been given relatively little attention?

3 How does Marshal Foch's view (Source 52) of the British leadership compare with your own earlier opinions?

Armistice

By November, Germany was no longer able to hold on to its own positions or retain its allies. The German people became more interested in food than fighting and leaders turned to face revolutionaries within Germany, instead of the lost cause of continuing the war.

The end came quite suddenly. On 8 November, the Kaiser fled to neutral Holland. News of an armistice filtered through to the troops, but as Source 53 describes, the fighting continued right up until the eleventh hour of the eleventh day of the eleventh month. When the Armistice was officially declared, the millions of survivors were left with feelings of relief and celebration mixed with a sense of loss.

101

In this unit you will first of all find out about the causes of the Second World War. We will look at who was to blame for a new world war only 21 years after the end of the first one.

At the centre of this story is Adolf Hitler. The unit goes on to a depth study of life in Hitler's Germany. It ends with an overview of Hitler's treatment of the Jews, the Holocaust.

Between the wars

Is there a war memorial in the place where you live? Is it like the one in Source 1?

Almost every city, town or village in Britain has a war memorial. They were put up just after the First World War to commemorate those who had died by recording their names. You can tell quite a lot about your community and about the war from a study of your local war memorial (see the Activity on page 103).

In Unit 1 we saw that the First World War caused greater slaughter than any previous war in history. It was called 'A war to end wars'. No wonder that the people in Source 2 are celebrating its end. Now look at Source 3. It shows children sheltering in a trench from a bombing raid in 1939. Only 21 years after the end of the First World War a second great conflict had broken out. This time more people, from more countries, were involved and many more civilians were killed. How could this happen?

SOURCE 1
A local war memorial.
Bellingham, Northumberland.

SOURCE 2
People in London celebrate the end of the First World War.

SOURCE 4
German sailors surrender to the British after sinking their own ship, the *Nurnberg*, at Scapa Flow in the Orkney Islands in 1919.

SOURCE 3
Children taking shelter at the beginning of the Second World War, 1939.

"MY FRIENDS, WE HAVE FAILED. WE JUST COULDN'T CONTROL YOUR WARLIKE PASSIONS."

DISARMAMENT CONFERENCE

COMMON PEOPLE OF THE WORLD

SOURCE 5
Newspaper cartoon, 1932, following the failure of disarmament talks. The cartoonist blames world leaders for failing to disarm when the people of the world only wanted to live in peace.

The answer mainly lies in the attitudes of the people of the world to each other in the years after the war. Look at Source 4. What do you think the sailors on the British battleship are thinking? Are their thoughts full of victory, crushing the enemy, forcing the Germans to scuttle their fleet of battleships, the pride of their navy? Or are they thinking 'good, now we can lay up our ships too, now that we don't need to feel threatened and this should make war almost impossible in the future'?

And what of the sailors from the German battleship? Are they thinking 'now we can live in peace together, without rivalry'? Or are they thinking that if Britain can have a navy, why shouldn't we? Are their thoughts full of revenge and a determination to come back and fight again?

Almost everyone who took part in the First World War was determined to avoid war again at almost any cost. Several disarmament conferences were held, but the results were disappointing, as Source 5 shows. By the late 1930s nations were once again arming themselves.

ACTIVITY

Look at your local war memorial.

1 What does it show? How does its design compare with other memorials locally?

2 What surnames are there? Are these names still common locally?

3 How many names are shown? What was the population of this place at the time? (Try the 1911 census.)

4 Which of the services were the people in (Army, Navy, etc.)? Which regiments of the Army? Were these local regiments? What ranks did they hold?

5 Are names from the Second World War added? What about any other wars?

The Treaty of Versailles

In 1919 the leaders of the victorious countries met at Versailles, near Paris, to agree a peace treaty for those countries defeated in the war to sign.

The attitudes of the winners varied depending on the national damage and destruction they had suffered. Countries like Britain and the USA, although providing men and weapons, did not suffer the direct results of enemy invasion as did France and Belgium. This degree of involvement became an important factor in shaping the attitudes of civilians and the allied leaders towards Germany after the war.

The winners

Each of the main allied leaders brought a different agenda to the lengthy peace discussions. They had different short- and long-term views. These are summarised in Sources 6, 7 and 8.

The losers

The German people, like millions of civilians across Europe, were war weary. There were shortages of food and other goods. There were also political problems: with the Kaiser gone, who was to lead the nation? A new republic had been created, called the 'Weimar Republic', but the recently elected political parties formed an uncertain government.

Within Germany bitter struggles for power broke out. The new government was attacked by the Communists on the left, and by right-wing groups. Many returning German troops were angry. They had been kept in ignorance of conditions at home. They felt betrayed that the war had ended while they still held allied territory. Some blamed politicians in Germany for ending the war before the German army was defeated. They claimed they had been 'stabbed in the back' by the new government.

President Wilson thought that America should stay involved in future events in Europe and that there should be a World Peace Treaty based upon his earlier 'Fourteen Points' offered to the Germans in 1918. The winners should think beyond mere revenge on Germany. An international peace-keeping organisation should be set up to avoid future wars.

SOURCE 6
The aims of the USA.

The French Prime Minister, Clemenceau, wanted revenge on Germany. France had been invaded twice in his lifetime by the German army, and he wanted to make Germany so weak that it would never be able to attack France again. He also wanted Germany to pay for the damage France had suffered in the war.

SOURCE 7
The aims of France.

The British Prime Minister, Lloyd George, also wanted revenge on Germany. 'Hang the Kaiser' and 'Squeeze Germany Until the Pips Squeak' were slogans with which he had won a general election in 1918. He also wanted Germany to be weakened and made to pay for the war. The British Empire could be expanded at Germany's expense.

SOURCE 8
The aims of Great Britain.

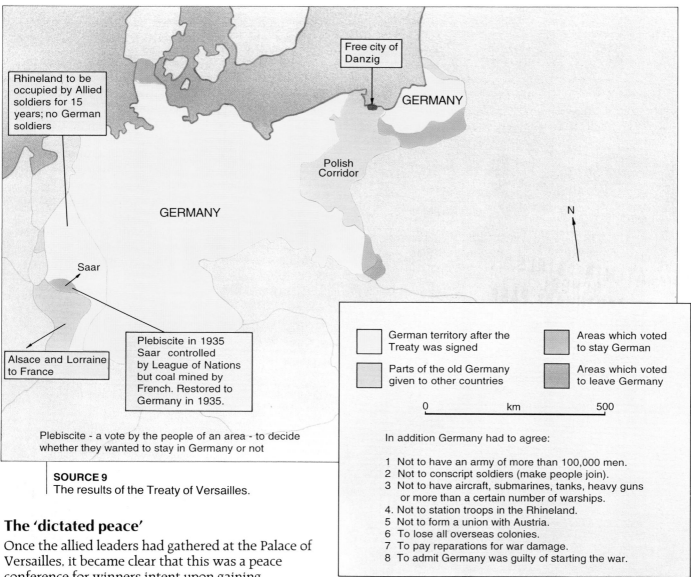

The map includes the following labels:

- Rhineland to be occupied by Allied soldiers for 15 years; no German soldiers
- Free city of Danzig
- GERMANY
- Polish Corridor
- GERMANY
- Saar
- Alsace and Lorraine to France
- Plebiscite in 1935 Saar controlled by League of Nations but coal mined by French. Restored to Germany in 1935.
- N

Plebiscite - a vote by the people of an area - to decide whether they wanted to stay in Germany or not

Key:
- German territory after the Treaty was signed
- Parts of the old Germany given to other countries
- Areas which voted to stay German
- Areas which voted to leave Germany

0   km   500

In addition Germany had to agree:

1 Not to have an army of more than 100,000 men.
2 Not to conscript soldiers (make people join).
3 Not to have aircraft, submarines, tanks, heavy guns or more than a certain number of warships.
4. Not to station troops in the Rhineland.
5 Not to form a union with Austria.
6 To lose all overseas colonies.
7 To pay reparations for war damage.
8 To admit Germany was guilty of starting the war.

SOURCE 9
The results of the Treaty of Versailles.

The 'dictated peace'

Once the allied leaders had gathered at the Palace of Versailles, it became clear that this was a peace conference for winners intent upon gaining maximum revenge upon Germany. German leaders were not even allowed to be present at any of the discussions. Source 9 shows the results of the Treaty, both in the land Germany had to surrender, and the other terms she was presented with.

Once these terms were published, Germany faced a stark choice: either sign the Treaty or face invasion by Allied forces. Germany felt that the Treaty was unfair. The Treaty created immediate bitterness and stored up problems for the future.

The issue most resented was the War Guilt clause. This stated that Germany was 'solely responsible' for the outbreak of the Great War in 1914. Because of this, Germany should pay for all the war damage as REPARATIONS to the allies. Reparations took years to sort out. Eventually an amount of £6,600 million was fixed, to be paid in instalments.

1 Look back to the motives of the three main leaders (Sources 6, 7 and 8). Compare them with Source 9. How might
   a Clemenceau
   b Woodrow Wilson
   c Lloyd George
   view the outcome of the Treaty?

2 Do you feel the Treaty was fair to Germany?

3 How do you think Germany should have been treated?

TIMELINE

1919	Treaty of Versailles
1922	Mussolini becomes ruler of Italy
1923	Hitler fails to seize power in Munich
1924–29	Years of relative calm and prosperity
1929	Wall Street Crash
1931	Japan invades Manchuria. League of Nations fails to stop Japan
1933	Hitler becomes Chancellor of Germany
1935	Italy invades Ethiopia. League of Nations fails to stop Italy
1936	German forces re-occupy Rhineland. Spanish Civil War starts. Hitler and Mussolini support General Franco's fascist rebellion
1937	Japan invades China
1938	March: Germany takes over Austria (the 'Anschluss'). September: Hitler seizes the Sudetenland, part of Czechoslovakia
1939	March: Germany takes over the rest of Czechoslovakia, breaking Hitler's agreement with Britain. August: Hitler makes agreement with Stalin (the Nazi-Soviet Pact) to divide Poland between them. September: Hitler invades Poland, Britain and France declare war on Germany.

AYLWIN GIRLS'
SCHOOL
SOUTHWARK PARK
ROAD SE16 3TZ

Between the wars

There were some key features of the years between the wars which affected events in several countries:

1 The terms of the Treaty of Versailles had to be changed. Several countries felt this: those which had been defeated in the First World War, like Germany, felt they had been unfairly treated. Some of those which had won, like Italy and Japan, felt they had not received enough rewards.

2 Communism was an international menace. The revolution in Russia in 1917 had led to the overthrow of the Tsar and the setting up of a totally new system. Other rulers and business leaders feared that Communism would spread (see Source 10).

3 The League of Nations was too weak to work. The League had been set up at the Treaty of Versailles to keep peace between nations. The USA never joined (hence the cartoon in Source 11). Germany was not a member until 1926 and Russia not until 1934. The League moved too slowly and was often ignored.

SOURCE 10
Anti-Communist poster from Germany in 1919. It says: 'Bolshevism will drown the world in blood.' The Bolsheviks were the Russian Communists who carried out the revolution in Russia in 1917.

THE GAP IN THE BRIDGE.

SOURCE 11
A British cartoon from 1919 about the refusal of the USA to join the League of Nations.

SOURCE 12
Hitler speaking at a Nazi meeting.

4 Democracy was replaced by dictatorships. In Italy, Mussolini became Prime Minister in 1922. He gradually made himself DICTATOR.

In Japan, the generals often ignored the wishes of the Japanese Parliament.

In Germany, an ex-soldier, Adolf Hitler, joined the National Socialist German Worker's Party, called the Nazis. In 1923 he tried, but failed, to take over the government in Munich. He was imprisoned and wrote his book, *Mein Kampf* (My Struggle), explaining his ideas. These are summarised in Source 14. Although he was a powerful speaker, see Sources 12 and 13, he attracted little support in the 1920s although he was convinced he had the answers to Germany's problems.

5 Economic Crisis. The world economy never recovered from the First World War. Unemployment remained high in many countries throughout these years.

'In the Circus Krone, Hitler spoke. He was an evangelist speaking to a camp meeting . . . His converts moved with him, laughed with him, felt with him. They booed with him the French. They hissed with him the Republic . . . The 8,000 were an instrument on which Hitler played a symphony of national passion.'

SOURCE 13
Extracts from the writings of a New York reporter in Germany between the wars.

- Germans were best. The Germans were a superior race of people, called 'Aryans'. Other races – Jews, Poles, Russians – were inferior.
- War is right. Because Germans were superior, they had the right to seize land, by force if necessary, from other countries, particularly those in the East occupied by inferior people.
- Versailles is wrong. The Treaty of Versailles was wrong and its terms should be ignored.
- Communism was wrong. Communism said that the class you belonged to was more important than your nation. It was therefore dangerous and should be opposed.

SOURCE 14
Hitler's beliefs.

	Number of unemployed	Seats in Reichstag
1929	1.3 million	13
1930	3.0 million	107
1931	4.4 million	107
1932	6.0 million	230

SOURCE 15
Unemployment in Germany and number of Nazis elected to the Reichstag (German Parliament).

Germany faced economic crisis in 1923. Inflation, caused by the reparations payments demanded by the Treaty of Versailles, ruined the currency and many people lost all they had. In 1929 a world-wide crisis followed the US Wall Street Crash. Unemployment soared in many countries. In Germany, voters turned to the Nazis (Source 15). Hitler was asked to become Chancellor (Prime Minister) in 1933.

'When the territory of the Reich embraces all Germans and finds itself unable to assure them of a livelihood, only then can the right arise, from the need of the people, to acquire foreign territory. The plough is then the sword and the tears of war will produce the daily bread for the generations to come.'

SOURCE 16
From Hitler's book *Mein Kampf*.

Was Hitler to blame?

It seems easy to say that Hitler was entirely to blame for the Second World War. He said he would go to war in his book about his beliefs, *Mein Kampf*, written in 1924. He claimed that the German people, because they were a superior race, had the right to seize land from other, inferior, peoples, by war if necessary. In 1937 he told his generals that he would expect to attack Czechoslovakia and Austria quite soon (look at the timeline on page 106 for when he actually did this).

He began to build up German armed forces as soon as he came to power in 1933. In 1935 he openly announced that he was rejecting the terms of the Treaty of Versailles restricting German armed forces and rearmament began (see Source 17).

SOURCE 18
A column of German cavalry on the streets of a Rhineland city during Hitler's reoccupation of the Rhineland in March 1936.

SOURCE 17
German rearmament: tanks.

In 1936 he committed his soldiers to their first action: occupying the Rhineland, part of Germany but supposed to be free of all military forces by the terms of the Treaty of Versailles (Source 18). The troops in Source 18 do not look as if they could put up much of a fight against a serious modern army (see Source 19). In fact, the French and the British did nothing. Nor did they do anything in March 1938 when Germany and Austria were united (the 'Anschluss') even though this was forbidden at Versailles.

By late 1938, Hitler was much more confident than he had been in 1936. His army was now much larger and better equipped. His next move was to demand the Sudetenland, the border areas of Czechoslovakia which had many Germans living there. Neville Chamberlain, the British Prime Minister, asked for talks with Hitler. Hitler promised that if he took the Sudetenland he would have 'no more territorial demands'. Chamberlain believed him, and the Sudetenland was his. Six months later, in March 1939, Hitler marched into the rest of Czechoslovakia (Source 20). The map, Source 21, shows how he had extended his borders without going to war.

SOURCE 20
Czechs, forced to give the Nazi salute, watch German forces march into Prague, March 1939.

'The 48 hours after the march into the Rhineland were the most nerve-racking of my life. If the French had opposed us then we would have had to withdraw. Our forces were not strong enough to even put up a moderate resistance.'

SOURCE 19
Hitler, speaking to friends several years later.

The next victim was Poland. After Czechoslovakia, Hitler did not believe Britain and France would go to war with him over Poland. The only country which could stop him was the USSR, so in August 1939 the Nazi–Soviet Pact was signed, in which the two countries agreed not to attack each other. In a secret agreement Germany and the USSR agreed to divide Poland between them. Poland was attacked in September 1939. For once Hitler had misjudged the reactions of Britain and France. War was declared.

1 Do you think Hitler was to blame for the Second World War? Support your argument by referring to: his ideas; German rearmament; the Rhineland; the Anschluss; the Sudetenland; Poland.

2 How much did other countries let Hitler get away with things? Think about: Britain and France in 1936 and 1938; the USSR in 1939.

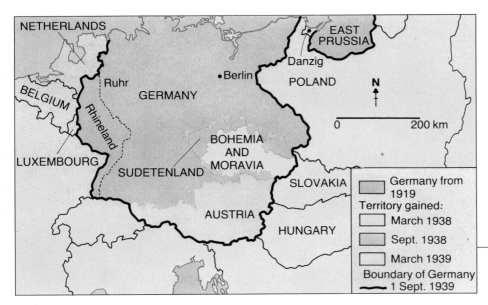

SOURCE 21
Changes to European borders as a result of Hitler's policies.

Who else was to blame for the war?

Who else might carry some of the blame for the Second World War?

- The peace-makers at Versailles drew up a treaty that the Germans resented. Hitler played on this resentment to gain popularity.
- The USA did not get involved. Its ISOLATIONIST policy, from 1920–41, prevented the USA from playing any part in peace-keeping.
- Britain felt that the Versailles terms were too harsh and that Germany had a right to have an army like everyone else. The British were deeply opposed to war (see Sources 24 and 25). Many in Britain felt that the Communist USSR was a worse danger than Hitler.
- France clung to the terms of Versailles and regarded Germany as an enemy.
- The USSR feared Hitler but was also suspicious of other countries. The Nazi–Soviet pact allowed Hitler to start the events which led directly to war: the invasion of Poland.

Let us look at three examples to see how everyone behaved.

Case Study 1: Alliances in Europe

Look at the map, Source 22. What does it show? France insisted that alliances with Eastern Europe were defensive only, to stop German advances. Germany insisted that the alliances were a threat. Germany was surrounded by hostile neighbours, so re-armament was necessary. This atmosphere of mistrust was typical of the 1930s.

SOURCE 22
Europe in 1936.

Case Study 2: Ethiopia

In 1935, Mussolini, dictator of Italy, ordered his troops to invade Ethiopia (then usually called Abyssinia). They used modern weapons, including poison-gas, against badly armed Ethiopians. The attack was completely unjustified: Italy wanted to make Ethiopia a colony. It was just the kind of event the League of Nations was set up to prevent. The Emperor appealed to the League (Source 23). What would it do?

The League reacted slowly. Eventually members of the League were asked not to trade with Italy, but essential supplies like oil were not included in the ban. Several countries carried on trading and the SANCTIONS had little effect. Britain and France tried to come to a private deal with Mussolini. As Source 24 shows, Britain would not go to war over the issue.

The League of Nations was seen to be completely ineffective. Mussolini got away with his invasion. Hitler watched with interest.

> I . . . am here today to claim that justice which is due to my people . . . I assert that the problem is a much wider one . . . It is the very existence of the League of Nations. It is the promises made to small states that their independence be respected and ensured. God and history will remember your judgements.

SOURCE 23
Haile Selassie, Emperor of Ethiopia (Abyssinia), speaking to the League of Nations in 1936.

'The British have such a horror of war that they will never support a policy which involves the slightest risk of it. They were very angry with Mussolini and very sorry for Abyssinia, but they were not willing to go to war.'

SOURCE 24
The British Secretary of State for War in 1935, Duff Cooper, wrote this, much later.

Case Study 3:
Sudetenland and appeasement

Hitler's threats to Czechoslovakia over the Sudetenland in 1938 seemed likely to lead to war. Hurried preparations were made in Britain for war. Chamberlain flew to meet Hitler three times and eventually gave him everything he wanted. This policy of giving in to Germany, hoping that Hitler's demands would cease, is called appeasement. Chamberlain was a hero at the time (Source 26) but has been criticised ever since.

It should be said in Chamberlain's favour that he was sincerely trying to avoid war (Source 25). Appeasement also gained Britain 12 precious months to build up her armed forces. However, this was done at the expense of the Czechs (look at Chamberlain's attitude to Czechoslovakia in Source 25). Hitler came to think that Britain never would go to war, so moved into Poland. The USSR was also disgusted at appeasement and made the Nazi–Soviet Pact in 1939. In these ways appeasement did not prevent war but made it more likely.

'How horrible, fantastic, incredible it is that we should be digging trenches and trying on gas-masks here, because of a quarrel in a far-off country between people of whom we know nothing. I am a man of peace to the depths of my soul. But if I were convinced that any nation had made up its mind to dominate the world by fear of its force I should feel that it must be resisted.'

SOURCE 25
Chamberlain, speaking in 1938 before meeting Hitler.

SOURCE 26
Chamberlain shows the Munich agreement at the airport on his return from Munich to Britain, September 1938.

attainment target

1 A. 'Hitler was to blame for the war.'
   B. 'Hitler was not to blame: he just took the opportunities handed to him. Other countries did not try hard enough to keep the peace.'

   Which of these two views do you think is more accurate?

2 Do you think anyone after 1935 could have stopped the Second World War breaking out? If so, who, and what should they have done?

3 Throughout the 1930s Stalin and Hitler had been hostile to each other. Why did they make the Nazi–Soviet Pact?

4 One interpretation of the causes of the Second World War is that they all had their roots in mistakes made at Versailles. How far do you agree with this interpretation? Draw on the events described in this unit to explain your answer.

This depth study is about what it was like to live in Nazi Germany during the 1930s, before the Second World War started in 1939. In particular, it looks at how popular Hitler and the Nazis were.

Hitler and the law

For ordinary Germans one of the most frightening things about Nazi rule was the speed with which Hitler made himself dictator and destroyed his opponents. At the beginning of 1933 Hitler had never held any position of power; by the end of the summer he was undisputed master of Germany, democracy was dead and his opponents silenced. How did he do this?

In 1923 Hitler had failed to seize power in Munich by force (The Beer-hall Putsch, see page 106). He decided that in future he would have to gain power through Parliament. (This is explained in Source 27.) He could then pass laws to set up his dictatorship and could not be stopped. This is exactly what he did in 1933.

In January 1933 Hitler became Chancellor (Prime Minister) of Germany by means of a deal made in secret with other parties. He immediately called for new elections and had laws passed which made it very difficult for his opponents to fight them. Opposition newspapers were banned; their meetings forbidden. The Nazis were in charge of many police forces and recruited 50,000 SA members as special police. Many of their opponents were arrested, see Source 28.

Then, when an attempt was made to burn down the Reichstag (Parliament) building, Hitler blamed it on his hated rivals, the Communists. The election was held amid violence and intimidation in March. The Nazis, with 44 per cent of the vote, were the biggest single party, and, with their allies, held 288 seats. Even so, the other parties altogether had 295 seats.

By banning the Communists and several socialists Hitler was able to pass the laws he wanted:

- March, 1933: The Enabling Law. Hitler could pass laws without consulting Parliament.

- May, 1933: trade unions abolished, their offices occupied, their officials arrested and imprisoned.

- July, 1933: all other political parties abolished – the Nazis were now the only legal party. This ended democracy in Germany for 12 years.

The Nazis also took control of the courts and the judges (Source 29). From now on, the German people could not hope for a fair trial: the law was just what Hitler wanted it to be.

'We will have to hold our noses and enter Parliament against the other parties. If out-voting them takes longer than out-shooting them, at least the result will be guaranteed.' Hitler, 1923

'We are not on principle a parliamentary party.' Hitler, 1930.

'We enter Parliament in order to supply ourselves with its weapons. We come as enemies; as the wolf bursts into the flock, so we come.' Goebbels, 1928

SOURCE 27
Nazi attitudes to Parliament.

SOURCE 28
A SA member, enrolled as a special policeman, arrests political opponents, 1933.

SOURCE 29
Nazi judges.

> In a cafe a 64-year-old woman remarked to her companion at the table: "Mussolini has more political sense in one of his boots than Hitler has in his brain." The remark was overheard and five minutes later the woman was arrested by the Gestapo who had been alerted by telephone.

SOURCE 30
An incident in Germany in 1938.

> 'Where would Hitler be without me? He had better look out – the German revolution is only just beginning. If he thinks he can squeeze me for his own ends and some fine day throw me on the ash-heap he's wrong. The SA can also be an instrument for checking Hitler.'

SOURCE 31
Ernest Roehm, leader of the SA, talks about Hitler in 1933.

Hitler and terror

Violence had always been an important part of Nazism. The SA had been formed to fight the Nazis' opponents on the streets. In 1933 opponents had been arrested and supporters frightened in order to win the election.

Terror affected people beyond those who actually opposed the Nazis. The incident in Source 30 may or may not be true; the point is that many Germans thought it was true and learnt to keep their thoughts to themselves.

The Night of the Long Knives

Hitler was prepared to use any means, including violence, to make himself ruler of Germany. He had only one rival: Ernst Roehm, leader of the *Sturm Abteilung* or SA. These were the brown-shirted storm-troopers who had supported Hitler from his early days. There were 2,000,000 of them, ten times the size of the army. Roehm wanted to turn the SA into the regular German army. He felt that Hitler had lost touch with his old friends and the ideas they had shared for changing Germany. He made no secret of these views (see Source 31).

Hitler, for his part, found his street-fighting past an embarrassment now that he was trying to appear respectable. He realised the one organisation which could stop him becoming dictator was the army and the army was worried about being replaced by the SA. Hitler was going to have to choose between them. On 30 June 1934, he did. In a series of planned raids by the SS, Roehm and 400 of his followers were arrested and executed. The SA was finished and Hitler's alliance with the army was secure. This attack on his former allies was known as the Night of the Long Knives. To many German and foreign observers it showed Hitler's utter ruthlessness, see Source 32.

In August 1934 old President Hindenburg died. Hitler took over the post of President as well, calling himself simply *Der Führer* (The Leader).

SOURCE 32
British cartoon after the 'Night of the Long Knives', 30 June 1934.

ACTIVITY

Some governments today use the law to terrorise their citizens. Their police arrest and torture people. Opponents disappear without trace. Contact your local Amnesty International Group to find out about examples of the kinds of things Hitler did happening in the world today. Compare the information they give you with what you have discovered on these pages.

1 The Nazis had always used violence against their opponents. What difference did it make that from January 1933 they were part of the government?

2 The Nazis liked to claim that they were swept to power by the mass of the German people. Is this true? Look at: how Hitler became Chancellor; the results of the March 1933 elections.

How did the Nazis try to control the lives of women and children?

The Nazis actively opposed women's equality. Hitler's view of women is made clear in Source 33: they were expected to stay at home and look after their husbands and children. If a woman gave up her job on getting married the couple could qualify for a loan. The Nazis believed in the superiority of their Aryan race, so having lots of children was important, boys especially, as they would become the soldiers of the Nazi armies of the future.

Women like the one shown in Source 34 were admired. A special medal, the Mother's Cross, was started in 1939: bronze for those with four children, silver for six and gold for eight. Source 35 shows the attitude towards women held by many Nazis.

'If the man's world is the state . . . then the woman's is a smaller world, for her world is her husband, her family, her children and her home. We do not consider it correct for women to interfere in the world of men. The programme of the Nazi women's movement has in reality but a single point and that point is the child.'

SOURCE 33
Hitler explains his views on women's roles, 1934.

'Aryan doctor desires male child through a registry office marriage with a healthy aryan, virginal, young, unassuming, economy-minded woman, adapted to hard work, broad-hipped, flat-heeled and earringless.'

SOURCE 35
Advertisement in Nazi newspaper.

Children

Adults could remember a time when there was democracy in Germany, when there was an alternative to Nazism. But children would grow up knowing nothing else but Hitler's one-party state. The Nazis therefore paid special attention to children.

First, in school. All teachers had to belong to the Nazi Teachers' Association. Their past was investigated and they could be sacked for having opposed Nazism. They had to show enthusiasm for Nazism in their teaching. If they did not, the children of Nazis in their class would report them and they could lose their jobs. The curriculum was controlled, especially History, see Source 36.

Pupils had to read Hitler's book *Mein Kampf.* Even maths problems had a racial or military theme, for example: 'A bomber can carry 1,800 incendiary bombs. If it drops a bomb every second, over how long a path can it distribute these bombs if it is flying at 250 km per hour?'

SOURCE 34
Wife of a Nazi official and her seven children.

Outside school most young people were expected to join the Hitler Youth. There were separate organisations for boys and girls from 10 to 18. In 1933 the Hitler Youth had 2.3 million members, or 30 per cent of young people; in 1939 there were 7.3 million members, or 82 per cent of young people.

The Hitler Youth took up most of your spare time. There were parades and marches, see Sources 37 and 38. There were camps and outdoor activities. Alongside all these were long sessions of INDOCTRINATION into Nazi ideas. Girls were taught to expect to fill the women's role described above. Hitler described his expectations of boys in a speech in 1935: 'slim and slender, swift as a greyhound, tough as leather and hard as Krupp steel.' Both boys and girls were expected to be obedient without question.

Some of the positive and negative sides of the Hitler Youth are described in Source 39. Some girls found that it gave them more freedom than they had at home. Many young people found that it took up time which they wanted to devote to their school work. There is also no doubt that many were reluctant to join in what were almost compulsory activities.

SOURCE 38
Poster for the Hitler Youth.

KOMM ZU UNS!

DEUTSCHES JUNGVOLK IN DER HITLER-JUGEND

SOURCE 39
The appeal of the Hitler Youth, as described in 1982 by A. Klonne.

'What I liked about the Hitler Youth was the comradeship. What boy isn't fired by loyalty, honour, trips to the countryside, making campfires, having a sing-song and telling stories? Sport had an important place.

Later, when I became a leader the negative aspects became more obvious. I found the requirement of absolute obedience unpleasant. The Hitler Youth interfered in everyone's private lives. There was too much military drill.'

The German nation in its greatness is the subject of the teaching of history, educating young people to respect the great German past, the basic racial forces of the German nation. Only important events should be portrayed; the powerless and insignificant have no history.

SOURCE 36
From the German Institute of Education guidelines for the teaching of History, 1938.

SOURCE 37
Girls of the Hitler Youth marching through their town.

attainment target

1 What was the Nazis attitude towards women? Why did they hold these beliefs?

2 How did they try to influence women to follow their ideas?

3 Why did the Nazis put so much effort into their policy for children?

4 How did they try to influence children?

5 What problems were there in forcing every child and young person to follow the Nazi ideal?

Jobs for the people: Hitler's greatest success?

It was the mass unemployment in Germany during the early 1930s that had helped Hitler to come to power (see page 107). Nazi promises of jobs brought them votes (see Source 40). Source 41 seems to suggest that the Nazis kept their promise. How was it done?

Creating jobs

Before the Nazis took over, nearly a million unemployed Germans had been given jobs on government schemes. Hitler removed all these people from the unemployed list. He continued the policy of job creation using government money, planning 7,000 km of *autobahns* (motorways). In typical Nazi fashion, the policy was described as if it were a war: it was called 'The Battle for Work', and all unemployed workers had to join the German Labour Corps (Source 42). The work these schemes offered was hard manual labour at very low wages.

SOURCE 40
Nazi poster promises 'Work, freedom and bread'.

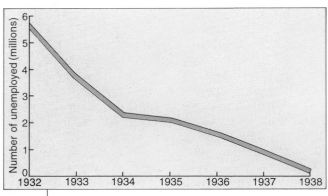

SOURCE 41
Unemployment figures, 1932–1938.

SOURCE 42
Workers in the German Labour Corps.

Military spending

The Treaty of Versailles required Germany to restrict its armed forces (see page 105). Hitler was determined to break this restriction.

He increased military spending from 1,900 million marks in 1933 to 5,800 million marks in 1936. This was 13 per cent of Germany's income; in the same year Britain spent 5 per cent and the USA 1 per cent. By 1939 Germany's military budget was 32,300 million marks. The army was increased in size from 100,000 (the limit imposed at Versailles) to 550,000 in 1936 and 850,000, with 900,000 in reserve, by 1938. In 1936 he told his generals to be ready for war in four years.

Rearmament met two of Hitler's aims: he wanted Germany to be a strong military power again. The growth of the armed forces also solved the unemployment problem. Many jobless men simply joined up. Military service was made compulsory in 1935. But the new armed forces also had to be armed and equipped.

SOURCE 49
Poster showing Hitler as the saviour of Germany.

In March 1933, Hitler appointed Goebbels as 'Minister of People's Enlightenment and Propaganda'. Goebbels used all the methods of 20th-century communication to get his message across. He took over control of all newspapers, radio stations, book publishing, theatre and cinema. Nothing could be shown, read or broadcast which his ministry had not agreed. At the same time, Goebbels could use all these MEDIA for his own propaganda. Radio was particularly popular: the number of sets in Germany went up by four times between 1933 and 1939. It told the German people of Hitler's 'successes': falling unemployment, military strength and his efforts to rid Germany of her 'enemies'. The poster, Source 49, shows the kind of image of Hitler that Goebbels put out.

It is hard to tell exactly how popular a government is in a country with no free elections and no free speech. However, Source 50 suggests that Hitler was genuinely quite popular at the end of the 1930s.

Resistance

Opposition to Nazi rule was extremely difficult. Anyone who spoke out openly faced arrest and imprisonment. Nevertheless some Communists and Socialists continued to publish anti-Nazi material in secret. The 'White Rose' group of students at Munich University were executed for publishing PAMPHLETS critical of Hitler. Other young people, the 'Edelweiss Pirates', held their own meetings and secretly published anti-Nazi leaflets. Some church leaders, both Protestant and Catholic, spoke out against Nazism at great personal risk. Many Germans undoubtedly never supported Hitler but kept quiet, like Mathilde Wolff-Monckeburg, who explains her reasons in Source 51.

Although the regime used terror, it is clear that it was also based on a large measure of consent from broad sections of the population. The fact that Hitler had solved the unemployment problem, restored Germany's position as a European power, seemed to confirm the message of Goebbels' propaganda.

A crucial element in popular consent was the fact that Nazism embodied, in an extreme form, many of the basic attitudes of a large section of the German people. They approved of the regime's hostility towards, not just Jews, but also gypsies, and of its harsh attitude towards homosexuals, tramps, habitual criminals and the "workshy". They welcomed the fact that such people were now being locked up in concentration camps.

SOURCE 50
From a book by the British historian, Jeremy Noakes, published in 1984.

'We hated the Führer from the very beginning but it was totally impossible to form an opposition, spied on as we were from all sides, telephone conversations listened to. It would have cost us our lives.'

SOURCE 51
From the diary of Mathilde Wolff-Monckeburg, written in Hamburg during the war for her children who were in Canada and Britain.

attainment target

1 What impression of Hitler and Nazism is given by Sources 47, 48 and 49?

2 How do these impressions fit in with what Hitler says about propaganda in Source 46?

3 What reasons does the historian who wrote Source 50 suggest for the German people's consent to Hitler's rule in the late 1930s?

4 What part did the following play in Hitler's popularity: his policies? propaganda? terror?

5 Look back over pages 112 to 119. What evidence is there that the German people agreed or disagreed with the actions of the Nazi government of the 1930s?

SOURCE 53
A Nazi stormtrooper outside a Jewish-owned shop. The notice says: 'Germans! Beware! Don't buy from Jews!'

SOURCE 52
Frank S. describes a lesson in 'Race Science' at his school in Breslau, Germany, in the 1930s. He was born in 1921 and was one of two Jewish students in his class.

'The teacher ordered him to the front of the room as the example of a Jew. The teacher pointed to Frank's features, explaining that they marked him as an inferior being, while the features of the blond-haired, blue-eyed student represented the perfect Aryan. Frank encountered repeated insults from non-Jewish students who wanted to pick a fight with him.'

Like many extreme nationalists, the Nazis had racist ideas (see page 107). In the next six pages we shall see how they put their racism into effect.

Anti-Semitism in history

Hatred of Jews – ANTI-SEMITISM – was not invented by the Nazis. It has been present in Europe for centuries. At various times Jews had been expelled from France, Hungary, Germany, Portugal, Spain and Russia. They were expelled from England from 1290 to 1655. In the late 19th century, the Tsars had encouraged attacks ('*pogroms*') on Jews in Russia. Anti-Semitic ideas were common in Europe in Hitler's youth. The difference in 1930s Germany was that the Nazis turned the ideas into government policies. Millions of Jews were now officially discriminated against with terrifying results.

In the 1930s

The subject of 'Race Science' was invented by the Nazis, and introduced into German schools. Source 52 describes the kind of lessons it led to.

Victimisation of Jews began with government and Nazi-organised boycotts of Jewish shops (see Source 53). Many German Jews had fought and died for their country in the First World War. However, the Nuremberg Laws, 1935, ruled that Jews could not be German citizens, or marry or have sexual relations with a German. Four hundred anti-Semitic laws were passed over the next few years. Some took away basic civil rights, such as voting, going to university or travelling. Others limited personal freedoms, such as the right to own a pet or a radio or telephone.

Jews were encouraged to leave Germany. Some were just dumped across the border. Anger at this provoked a young Jew to assassinate a German diplomat in Paris in November 1938. This led to a night of massive retaliation against Jews in Germany. On 9–10 November 1938, Jews' shops, houses and synagogues were smashed and burnt by Nazis with full government support and no police intervention (see Source 54). Broken glass lay all over the streets leading to the night being known as *Kristallnacht*, the Night of Broken Glass.

The first German concentration camp was set up at Dachau in 1933. People whose lives, beliefs or 'race' did not conform to Nazi ideas were sent there. Source 55 shows the badges each group had to wear. Gypsies were persecuted too (see Source 56). There were very few black people in Germany, but in 1937, 385 black children were STERILISED in German hospitals. Some mentally and physically disabled people were put to death.

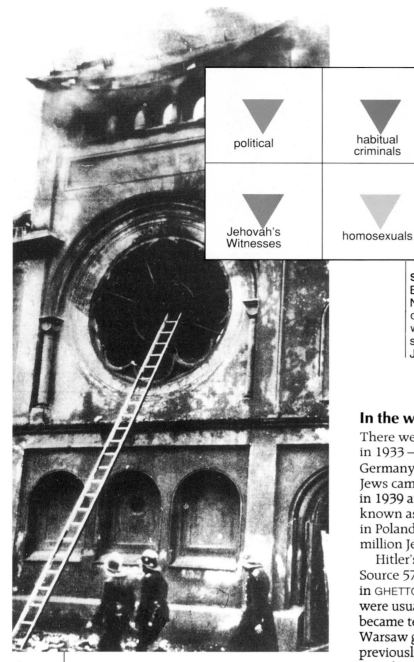

SOURCE 54
A synagogue in Berlin, set on fire by Nazis during Kristallnacht, 9 November 1938.

political	habitual criminals	emigrants	
Jehovah's Witnesses	homosexuals	vagrants	Jews

SOURCE 55
Badges worn in the concentration camps. The Nazis imprisoned people in the camps for very different reasons. As this source shows, some were there for their political or religious beliefs, some for what they had done and some, like the Jews, simply for who they were.

In the war

There were only half a million Jews in Germany in 1933 – 1 per cent of the population. When Germany took over western Europe in 1940, more Jews came under Nazi rule. But the attack on Poland in 1939 and on the USSR in 1941, brought the area known as 'The Pale' into German hands. Here, living in Poland, Lithuania, Ukraine and Bielorus, were four million Jews.

Hitler's instructions to his troops can be read in Source 57. Jews were forced from their homes to live in GHETTOES in certain towns and cities. Ghettoes were usually in a run-down part of the city and soon became terribly over-crowded. The largest was the Warsaw ghetto, where 450,000 lived in the space previously occupied by 100,000. Each ghetto was completely cut off from the rest of life. A special Council formed by the Nazis (the *Judenrat*) ran each one. These organised health, education and police. They also had to supply money and workers to the Nazis. Soon they faced more serious demands.

It all began to happen in 1937, 1938. First with the Jews, then we noticed on our travels that we were more and more discriminated against. Despite this we went on hoping that we travellers would be safe. After all, we were still Germans.

SOURCE 56
A German gypsy, Bernhard Stembach, describes his experiences.

'Be merciless! Be brutal! I have sent to the east only my Deaths Head Units, with orders to kill without mercy all men, women and children of Polish race or language.

SOURCE 57
Hitler, speaking in September 1939.

The 'final solution'

Read Source 58. It shows how far Nazi anti-Semitism had gone. The right of the Jews to exist at all under Nazi rule had become a 'question', needing a 'solution'. The final solution proposed by Göring, with Hitler's full support, and carried out by Heydrich and Himmler, was to kill everyone.

It is impossible to comprehend what this scale of organised death means. Sources 59, 60, 61 and 65 describe different aspects of the 'final solution', as seen by four individual victims.

Finding a way of killing so many people was not easy. At first they were shot. Special squads, *Einsatzgruppen*, ordered Jews to dig a trench. They were then shot and fell into the trench which became a mass grave (see Source 59). At Babi Yar, in the Ukraine, 30,000 Jews were killed and buried in this way.

Shooting proved to be an inefficient way of killing so many people however. The Nazis therefore employed 20th century technology to find a way of killing as many people as possible at one time. The gas chambers, built at Auschwitz by the end of 1941, were the result. They could kill 2,000 people at once. Other death camps were built at Chelmno, Belzec, Maidenek, Sobibor and Treblinka. Auschwitz was the biggest because its position on the railway network meant that Jews could be brought there by train from all over Europe (see Sources 60 and 61).

'I hereby charge you with making all necessary preparations...for bringing about a final solution of the Jewish question within the German sphere of influence in Europe.'

SOURCE 58
Göring's order to Himmler and Heydrich of 31 July 1941.

'All around and beneath her she could hear strange sounds, groaning, choking and sobbing. Many of the people were not dead yet. Then she heard people walking near her, actually on the bodies. They were Germans who had climbed down and were taking things from the dead and occasionally firing at those which showed signs of life.'

SOURCE 59
Dina Pronicheva, who survived the mass shootings of the Einsatzgruppen, describes her experiences.

'We are lined up beside a railway cattle wagon. Once we are inside there is no room to sit . . . There is no roof. Suddenly the door is slammed shut and sealed. A bucket is tossed in as a container for human waste. Terrible cries pierce the air. An old lady near me has just died. A little boy is screaming for his mother.'

SOURCE 60
A Polish Jew named David describes the train journey to Treblinka camp.

SOURCE 61
Jews being taken by train to a concentration camp.

The Nazis were proud of this efficient death machine. Lists of Jews from all over Europe were drawn up. They were taken from their homes and put on trains. Three hundred and twenty thousand Jews died on the trains.

On arrival at the camp, families were separated (see Source 62). Most women, all children and the old and sick – about 80 per cent of each train load – went straight to the gas chambers. They were told it was a communal shower, as Source 63 tells us. The relatives of these people, working in separate parts of the camp, often did not find out until months later that members of their families had been put to death.

Special prisoners – *Sonderkommando* – opened up the doors of the gas chambers. Gold teeth and rings were taken from the bodies (see Source 64) as well as hair to fill mattresses. They then burnt the bodies in special ovens.

Those who had been selected to work were sent to special factories at the camps. Workers were treated as non-humans, and usually died after a few months. Source 65 describes one man's attempt to cling to his humanity. In some camps painful, often fatal, medical experiments were carried out.

The process continued to the end of the war. In fact, transporting victims to the camps actually hindered the war effort by using locomotives, men and fuel. By 1945, six million Jews as well as about five million others including Slavs, gypsies and homosexuals had been killed.

> An SS Officer came to meet us, a truncheon in his hand. He gave the order: "Men to the left, women to the right"…Eight short, simple words. Yet that was the moment when I parted from my mother. I glimpsed my mother and my sister moving away to the right. My mother was stroking my sister's fair hair as though to protect her, while I walked on with my father and the other men and did not know that in that place at that moment I was parting from my mother and sister for ever.

SOURCE 62
A Jewish boy, Elie, aged 15, describes the 'selection' on the platform at Auschwitz.

SOURCE 65
Primo Levi, an Italian Jew, who was in Auschwitz, describes how their treatment almost destroyed their humanity.

> 'Before entering the gas chamber prisoners were told to leave their clothes neatly together and remember where they had put them so that they would be able to find them again quickly after their shower.
> The women went in first with the children, followed by the men who were always fewer in number. The door would be closed and the gas discharged through vents in the ceilings. About one-third died straight away. The remainder began to scream and struggle for air. The screaming, however, soon changed to the death rattle and in a few minutes all lay still.'

SOURCE 63
Rudolf Höss, commandant of Auschwitz, describes the gassing.

SOURCE 64
Wedding rings taken from the dead.

> 'Nothing belongs to us any more. They have taken away our clothes, our shoes, even our hair… They took away our name. If we want to keep it we will have to find the strength to do so, so that behind the name something of us still remains.'

Questioning the Holocaust

Several questions will probably have occurred to you as you read the last four pages: for example, why didn't the Jews resist what was happening? Couldn't the Allies help? What about individuals who witnessed what was going on? Did the German people know what was going on? Did they do anything?

Why didn't the Jews resist?

Some did resist. Source 66 portrays the Warsaw ghetto uprising of April 1943. When 2,000 armed SS troops entered the ghetto to round up remaining Jews, 700 fought back with grenades and guns. The Germans were forced to retreat and 200 of them were killed or wounded. For 42 days the Jews resisted German forces until they ran out of food, water and ammunition. Clashes between Jews and Germans continued until June 1944.

In October 1943, 600 prisoners attacked the guards at Sobibor camp (in Poland) and escaped. There were personal acts of resistance. Once, at Buchenwald (in East Germany) as the women were going into the gas chamber, the commanding officer found out that one was a dancer. He ordered her to dance for him. She did, and as she came near him, seized his gun and shot him.

SOURCE 66
A poster celebrating Jewish resistance in the Warsaw ghetto.

SOURCE 67
Jewish refugees being refused entry into Britain, 1938.

SOURCE 68
A Jewish surivivor describes support he received from German citizens at the time of Kristallnacht (November 1938).

'The mood among the Christian population in Munich is wholly against the action. German people offered to put up my family for the night. Despite the ban on sales to Jews, grocers asked Jews whether they needed anything, bakers delivered bread irrespective of the ban. All Christians behaved impeccably.'

There were many reasons why mass armed Jewish resistance was impossible. At first they could not believe what was happening. By the time they did, they had been isolated in ghettoes, out of touch with each other and with no weapons. Only when death seemed certain, when there was no choice, was resistance planned, and by then many people were terrorised and starved. In that situation even little acts, like studying, painting or making music was a kind of resistance. All of these things happened in the camps.

Why didn't the Allied governments help?

In the 1930s, many people all over the world put pressure on their governments to take German Jewish refugees. Many did, but never all those who wanted to come (see Source 67). Most governments limited IMMIGRATION by law, partly because of the economic depression, and partly because of hostility to foreigners.

When the 'final solution' began in 1941, the Allied governments heard about it almost at once. By 1944, Allied leaders knew the scale of what was happening, but little was done. Some suggest that the Allies could have bombed the railways leading to the camps. However, they seemed reluctant to divert their war efforts. The general public was given little information until early 1945 when Allied forces, with journalists, reached the first camps.

What could individuals do?

Individuals can make a difference. Source 68 illustrates this. In 1938 to 1939, 2,500 Jewish children were rescued from Germany and brought to England. The Quakers were particularly active in this 'Kinder-transport'. When the Germans overran Denmark, the Danes helped almost all the Jews to escape (see Source 69). Raoul Wallenberg, a Swedish diplomat, helped Jews to escape from Hungary. Selahattin Ulkumen helped to save Jews on the Greek island of Rhodes. Miep Gies hid Anne Frank in her house in Amsterdam. Oskar Schindler, a Sudeten German, protected 1,200 Jewish workers at his factory in Poland. Many unknown individuals risked their lives to hide or assist Jews.

It was the natural thing to do. I would have helped any group of Danes being persecuted. The Germans picking on Jews made as much sense to me as picking on redheads.

SOURCE 69
The words of Dr Koster, a Dane who helped Danish Jews escape to Sweden.

Why didn't the German people do more?

They knew that any opposition or criticism of the Nazis would be dealt with ruthlessly. Some German people have claimed that they did not know about the camps, because the Nazis controlled the press and the radio.

This is almost certainly an excuse. The persecution of Jews in the 1930s was done openly. There were 100 concentration camps. Jews were transported along railway lines and roads. Source 70 gives the view of one German, Speer, with great honesty. Speer knew something terrible was going on, but he did not ask any questions. He did not want to know. This is probably how many Germans felt.

When the Allies freed the camps in 1945, they wanted to force German officials to see what conditions were like (see Source 71).

'I did not query him. I did not query Himmler. I did not speak about it with personal friends. I did not investigate, for I did not want to know what was happening there.'

SOURCE 70
Albert Speer, Hitler's economic adviser, was told by a friend not to go to see the camps, which many leading Nazis did. This is how Speer reacted.

SOURCE 71
German officials from the nearby town of Celle were made to witness the mass burial of the dead at Belsen camp, April 1945.

In this unit you will find out about the Second World War. It starts with an overview of the war itself. The focus here is on technology and people: what weapons were used and what the human experience of war was like. The overview ends with an investigation into the dropping of the atomic bomb on Japan.

The unit then goes on to two depth studies. One looks at the Home Front in Britain during the war. The other looks at the experience of women in Britain over the 20th century and how far the world wars changed women's lives.

The unit ends with an overview of the legacy of the Second World War on Britain, Europe and the world after 1945.

The Second World War

In Unit 1 you found out what the First World War was like. The Second World War was different in several ways.

World War   Fighting took place on land, in and under the sea and in the air: in Europe, Africa and Asia; in deserts, in jungles, in snow, in the warm Pacific and the freezing Arctic.

Different weapons   Look at Sources 2 and 3. Using aeroplanes and tanks in war was not new but both had developed a great deal in the 20 years since the First World War. Using these weapons meant that the Second World War was to be a war of rapid movement, unlike the First.

The human side   Civilians were much more involved (see the depth study on pages 138 to 151). Because it was a world war, with fast-moving weapons, the experiences of those fighting were more varied, as we shall see. Source 1 reminds us that it was not just a white person's war either.

SOURCE 1
Members of the Caribbean Regiment in action, 1945.

SOURCE 2
Stuka dive bombers in action, 1940.

SOURCE 4
After the war a German describes the military strength of the Americans.

> He looked at me and said, "Well it's like this. I was on the hill as a battery commander with six 88-millimetre anti-tank guns, and the Americans kept sending tanks down the road. We kept knocking them out. Every time they sent a tank we knocked it out. Finally we ran out of ammunition and the Americans didn't run out of tanks."

Industry

Production of weapons was by far the most important factor in winning this modern war. Germany and Japan had hoped for short, sharp wars. In the end, the USA and the USSR could turn out more tanks, more planes and guns than their enemies.

Source 4 gives an example of what this superiority meant. It is a theme you will find running through this overview.

Blitzkrieg

At first, the new weapons were used most effectively by the Germans. Panzer divisions, made up of tanks and soldiers in lorries or on motorbikes could strike deep into enemy territory quickly, causing chaos. Dive-bombers worked with the ground forces, destroying key targets such as airfields or petrol dumps.

The Germans called this 'lightning war' (*Blitzkrieg*). It was used effectively in September 1939 against Poland. It was used again in May 1940 when German forces attacked Holland, Belgium and France.

Dunkirk

Within 10 days German Panzer divisions had reached the Channel coast. British troops were sent reeling back to the port of Dunkirk. Source 5 shows troops waiting on Dunkirk beach to be evacuated. From 28 May to 16 June 338,000 soldiers (139,000 of them French) were evacuated. Over 68,000 soldiers were killed, while 2,500 guns, 90,000 rifles, 64,000 vehicles and 51,000 tons of ammunition had to be left behind.

SOURCE 5
A painting of the withdrawal from Dunkirk, by Charles Cundall, commissioned in 1940.

SOURCE 6
RAF pilots run for their parked aeroplanes (Hurricanes).

Why did the Germans lose the Battle of Britain?

In the summer of 1940, Hitler made plans to invade England. This was called Operation Sea-lion. But the invasion of Britain posed a different problem from the Blitzkrieg attack on France. There were 30 to 40 kilometres of English Channel to cross. Fleets of barges would be needed to ferry thousands of troops to the English coast. They could easily be attacked from the air. Hitler's first step, therefore, was to win control of the skies. The Battle of Britain, which lasted through August and September 1940, was the battle between the RAF and the Luftwaffe to achieve this.

The Luftwaffe sent bombers with fighter escorts to bomb airfields and destroy fighters on the ground. At the beginning of the battle the Luftwaffe had about 930 fighters to the RAF's 650.

The voice of the controller came unhurried over the loudspeaker telling us to take off and in a few seconds we were running for our machines. I climbed into the cockpit of my plane and felt an empty feeling in my stomach. I knew that that morning I was to kill for the first time. We ran into them at 18,000 feet, 20 yellow-nosed Messerschmitt 109s. As they came down we turned head on to them. I saw B. . . . let go a burst of fire at the leading plane, saw the pilot put his machine in a half-roll and knew that he was mine. I turned the gun-button to fire and let go a 4-second burst. I saw the bullets from all eight guns thud home. For a second he seemed to hang in the air, then a jet of flame shot upwards and he spun out of sight.

SOURCE 7
Richard Hillary, a Spitfire pilot, describes his first battle.

'Finally my chance came. I saw a Messerschmitt 109 and 200m behind him, a Spitfire. I peeled off and dived, turning in behind him. Be calm! Don't fire yet! I applied full power and closed the gap. Suddenly the Tommy opened fire. I pressed the gun button at the same instant. My first shot hit. The Spitfire streamed a long grey smoke train and dived steeply into the sea. My first Tommy was down.'

SOURCE 8
Max-Helmuth Ostermann, a German pilot, describes the battle.

As the battle developed a number of factors became important:

- **Radar** (Radio Detection And Ranging). A chain of radar stations gave the RAF information on German aircraft up to 25 kilometres away. Pilots then rushed to their planes (see Source 6) and were rarely caught on the ground.
- **Aircraft**. British Spitfires were more manoeuvrable than Messerschmitts, and were heavily-armed. The German aircraft also did not have much flying-time left by the time they were over England.
- **Pilots**. The RAF was desperately short of trained pilots. However, at least British pilots who survived being shot down could go back to the battle. Shot-down German pilots were prisoners until the war ended.
- **Aircraft production**. This was crucial. By working at full capacity, British factories could produce more planes, as Source 10 shows. It was these figures that led Hitler to call off Operation Sea-lion on 17 September.

The human side

The Battle of Britain was a most unusual battle. For one thing the fighting could be seen in the skies over southern England by millions of people (Source 9). For another, the numbers of men involved were, by 20th-century standards, very few. They fought one-to-one, as in battles of the past, although, of course, thousands of people were involved in keeping the planes flying.

Sources 7 and 8 are two personal experiences of the battle. In what ways are they similar? What do you think the men in Source 6 would be feeling as they rush to get airborne?

	Germany	Britain
Fighters lost	470	769
Fighters built	391	943
Bombers lost	734	*
Bombers built	642	*

*British bomber production and losses were not relevant to the outcome of the battle.

SOURCE 10
Aircraft losses and production, August–September 1940.

1 Choose one of the following items and explain how it led to the German defeat in the Battle of Britain:
   a Radar,
   b Aeroplanes,
   c Pilots,
   d Aircraft production.

2 Which do you think was the most important reason for the German defeat? You should compare at least three of the items in the answer.

3 Some of the items listed in 1 above are about technology, and some are about people. Choose one example of each and explain them.

Why were the Russians unbeatable?

Hitler had always said he would attack Russia. The invasion, Operation Barbarossa, began in June 1941. Stalin did not believe reports that it would happen and the Red Army was unprepared. By November the German army, expert in motorised war, had advanced deep into Russia reaching Leningrad and the outskirts of Moscow. Nearly 3 million Russian prisoners had been taken. Yet Russia was not defeated.

Problems for the Germans

Invading Russia was not like invading France the previous year, see page 127. Distances were much greater; Berlin to Moscow is 1,800 km, Berlin to Paris just over 800 km. Roads were much worse, as Sources 11 and 12 show. Supplying their forces in these conditions became a huge problem for the Germans. Nor could they live off what they could seize: see Stalin's orders in Source 14.

Then came the winter. Transport ground to a halt. Petrol froze in the tanks. German soldiers, in summer uniforms for a short, sharp war, were ill-equipped. Thousands suffered from frostbite. Desperate measures were used (Source 13).

The Russian response

In Bielorus and Ukraine Stalin's rule was hated and the Germans were welcomed. However, Hitler's ideas of the racial inferiority of these people replaced any friendship with harsh cruelty. Civilians were massacred. Very few Russian prisoners of war survived. Russian soldiers and people knew what their fate was if they lost. The war became desperate and bitter (Source 17).

SOURCE 12
German transport in Russia, in the mud.

SOURCE 11
General Blumentritt describes the German advance into Russia in 1941.

It was appallingly difficult country for tank movement – great forests, wide swamps, terrible roads and bridges not strong enough to bear the weight. The great motor highway leading from the frontier to Moscow was unfinished – the one road a Westerner would call a road. On our maps all the supposed main roads were marked in red, but they often proved to be merely sandy tracks.

Such country was bad enough for the tanks, but worse still for the transport accompanying them – carrying their food and supplies. Nearly all this transport consisted of wheeled vehicles which could not move off the roads, nor on them if the rain turned them to mud.

'The bodies (of dead Russian soldiers) were frozen stiff. And their boots were frozen to their legs. "Saw the legs off" ordered Kageneck. The men hacked off the dead men's legs below the knee and put the legs, with the boots still attached, in the ovens. Within 10 or 15 minutes the legs were sufficiently thawed for us to strip off the vital boots.'

SOURCE 13
A German soldier describes what they were driven to do to get decent boots to cope with the fierce Russian winter.

'All citizens of the Soviet Union must defend every inch of Soviet soil, fight to the last drop of blood. In the event of a retreat by the Red Army all railway rolling stock must be brought away. We must not leave the enemy a single railway coach, a single engine. We must not leave a single pound of grain or a single gallon of petrol. All valuable materials which cannot be taken away must be destroyed.'

SOURCE 14
Stalin addresses his people as the German army advanced.

SOURCE 15
Soviet tanks on a production line at a factory in the Urals. On the first tank is the name of the popular Leningrad communist, Kirov.

SOURCE 16
Soviet soldiers at Stalingrad.

'The Russian soldier is immune to the most incredible hardships. He can stand up to the heaviest artillery fire and air bombardment, while Russian commanders remain unmoved by the bloodiest losses. To step on walls of dead, composed of the bodies of his former friends and companions makes not the slightest impression on him.'

SOURCE 17
German General Mellenthin describes Russian soldiers.

Stalingrad

In 1942 a German advance reached Stalingrad. Here Soviet and German troops fought for the city, building by building, room by room (see Source 16). In the end German efforts failed for lack of supplies and they surrendered. Over 240,000 German soldiers were killed or captured.

When the Germans advanced, thousands of factories were packed up and moved east, out of their reach. Source 15 shows a Soviet tank factory in the Urals. By 1942 Soviet production of aircraft outstripped German production by 3 to 2, of tanks by 3 to 1 and of guns by 10 to 1. The Soviet Union was larger, with a bigger population and greater resources than Germany. When these were mobilised the Red Army could not be stopped. At the huge battle of Kursk, in 1943, Soviet forces numbered 6.4 million men, 103,000 guns, 9,900 tanks and 8,400 aircraft.

> **attainment target**

1 Which of the sources here would you use to find out about the technology of the war in Russia?

2 What else would you like to see to find out more about this?

3 Which of the sources here would you use to find out about the human side of the war in Russia?

4 What else would you like to see to find out more about this?

5 Which do you find the more useful source for showing the German transport difficulties, Source 11 or Source 12?

6 Write an account of the war on the Russian Front using the sources on these pages.

SOURCE 18
Pearl Harbor. 8.40 a.m. on 7 December 1941. Japanese bombers blow up US ships.

The Pacific War

Japanese troops had seized Manchuria in 1931 and attacked China in 1937. After 1939, the war in Europe meant that the British, French and Dutch empires in the East could not be defended properly. The Japanese saw this as a chance to take the raw materials their industry needed: rice, coal, rubber, tin and oil. Only the USA could stop them taking them.

Pearl Harbor

Japanese leaders calculated that if they could knock out the US Pacific fleet, they would gain enough time to take all the lands they wanted. After that they would be too strong for the US to stop them. They therefore planned a surprise raid on the US fleet in Pearl Harbor, Hawaii. Early on Sunday, 7 December 1941, Japanese aeroplanes took off from the decks of their aircraft carriers 500 kilometres from Pearl Harbor. The US fleet was caught completely unprepared. Eight battleships were sunk or damaged (see Source 18), ten other ships, 188 aircraft were destroyed and 2,403 people killed. President Roosevelt called it 'a day of infamy'.

However, some of the fleet was safe as it was out at sea. Even more important, this was the end of US isolation. From now on US wealth, resources and industry were poured into the fight against Japan, Italy and Germany. Churchill was delighted. The important differences in industrial capacity can be seen in Source 19.

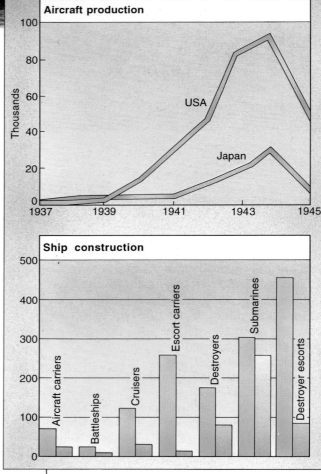

SOURCE 19
Japanese and US production of ship and aeroplanes during the war.

SOURCE 20
Fighter aircraft on the deck of the US carrier *Yorktown* during the battle of the Coral Sea, May 1942.

SOURCE 21
Australian troops disembarking from landing craft, New Guinea, 1943.

Aircraft carriers

Sea battles were fought between fleets of aircraft carriers with their supporting battleships. The fleets were hundreds of kilometres apart and used their aircraft (Source 20) to attack the enemy. Major battles took place at the Coral Sea, May 1942 and Midway, June 1942.

The US General MacArthur could not hope to fight the Japanese on every one of the many islands in the Pacific. His strategy of 'island-hopping' meant landing on important bases (see Source 21), cutting Japanese supply lines and mopping up afterwards.

The human side

Two things made the life of a soldier in the South Pacific difficult: the jungle, and the fanaticism of the Japanese. The jungle was the one place where the 20th-century technology of this war broke down. It could not be crossed by any tank or motorised vehicle. Japanese soldiers were skilled in using bikes. Source 22 describes the climatic conditions.

The Japanese made up for their lack of resources by their bravery and stamina. On a few ounces of rice, some water and some pickles they would fight for days, often to the last man. They believed that it was far better to die honourably, fighting for their Emperor, than to surrender. Towards the end of the war, suicide pilots, 'Kamikazes', would attack US ships by flying their planes, loaded with explosives, on to their decks, see Source 23.

'The moist humidity was so overpowering, and hung in the air so heavily, that it seemed more like a material object than a weather condition. It brought the sweat starting from every pore at the slightest exertion. Unable to evaporate in it, the sweat ran down over the bodies soaking everything to saturation. When it had saturated their clothing, it ran down into their shoes, filling them, so that they sloshed along in their own sweat as if they had just come out of a river.'

SOURCE 22
The unbearable climate of the tropics is described by a US marine, James Jones.

SOURCE 23
US carrier *Bunker Hill* after being hit by two Japanese 'Kamikaze' pilots, April 1945.

---

1 From a naval commanders' point of view, what are the advantages and disadvantages of fighting in battle against an enemy hundreds of kilometres away?

2 Why was the jungle the one place where 20th-century technology was almost useless?

The Desert War

In September 1940 Italy, taking advantage of Britain's plight at that time, invaded Egypt, a British colony. The Italians were soon driven back, however, and in early 1941 Hitler sent General Rommel to help his ally.

The North African desert seemed ideally suited to tank warfare. It was open, with few natural obstacles (see Source 24). The war was waged over hundreds of kilometres as each side advanced or retreated. Each advance brought supply problems; the further you were from your base, the further supplies had to be brought out into the empty desert (see Source 25). Food, ammunition and spares all had to be transported to the armies.

Eventually, after getting to within 95 km of the main British base at Alexandria, Rommel was defeated at El Alamein in October 1942 by General Montgomery. It was the first serious setback Hitler had suffered. From then on the Germans were driven back across North Africa. The Allies landed in Sicily in 1943, then began to move north through Italy. As Churchill said, 'It may almost be said, before El Alamein we never had a victory. After it we never had a defeat'.

The human side

The desert might have been good for tanks, but it was awful for people, as Source 26 describes. The nights could be freezing cold, the days very hot. There were flies everywhere and always a shortage of water.

1 Make a list of all the things tanks and lorries need to keep them fighting.

2 Make a list of all the things people need in the desert to keep them fighting.

3 Use these lists to explain why the supplies problem was so important in the desert war.

SOURCE 24
German tanks moving through the desert.

> The sun was a burning metallic monster in a cloudless blue sky under which you perspired until the moisture dripped from nose, chin and elbows, and turned your shirt or shorts black and clinging. And the sand – the sand that blew about nearly all the time and penetrated your throat and eyes and truck carburettor – caked itself upon the sweaty wetness of your face and whole head.

SOURCE 26
A description of conditions in the desert by G. Talbot.

SOURCE 25
German supplies and transport aircraft.

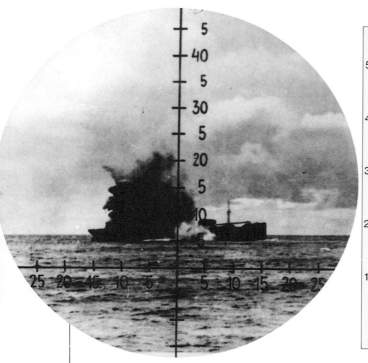

SOURCE 27
A British merchant ship torpedoed, seen through the periscope of a U-boat.

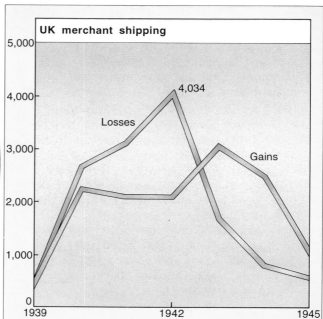

SOURCE 28
British merchant shipping: gains and losses, 1939–1945.

The Atlantic War

After the war Winston Churchill wrote: 'the only thing that ever really frightened me was the U-boat peril.' He knew that Britain was utterly dependent on imports of food and other essential supplies, mainly from the US. If these failed, the country could not go on fighting. The Battle of the Atlantic was between the German U-boats and the Allied aeroplanes and warships. From 1941 the merchant ships travelled in convoy protected by several fast escort vessels.

At first the U-boats were highly successful, hunting in 'wolf-packs' of about ten, particularly after they took over French ports in 1940. Convoys of 20 to 50 merchant ships, travelling slowly, were easy targets for the U-boats' torpedoes. Sometimes less than half of the convoy reached Britain. In 1942 over 1,600 merchant ships were sunk. Then the tide turned. Long-range aircraft could patrol far out at sea, protecting the convoys. Allied technology improved, so that they could detect U-boats better. They could also decode their radio messages. As Source 28 shows, more ships were being built than were being lost.

The human side

Casualties were high on both sides (see Source 29). A quarter of all merchant seamen died. By the end of the war U-boat losses were even higher: 27,000 out of 39,000 German U-boat crewmen were killed.

(a) British merchant seaman S. Champion:

'They sank four ships the first night. There seemed to be fires and explosions everywhere. Then we copped it. It must have been about two in the morning. The blast knocked me flying and she lurched and began to go down right away. We had no time to get the boats away, or get me up from below. A few of us were struggling in the water for a life-raft. In a few minutes the ship had gone down with most of my mates, and only seven of us left on the rafts.'

(b) German U-boat captain during a depth-charge attack in his submarine:

'Had they spotted us? We dived to 75 fathoms. We had never known the charges to fall with such uncomfortable accuracy as these did. All the glass panels on our controls were shattered. Valve after valve was loosened and before long the water came trickling through. Faces are pale and every forehead sweating. The steel bulkheads are buckling and may give way at any minute. "Well it's not everyone who gets such an expensive coffin", someone remarks. "Four million marks it cost".'

SOURCE 29
Two experiences of the Atlantic War.

Why were the atomic bombs dropped?

In June 1944, on D-Day and the days that followed, nearly 2 million men and all their weapons and equipment were landed in northern France. Source 30 shows some of the massive amount of war material the Allies could use – one of the main themes of this overview. The Red Army, from the east, and the Allied forces, from the west, closed in on Germany. Hitler committed suicide on 30 April 1945 and Germany surrendered on 8 May.

Ending the war against Japan was the next goal. Truman knew that invading Japan would not be easy. Even though the US had almost total control of the air and sea, the Japanese forces would fight desperately. Already US casualties were rising: in the attack on Saipan, in 1944, 14,000 Americans (20 per cent of forces) were killed. At Iwo Jima 23,000 (29 per cent of forces) and at Okinawa 66,000 (43 per cent of forces) had lost their lives.

Truman was told that his scientists, working on what was called 'The Manhattan Project' had produced two samples of a new powerful bomb. The Manhattan Project had cost $2,000 million. At the same time some of his advisers were thinking about the world after the war and were worried about the growing power of the USSR (Source 31).

As you know, Truman ordered the dropping of the bomb on Hiroshima. The single bomber, *Enola Gay*, carried out the mission on 6 August 1945. The results can be seen in Source 32. Source 33 gives an exact description of how the city was affected. Three days later the second bomb was dropped on Nagasaki. Over 70,000 people died instantly at Hiroshima, but people have been dying of radiation sickness ever since. So far ¼ million people have died.

SOURCE 30
Tanks and other vehicles being unloaded on to the Normandy beaches. Barrage balloons above the ships protect them from low-flying aircraft.

> Gentlemen, can I tell you what really worries me? Russia's influence in Eastern Europe. Rumania, Bulgaria, Czechoslovakia, Yugoslavia, Hungary are all living under a Soviet shadow. It will be impossible to persuade Russia to remove her troops from Poland unless she is impressed by American military might. Now, our demonstrating the bomb will make Russia more manageable.

SOURCE 31
Truman's personal adviser, James Byrnes, said this in 1945.

Was it justified?

Your answer to this question will depend on which option you choose, and for what reasons. Truman was clear that it was justified because it saved American lives – see Source 34. But was it right to do this in order to impress the Russians? Or to justify the cost of the Manhattan Project? (see Source 35). Why didn't Truman choose option (iii), which many of his top scientists suggested? Was revenge for Pearl Harbor part of the motive? What do you think?

ACTIVITY

Get into groups of three or four. One is President Truman, the rest are his advisers. In the light of what you have just read, which option should you choose:

i)   Invade Japan
ii) Call on Japan to surrender
iii) Demonstrate the atom bomb on a desert island and then call on Japan to surrender
iv) Use one of the bombs
v)   Use both bombs.

When you have made your decision, explain your reasons, noting why you rejected the other options.

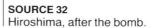

SOURCE 32
Hiroshima, after the bomb.

'Suddenly a glaring pinkish light appeared in the sky, accompanied by an unnatural tremor, which was followed almost immediately by a wave of heat and wind which swept away everything in its path. Many were killed instantly, others lay writhing on the ground screaming in agony from the intolerable pain of their burns. Everything standing upright in the way of the blast – walls, houses, factories and other buildings – was annihilated. Trams were picked up and tossed aside. Horses, dogs and cattle suffered the same fate as human beings. Trees went up in flames, the rice-plants lost their greenness, the grass burnt on the ground like dry straw.

Up to about three miles from the centre of the explosion lightly built houses were flattened as though they had been made of cardboard. Those who were inside were either killed or wounded. The few who succeeded in making their way to safety generally died some 20 or 30 days later of the deadly gamma-rays.'

SOURCE 33
A Japanese journalist describes what happened when the bomb dropped.

'The world will know that the first atomic bomb was dropped in Hiroshima – a military base. We wished to avoid the killing of civilians. We have used this in order to shorten the agony of war, to save the lives of thousands and thousands of young Americans.'

SOURCE 34
Truman defends his decision to drop the bomb.

SOURCE 35
British cartoon, 1945.

137

Read Source 36. Churchill is describing how the Second World War affected everyone in the country, not just the armed forces. For this reason many people in Britain called it 'The People's War'. In this depth study we will find out if it really was a 'People's War' and, if so, in which ways the war changed the lives of different groups of people.

How were ordinary people involved?

In one obvious way ordinary people were heavily involved: the bombing of towns and cities killed and injured people including young and old, male and female (Source 37). In all previous wars, soldiers had fought and killed each other while civilians were mainly unharmed. In the Second World War 60,000 British civilians were killed, over 15 per cent of all British casualties. Even preparing for the worst, like a gas attack, meant new and frightening things to do.

The pictures here show some of the other ways in which ordinary people were involved. Men, quite often old, joined the Local Defence Volunteers or LDV (see Source 38). This was 'Dad's Army', ready to defend their local area if the Germans invaded, which seemed quite likely in 1940.

We saw in the overview in this unit that producing weapons was as important for eventual victory as using them. This is what Churchill meant when he said (Source 36): 'The front lines run through the factories.' Women were recruited into factories to help with this skilled and important work (see Source 39). By 1944 60 per cent of the workforce was female.

'The whole of the warring nations are engaged, not only soldiers, but the entire population. The fronts are everywhere. Every village is fortified. Every road is barred. The front lines run through the factories. The workmen are soldiers with different weapons but the same courage.'

SOURCE 37
An air-raid warden holds a terrified child after an air attack on London, 23 June 1944.

SOURCE 36
From a speech by the British Prime Minister, Winston Churchill, in 1940.

SOURCE 38
Local Defence Volunteers ('Dad's Army').

SOURCE 39
A woman lathe operator making a gun – a painting by Laura Knight.

The KITCHEN FRONT

122 WARTIME RECIPES
broadcast by Frederick Grisewood, Mabel Constanduros and others, specially selected by the Ministry of Food.

6

A better Britain?

Even the regular, boring job of preparing food became difficult. Many kinds of food were in short supply – wasting it made shortages for others. Source 40 shows how much the government intervened in people's ordinary lives, with advice on all sorts of topics.

The name 'The People's War' meant more than just a war in which everyone was involved. The 1930s had been hard for many millions of British people. Unemployment stood at nearly three million in 1932 and there were still a million people unemployed in 1939. In some areas, unemployment and the poverty it brought were still widespread. Worst of all, many unemployed people felt their problems had been ignored by the government and the prosperous south-east of England.

In the war, no one could be ignored. The efforts of ordinary people all counted towards victory. Many hoped that this concern for all the people of Britain would be carried on after the war.

1 What do the pictures on these pages tell you about the part ordinary men, women and children played in the war?

2 Which of the war jobs shown in Sources 37, 38 and 39 looks hardest and which easiest?

3 In what ways do Sources 37 and 39 show the importance of women to the war effort?

4 Source 38 was censored, that is, the government did not allow it to be published. Why do you think this was?

SOURCE 41
Evacuees at Paddington Station, London.
London.

SOURCE 42
Four evacuees arriving at their new home, with their new foster-parents, in 1939. The man on the left is probably their teacher who arranged where they would stay.

Was evacuation successful?

In the First World War, German air-raids killed 1,413 people. By the 1930s, bombers were much bigger and British government planners expected far greater casualties. They estimated that 600,000 people would be killed in a few days. They also expected poison gas to be used. From as early as 1935, plans were made to evacuate all children, pregnant mothers, mothers with young children and disabled people from the cities of Britain to safer areas.

On 1 September 1939, as war became likely, these plans were put into action. Over four days, using buses and 4,000 special trains, one and a half million people were evacuated (see Source 41). All reached their destinations, tired and anxious, but safe. Parents who could afford to, made their own arrangements to send their children to the country or even to Canada, Australia or the USA.

'It was so entirely different to see rolling green hills, cows and sheep instead of the grim bricks and mortar that was Lambeth. My son was five years old and I was twenty-six. They were very kind to us. My son and I were never homesick, we were too happy enjoying the beautiful Dorset scenery. We were away almost six years.'

SOURCE 43
Ivy Moore describes her evacuation.

ACTIVITY

How would you organise an evacuation?
Divide the class into two halves. The first is responsible for getting the whole of your school successfully evacuated. The second is responsible for receiving and settling in a thousand evacuees. Work in committees of four.

Thoughts for the first group: What will you tell the children? What will you tell their parents? What can they take with them? How much can they carry? How will you travel? How will you keep their education going after they have arrived and settled in?

Thoughts for the second group: How will you welcome the evacuees? How will you decide how many evacuees each family can take? How will you match up evacuees and foster-parents so that both are happy? What will the children need – in the first few hours? – as time goes on?

For both groups: How could you manage evacuation better than in 1939?

> The foster-mother thought she was on to a good thing with me and the other 11 year old girl *billeted* with her. We were expected to shop and wash up and look after her whining three year old.

billeted: given accommodation

SOURCE 44
Mary Baxter talking about her evacuation.

That part of the plan was successful. But what was it like for one and a half million city children to be dumped suddenly in the countryside? (See Source 42.) Sometimes, not very much care went into choosing suitable foster-parents. Sources 43 and 44 show contrasting experiences of evacuation. For some, it was wonderful. They loved the countryside, got on well with their foster-parents and became friends for life. One boy wrote home, describing the countryside as winter ended: 'It's called spring, and they have one down here every year.' Others were horrified as they were lined up in a village hall while foster-parents looked them over and chose the ones they wanted, like a slave auction. Most missed their families and homes and the excitement of city life.

Reactions to the evacuees

It was not easy for the foster-parents either. Some people, often the better off, refused to take evacuees. The Association of Head Masters and Head Mistresses reported in July 1941 that 'the more well-to-do people have tended to shirk their

'One boy returned to his billet with a live hen under his arm and told his landlady he could "get plenty more" for her.'

'Their clothing was in a terrible condition, some of the children being sewn into their ragged garments.'

'Many of the children – and mothers – wet their beds and were not in the habit of doing anything else.'

'One boy, 13, refused to eat cereal and milk, saying, "I want some bloody beer and some chips."'

SOURCE 45
Comments on evacuees collected by Women's Institute all over Britain, 1940.

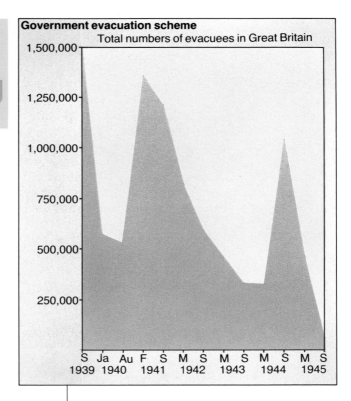

Government evacuation scheme
Total numbers of evacuees in Great Britain

SOURCE 46
Number of evacuees, 1939 to 1945.

responsibilities'. Those who did co-operate were often shocked by the evacuees for reasons illustrated by Source 45.

It was more than a clash of town and country. It was also a sight, for country people, of real poverty in some cities. Some children had no decent clothes, shoes, knickers or socks, because their parents could not afford them. Some didn't know how to use a bath or a toilet because many city houses or flats did not have them. Young mothers met in the village pubs because that was the only place they could meet.

Did evacuation work?

Source 46 shows that there were three evacuations: the first, and biggest, was in September 1939. In fact, no bombs fell on London for another eleven months. By the end of the year nearly 60 per cent of evacuees had gone home. The Blitz brought a second evacuation, nearly as large as the first, in the autumn of 1940. The flying-bombs of June 1944 led to a third evacuation, of over one million people. Although, as Source 46 shows, people drifted home quite quickly, evacuation undoubtedly saved many lives.

The lasting result of evacuation, however, was increased awareness of how bad life in Britain was for many families, especially the children.

The Blitz

At the end of August 1940 Hitler turned his attention from bombing British airfields to bombing the cities. It marked the end of the Battle of Britain, but the beginning of a horrendous period in the lives of many British people.

Liverpool was bombed for four nights at the end of August. Then on 7 September, there was a huge air-raid on the London docks and surrounding residential areas. INCENDIARY BOMBS caused fires over more than 100 hectares. Such a huge blaze caused a fire-storm, sucking in cold air like a gale. Tremendous heat was generated, causing the fire to spread rapidly. The Fire Officer's report, Source 47, explains that he had seen nothing like it before. The fire could be seen for nearly 50 kilometres. The contents of the warehouses caught fire and caused special hazards. Pepper fires loaded the air with stinging particles. Paint fires coated everything with varnish. Rubber fires caused huge clouds of black smoke.

'The flames were so long and their heat so great as to blister the paint on fire-boats that tried to slip past on the opposite bank of the Thames, 300 yards [0.7 km] away. Solid embers a foot long were tossed into streets far off to start fresh fires.'

SOURCE 47
The Chief of the London Fire Brigade, describing the fires at the Surrey Docks on 7 September 1940.

SOURCE 48
St Paul's Cathedral, London, during the Blitz of 29 December 1940.

SOURCE 49
Householders emerging from an Anderson shelter.

In the surrounding streets, thousands of homes were destroyed. Firemen struggled until they were exhausted. Air-Raid Precaution (ARP) workers tried to get people out of the ruins. Women's Voluntary Service (WVS) workers tried to look after homeless families. Four hundred and thirty people were killed and 1,600 seriously injured. The bombers returned every night for the next 76 nights and then most nights for the next six months (see Source 48).

On 14 November 1940, 400 German bombers dropped 30,000 incendiary bombs and 500 tonnes of other bombs on Coventry. The effect of heavy bombing on a much smaller city was, if anything, even worse than the Blitz on London. One-third of the houses in Coventry were destroyed, telephones, water, gas and electricity supplies were totally cut off. Five hundred and fifty-four civilians and 26 firemen were killed.

Other cities were devastated, including Birmingham, Hull, Manchester, Liverpool, Newcastle, Bristol, Sheffield, Portsmouth, Southampton, Plymouth and Leicester. In March 1941, Clydeside was hit and the town of Clydebank made almost uninhabitable.

SOURCE 50
Tube shelters visited by King
George VI and Queen
Elizabeth, November 1940.

SOURCE 51
A drawing of children in the
Tube by the artist and sculptor
Henry Moore.

Sheltering

Government plans to provide air-raid shelters were
not very effective. Brick shelters, with thick concrete
roofs, were built in many streets. They were cold,
damp, unhygienic and dangerous. Two and a half
million Anderson shelters had been issued, free, by
the government. They consisted of two curved steel
walls and were to be sunk three feet into the ground.
Even though they were liable to flooding, they gave
good shelter in a raid to those who had a garden to
put one in (as shown in Source 49).

London Transport had been told to stop people
using the tube stations as bomb shelters. The
government was afraid people would go into them
and never come up to go to work. In the event, the
people simply forced their way in and took over.
London Transport had to co-operate. Two white lines
were drawn on the platform. Until 7.30 pm shelterers
had to keep 8 feet (2.5 metres) from the edge. Then
until 10.30 pm they could move to the second line,
leaving 4 feet (1.2 metres) for travellers. Then the
current was switched off and hammocks or boards
were put across the tracks. Some people even slept on
the escalators.

At the height of the Blitz, 79 tube stations were
being used as shelters by 177,000 people. There were
no sanitation or washing facilities and the smell was
often terrible. Nor were people particularly safe in the
stations, as direct hits could kill hundreds. However,
they felt safe and preferred to be with others. They
became one of the sights of London. The King and
Queen visited them (as shown in Source 50), and
artists sketched them (see Source 51). Things were
very different at the Dorchester Hotel, however, as
Source 52 illustrates.

SOURCE 52
The air-raid shelter at the Dorchester
Hotel, London, described in 1941.

1 Why do you think Source 48 is such a famous
picture?

2 In what ways did the Blitz make the Second World
War truly a 'People's War'?

3 Artists like Henry Moore (Source 51) and Laura
Knight (Source 39, page 139) were paid by the
government to paint wartime scenes. Why do you
think the government did this?

'A neat row of beds, about two feet [61 cm] apart, each
with a fluffy eiderdown . . . The pillows were large and
full and white. There was a little sign pinned to one of
the curtains. It said "Reserved for Lord Halifax".'

Britain can take it

SOURCE 53
Fire-fighters in action during a raid on Manchester, 23 December 1940.

'East London paused for a moment yesterday to lick its wounds after what had been planned as a night of terror. But it carried on.'

SOURCE 54
From the *Daily Herald*, 9 September 1940.

SOURCE 55
Some people, such as this man, managed to remain patriotic even when things were at their worst.

Heroism

There were certainly heroes of the Blitz. Thousands of people faced death each night to deal with the results of bombing. The ARP and WVS workers, for example, described on the previous pages, risked their lives to save others. Most of them were volunteers, doing this work on top of their regular jobs. Source 53 shows the kind of conditions fire-fighters had to face, night after night. Eight hundred and twenty-three of them were killed in the war.

Some people rose to the occasion. In the London borough of Islington 'Mrs B.', a beetroot seller, took charge of a rest centre. She arranged a milk supply for the babies and got them and their mothers to sleep. Then the elderly were organised to sleep on the remaining beds while everyone else, up to 300 people, slept where they could. In the morning she organised the washing, bathed the babies, swept the floors, supervised breakfast and went home about eleven. Every evening she came back and did the same again.

SOURCE 56
'Trekking' from Southampton, December 1940.

The Blitz and morale

The German blitz on British cities had two purposes: to disrupt factories making weapons and to break the morale of the people. The first of these failed. Even the weapons factory at Clydebank kept on working after the raids, with hardly a hiccup. How near did the raids come to breaking the morale of the people?

Obviously the government did everything it could to keep up morale (see also pages 150 and 151). Newspaper articles like the one in Source 54 gave the impression that morale never faltered. At the time, and since the war, this view has been widely held. How far do Sources 55, 56, 57, 58 and 59 support this view?

Government instructions for an air-raid were to 'stay put'. In fact, thousands of people 'trekked' out of the cities. Some left each night, some more permanently; some went because they had been made homeless, some just to avoid the bombs (see Source 56). Sources 57 and 58 show just how bad the situation was after a heavy raid. Source 59 shows how people who worked through the Blitz felt about it years later.

attainment target

1 The *Daily Herald* (Source 54) said that the East End 'carried on'. Do Sources 57 and 58 support this view?

2 What problems are there in finding out exactly what life was like in the Blitz?

3 Many people think that life carried on, cheerfully, in the Blitz. Do Sources 58 and 59 support this interpretation?

4 Why do you think the view of Britain carrying on cheerfully is still so popular?

5 What is your interpretation of these events, based on this book and your own knowledge?

'Of the blitz I shall write little. We in 'S' Division were luckier than many London police, but we still had our fill of its cruelty and horror, its sickening destructiveness, its white dusty filth, and its peculiar stink of fresh decay. Just these few words and it begins to depress me again.

SOURCE 59
From the autobiography of T. Clarke, a Special Constable in the Blitz, published in 1974.

'The press versions of life going on normally in the East End are grotesque. There was no bread, no electricity, no milk, no gas, no telephones. There was every excuse for people to be distressed. There was no understanding in the huge buildings of central London for the tiny crumbled streets of densely massed population.'

SOURCE 58
A report from the East End of London, September 1940.

SOURCE 57
Bomb-damaged houses in Stepney, London, 9 September 1940, a censored photograph.

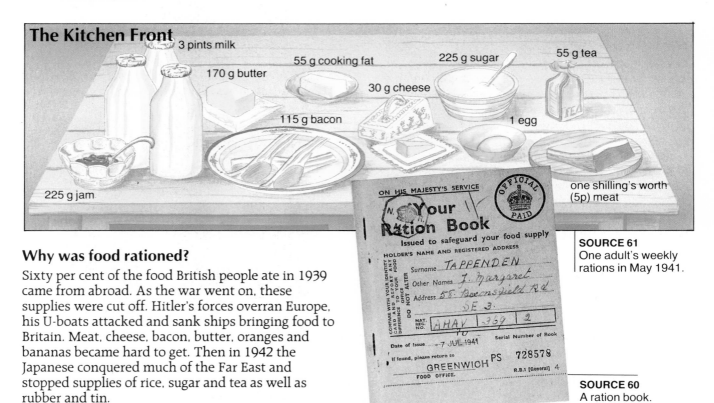

The Kitchen Front

3 pints milk

170 g butter

55 g cooking fat

225 g sugar

55 g tea

30 g cheese

115 g bacon

1 egg

225 g jam

one shilling's worth (5p) meat

SOURCE 61
One adult's weekly rations in May 1941.

ON HIS MAJESTY'S SERVICE

OFFICIAL PAID

Your Ration Book

Issued to safeguard your food supply

HOLDER'S NAME AND REGISTERED ADDRESS

Surname *TAPPENDEN*

Other Names *J. Margaret*

Address *58 Beensfield Rd*
SE 3.

NAT. REG. NO. *AHAV 369 2*

Date of Issue ....7 JUL 1941

Serial Number of Book

If found, please return to PS 728578

GREENWICH
FOOD OFFICE. R.B.1 [General] 4

SOURCE 60
A ration book.

Why was food rationed?

Sixty per cent of the food British people ate in 1939 came from abroad. As the war went on, these supplies were cut off. Hitler's forces overran Europe, his U-boats attacked and sank ships bringing food to Britain. Meat, cheese, bacon, butter, oranges and bananas became hard to get. Then in 1942 the Japanese conquered much of the Far East and stopped supplies of rice, sugar and tea as well as rubber and tin.

At first the shortages simply brought higher prices: a 50 per cent rise from 1939 to 1941. The result was food for the rich and shortages for the poor. This was obviously unfair in a 'People's War' and in January 1940 the government introduced a system of rationing. Everyone was supplied with a ration book (see Source 60). These had a number of 'coupons' for certain basic foods for each person. Everyone registered with a particular butcher and grocer, and always had to shop there with their ration books. The shopkeepers then got supplies according to how many customers had registered with them.

Source 61 shows the basic rations for an adult in May 1941. Of course there was other food available, but each individual only had a certain number of points to spend each month on items like dried fruit, canned fruit, cereals, condensed milk, syrup, biscuits or cakes. Many things were in short supply, so shoppers, mostly women, spent hours in queues hoping for some rarity, like fish (see Source 62).

'Sometimes you could get fish but it was always in short supply – first come, first served. You could wait half an hour in the queue and still not get any.'

SOURCE 62
A woman describes the problems of buying non-rationed food.

A Ministry of Food was set up to control supplies and advise the public. The government knew that the food supply was as serious a problem as the supply of bullets or aeroplanes. People had to be fed properly to carry on with their work. Scientists advised the Ministry of Food on healthy diets. Large numbers of leaflets and posters appeared, and there was a radio broadcast every morning after the 8 am news. They tried to tell people how to manage on the rations and how to cook interesting, healthy meals using non-rationed foods (see Sources 63 and 64). People were told to eat more vegetables. Brown bread was produced, because it was healthier, although many people hated it.

Did rationing work?

Most people felt that the system of rationing was fair. There were extra allowances for pregnant mothers, nursing mothers and babies. All children got one-third of a pint of milk a day at school. Many extra allotments were made, in parks, golf-courses and tennis courts. People were encouraged to 'Dig for Victory' by growing vegetables and keeping chickens or rabbits. Special supplies of dried egg, concentrated orange juice and canned meat came from the USA.

In spite of the calculations of the scientists at the Ministry of Food, some workers, doing heavy jobs like mining or steel-making, did not get enough food.

Big families were able to manage better, by pooling all their coupons, than single people living alone. Above all, many could still buy almost anything. The 'black market' (illegal supplies of food) flourished.

The worst aspect of rationing, for most people, was that it made life even more of a struggle, even more tedious. Calculating coupons and points, queueing for ages and wondering how to make interesting meals out of not very much, were daily problems. Many people worked hard, for long hours, and unappetising meals added to the monotony of life. People longed for an orange, or a chocolate bar.

The ration was nourishing, however, and most people had a more healthy diet than before.

SOURCE 63
Ministry of Food advice, featuring the cartoon character Dr Carrot.

'Dr Carrot says: "You need lots of Vitamin A. Call me in regularly and I'll guard your health."'

SOURCE 65
Utility fashions.

SOURCE 64
A Ministry of Food poster.

Other rationed items

Many factories had turned from producing goods for peace to producing goods for war. Crockery, furniture and clothes became scarce and expensive. Again, the government stepped in, with 'Utility' goods. To make the best of scarce resources, factories could only make a few designs, in simple styles. Furniture, for example, came in 22 items, with three designs for each, at two levels of quality. Clothes were put on 'points' too. Pleats, trouser turn-ups and long dresses were banned, to save cloth. Source 65 is a propaganda picture showing Utility fashions. Women – all the messages were targeted at women – were encouraged to 'make do and mend'. Last year's fashions were re-designed, clothes were made out of curtains, parachute silk and linen sacks.

1 Which items of food that you eat regularly come from abroad? Would you miss them if you couldn't have them?

2 Look at Source 61. Design a menu for a week using these items – note that you can add one of each of the items 'on points' and as many vegetables as you like.

3 Was rationing fair? Was it successful?

4 Do you think the government should do more nowadays to encourage people to eat sensibly?

The women's war

Although millions of women had worked in factories, transport and offices in the First World War, most of them returned to their traditional roles in 1918. In 1939, five million women in Britain had jobs. This was one of the highest figures in Europe but the jobs they had were mainly low-paid and unskilled. Their role was to be the wife, mother and home-maker. Did the Second World War change this?

Women at home

We have already seen women playing a big part in the 'People's War' (see Source 39 and pages 138–147). The war disrupted women's lives quite suddenly and drastically. Many children were evacuated, and hardly seen for six years. Some women were evacuated themselves (see Sources 43 and 44, pages 140 and 141). Husbands, brothers, sons and fathers went off to fight, to be seen only on occasional hurried leaves, or perhaps never again. Even the basic daily round of shopping and cooking was disrupted by rationing, let alone the Blitz. To men away fighting, the women's role was to keep their home life normal.

I remember three girls we put in charge of calves and they were marvellous. They became the most efficient tractor drivers... They got used to humping potato bags. I can't think of anything they couldn't do.

SOURCE 67
The wartime Cultivation Officer for Gloucestershire, a man, describes some of the Women's Land Army.

'We were working from drawings to make the very first Lancaster and I was amazed how many men couldn't read a drawing. I could.'

SOURCE 68
Barbara Davies, a wartime factory worker.

SOURCE 69
A woman munitions worker.

SOURCE 66
A poster encouraging women to work.

SOURCE 70
A painting by Laura Knight of WAAFs at a barrage balloon site in Coventry. Barrage balloons were flown above cities to force German bombers to fly high.

'The hand that held the Hoover works the lathe'

Britain needed far more from women than just keeping homes, however. Industrial output was crucial to winning the war, and men were being taken away to fight. As in the First World War, the factories turned to women. Posters like Source 66 encouraged them to take factory jobs.

Then, in December 1941, the government calculated that two million more people were needed for the war effort in factories and the forces. To achieve this, Britain, alone among the countries involved in the war, introduced conscription for women. If you were aged 20 (later 19) to 50 and did not have children or a husband at home, you could be 'called up'. You could choose to work, or to join the forces in a non-fighting role. By 1945, eight out of ten married women and nine out of ten single women aged 18 to 40 were doing one or the other.

---

attainment target

1 How did the war change women's lives:
   a in their jobs?
   b at home?

2 Which changes affected women early in the war? Which only affected them later?

3 Did the war affect women in the same way, or differently, from the First World War?

How did women react?

Many women enjoyed being able to develop new skills (see Sources 67 and 68). Some women moved away from home to work in factories far away (see Source 69). They lived in hostels and had more freedom, money and independence.

Many joined the armed forces: the ATS (Auxiliary Territorial Service), WAAF (Women's Auxiliary Air Force) (see Source 70), or the WRNS or Wrens (Women's Royal Naval Service). Some did important skilled work, such as code-breaking, delivering aircraft to airfields, or operating radios.

It wasn't all fun and excitement. Many women were killed. Many were bored and homesick. They were also paid less than men for the same work. For example at Rolls Royce men received £3.65 and women £2.15 a week. Women even received less injury compensation than men. They were often given the 'traditional' jobs: cooking, cleaning and washing.

What were the results?

Different women reacted differently, of course (see Source 71). Some things were changed for ever. Equal pay for equal work and married women working were both more widely accepted after the war. Neither of these causes is completely won, to this day, but the Second World War was a turning-point for both.

'When we get married I shan't want to work. I shall want to stay at home and have children. You can't look at anything you do during the war as what you really mean to do. It's just filling in time until you can live your own life again.'

'You've got money coming in at the end of the week and it's nice. It's a taste of independence and you feel a lot happier for it.'

'I'm going out to the WVS Centre in the morning. My husband is very silly about it. He said: "When the war got over, I thought you'd always be in at lunchtime." I said: "Well, you always have a good lunch left." He said, "Well, I like you there always." No thought as to my feelings or any service I could be doing.'

SOURCE 71
Three women describe their feelings about adjusting to peacetime when the war was over.

SOURCE 72
A description of a dance-hall in Southampton.

'It was difficult to get inside the door for people jammed in the tiny hall. Girls were young, many in jumpers and skirts. The floor was so crowded that most couples just shuffled and hugged.'

A better world

Look back over this depth study and see in how many different ways the people of Britain suffered during the war years. How did they keep going?

Smiling through

People felt they were all in it together. The bombs did not distinguish between the houses of the rich and those of the poor. The Queen was said to be glad when Buckingham Palace was hit because she 'could now look the East End in the face'. Rationing was the same for all. Everyone talked to each other. There was no point in clinging to traditional British reserve and the class distinctions of the 1930s.

Party conflict was called off during the war. Labour Leader Clement Attlee was Churchill's Deputy. Labour politicians were in the Cabinet. Trade unionists worked with employers to make sure industry worked well during the war.

One of the things all classes of people enjoyed and talked about was radio programmes. They enjoyed comedy programmes, like ITMA. They could all sing the romantic, but moving, songs of Vera Lynn and Anne Shelton. Even serious discussions, plays and classical music had enormous numbers of listeners.

For many, especially young people, the war brought change and excitement. Relaxation was important as an escape from shortages and long working hours (see Source 72). Romances flourished among men and women away from home, on the move, perhaps about to die. One-third of all births in 1944 were ILLEGITIMATE. Britain was full of soldiers from all over the world. American soldiers (GIs), well-paid, well-dressed and well-fed, were particularly popular. Twenty thousand British girls married American servicemen.

Winston Churchill

There was almost total support for the British Prime Minister from 1940, Winston Churchill. His speeches to the British people on the radio seemed to express why they were fighting and how they felt (see Source 73). He did not make light of the problems – he promised 'blood, toil, tears and sweat'. But he was also totally committed to victory. When the German invasion seemed likely, he promised: 'We shall fight on the beaches . . . we shall fight in the fields and in the streets. We shall fight in the hills. We shall never surrender.'

Making plans

The war demanded tremendous sacrifices from ordinary people. Posters such as Source 74 reminded people that they were making them for Britain. But what kind of Britain? Britain in the 1930s had not been a good place to live for many millions of people. During the war, understandably, people spent a lot of time talking about the future. In the army, the Army Bureau of Current Affairs held discussions about it.

On the radio, J.B. Priestley gave talks about it. They wanted life to be fairer, to turn the 'People's War' into a 'People's Peace'.

Even at the height of the war, committees worked on plans for the future. The Minister of Education, R. A. Butler, passed an Education Act in 1944 to give everyone education from the age of 11 to 15. A Ministry of Town and Country Planning was set up in 1943 to protect the countryside and build better towns. Most importantly, Sir William Beveridge produced a report in 1942 on health, employment and social security. His approach is shown in Source 75. He proposed a system of national insurance to protect everyone 'from the cradle to the grave'. The Beveridge Report struck a chord with the people.

'The purpose of victory is to live in a better world than the old world. Each individual is more likely to concentrate on his war effort if he feels that his government will be ready in time with plans for that better world.'

SOURCE 75
Sir William Beveridge describes his report.

SOURCE 74
A patriotic poster issued by the Army Bureau of Current Affairs.

ACTIVITY

There is great scope for oral history in your study of 'The People's War'. Oral history means people talking about their own past. This helps us to put what we read in books in a new light. Several sources from these pages are taken from oral history.

Work with a partner. Choose one topic from this depth study you would like to find out more about. Draw up some questions. It is better to have a few questions which really get someone talking than lots of questions which just require yes/no answers. It is also better to talk to someone yourselves rather than sending out a written questionnaire. A tape-recorder is a good idea: that way you can concentrate on the old

person and their memories and not worry about writing everything down.

Interview two or three people. Ask the same or similar questions, if you can, so that you can compare answers. It might work better to interview two old people together, so that one person's memories may remind the other of something.

When you have all your material, read through what this book says about the topic. Try and find some other books.

Then write up the oral history you have discovered, comparing your conclusion with textbook accounts.

What was the role of women in Edwardian Britain?

It is difficult to summarise the many different experiences of women's lives into a few pages. Not all women lived similar lifestyles. As with other aspects of life in Edwardian times, there were stark contrasts between rich and poor. These differences in income were closely related to issues of social class, lifestyles and status within society.

Source 76 reveals the relative numbers of upper, middle and working class people and their incomes in 1904. There was an increase in public and government interest in the problems of poverty in first decade of the 20th century. Despite this, however, many working-class women in towns experienced hardships similar to those of many earlier generations since the time of the Industrial Revolution (see pages 66 to 75).

Rich	Comfortable	Poor
1,250,000 persons	3,750,000 persons	38,000,000 persons
£585,000,000	£245,000,000	£880,000,000

SOURCE 76
Incomes in Britain, 1904, from *Money, Riches and Poverty* by L. G. Chiozza, 1905.

SOURCE 77
This picture was originally published as a poster as part of the campaign for women to get the vote. Later, in 1908, it appeared in a weekly London magazine. Its caption was 'The real head of the household – yet she has no voice in the nation's affairs.'

Her rights

Let us think about the woman in Source 77. The woman would be well aware that she was seen as inferior to men. Her duty would be to obey her husband's wishes. She knew of some recent changes in the law that gave women some rights of property ownership (see page 74). She also knew about the activities of the local SUFFRAGETTES and their campaign to win votes for women.

She thinks it is unfair that her drunken husband has voting rights simply because he is a man. She supports Mrs Pankhurst and the Women's Social and Political Union but does not approve of their law-breaking activities. She hopes that her baby will grow up able to vote in elections in the future, if she survives.

His rights

Her husband works as a docker – a casual labourer unloading cargoes from ships at the nearby docks. He has no guarantee of work. He has to turn up at the dock gates early each morning and hope to be picked by the foreman to work that day. If he managed a whole week's work he might bring home 27 shillings (£1.35). But . . . he might not.

ACTIVITY

Look at the man, woman and child in Source 77 carefully.

Divide into groups of three or four.
Each group should study one section of the text on these pages and note down two key reasons why the lifestyle of the woman in Source 77 was so limited.

Each group in turn will then be called upon to present their key findings back to the whole class. These should be recorded in a table.

He thinks that he should be the breadwinner and that his wife's place is to look after the home and the children. He disapproves of his wife's interest in the idea of 'votes for women'.

The baby

How old do you think the baby looks? Does it look healthy? In reality, a great many infants died before their first birthday. Infant deaths were caused by a combination of unhygienic living conditions and poor diet. This baby is likely to have other brothers or sisters since the average family size was three to four children. Her mother might have spent, on average, 15 years either pregnant or looking after babies under one year old.

Her education

How old do you think the woman looks? The woman would have been to a local school between the ages of five and twelve. She would have been taught the basic three Rs; reading, writing and arithmetic. She probably learnt to sew at school, as well as how to cook, so she could become a good wife and mother once she got married.

Her diet

What item of food is shown here? This poor family, like many others, would mainly live on a diet of bread and potatoes, along with cups of tea. They could only afford a little meat, perhaps pork or bacon at the weekend. As well as working, the woman would be expected to shop, cook and clear away all the meals. In this family, the man has spent too much money on beer!

Working hours and wages

What job is the woman doing? The woman is working from home making clothes as a seamstress. Perhaps she worked for a clothing shop. To obtain a 'living wage' she would have to work around 50 to 56 hours a week. In return for this effort her wages would be very low. For example, 1 shilling (5p) for 12 blouses, 8d (3.5p) for 12 children's shirts and 2s 9d (14p) for 12 nightdresses. Such work, common in Edwardian England, was known as 'sweated labour'.

Her pastimes and interests

Does the picture offer any clues to these? Even if she wanted to pursue any interests, she would find it impossible. Her limited education, lack of spare income, time, need to care for her children and lack of energy would all act as barriers.

A suffragette gave her a handbill whilst out shopping to publicise a mass rally for 'Votes for Women' in Hyde Park. She would quite like to go but the cost of the omnibus and getting someone to look after the baby are problems. Also, she would need the approval of her husband. It would be unusual for a married woman to appear in public without her husband.

Her health

Does the woman look healthy? Remember that this is a painting not a photograph. For a woman in a similar position, her poor diet, long working hours and the demands of raising a large family would take its toll. In 1901 the average life expectancy of women in the UK was 49 years. She might fall victim to a number of killer diseases, especially tuberculosis (TB), but also bronchitis and pneumonia. These were the diseases of poverty caused by unhealthy living conditions.

Housework

By its nature, sewing creates waste offcuts. As well as working, the woman would be expected to keep the house in order. The domestic chores, all without the benefit of labour saving devices, took up many hours of the woman's time.

Technology

What forms of technology are visible in the picture? For her work she would have purchased a treadle-operated sewing machine. The machine's power came from the woman rocking her feet to and fro.

The dingy room is poorly lit by an early gas lamp, which would give off smelly vapours if the room was not well ventilated.

---

1 Which background factors do you need to think about in relation to Source 77?

2 Which parts of the picture does the artist emphasise? Why?

3 Can we rely on this image of working-class life?

4 How can the picture still be useful evidence for this topic?

5 List the sorts of changes that are needed before the woman's life can be made any easier.

6 Are there any signs of changes coming in the future?

Women in the Great War

Before 1914, most women who worked outside the home were single (see pages 68 and 69). Once married, they were expected to take up domestic duties at home.

The two largest areas of employment for women who did work were in industry (such as the woman in Source 77) or in domestic service where over one and a half million women worked in 1914.

Responses to war

The Great War was not an all-male affair. It changed everyone's lives and forced society to reconsider the role of women. Women were expected to continue their traditional role of keeping the home together. In addition, millions of women volunteered to work in factories and on farms to help the war effort.

Women were active in many ways. When war was declared, recruitment propaganda exploited the patriotic 'duty' of women to encourage men to 'join up'. Women organised 'comforts' for troops in the trenches. Women also helped with refugees and joined organisations like the Voluntary Aid Detachment. Over 25,000 women from Britain served on the fronts.

Not all women supported the war. The Women's Peace Crusade protested against the fighting by holding meetings, distributing leaflets and making house to house calls. Often their ideas for peace were met by hostility from the authorities, the media and the public. Such women were thought of as unpatriotic and dangerous.

The 'right to serve'

Many other women demanded 'the right to serve' like the men. With shell shortages and a constant need for more men at the Front, the authorities were put in a difficult position. Should they relax the rigid working practices – backed by the male dominated trade unions – which excluded women from skilled employment?

From 1915 onwards, over 900,000 women were recruited into the factories. Many worked in munitions factories making armaments for the Front, as Source 78 shows. Although these women were quite well paid, it was always less than any men doing similar jobs. This led to issues of resentment and charges of discrimination. The work itself, which involved handling chemicals used for explosives, was unhealthy and dangerous.

Women took over a range of jobs which had previously been done by men. Through hard work and the introduction of new technology production levels were maintained and even increased. Women factory workers had to do shift-work, despite the special difficulties for mothers. Often the authorities set up pre-school nurseries for their children. Gradually, and grudgingly, women won the respect of men, as Source 79 reveals.

SOURCE 78
A poster used for recruiting women into the munitions factories.

> Saturday, 13th November. Mr James Caldwell called. He had talked with a foreman, who said the women-workers were doing splendidly. Lads were often selfishly thoughtless, and larked about. The women worked thoughtfully and steadily.

SOURCE 79
An extract from the Reverend Clark's diary for 13 November 1915.

SOURCE 80
'Land girl ploughing', a painting by Cecil Aldin.

Farm work

Women were also needed on the farms. Many men thought that farm work was 'too hard' for women. Nevertheless, in Britain over 260,000 women joined the Land Army to help provide food supplies, as Source 80 shows.

Attitudes in 1918

Most women were grateful for the new opportunities that the Great War opened up. They felt proud to have contributed to the war effort. Women began to value their new found independence and became more assertive. Their experience of a more liberated status during the Great War meant that after 1918 women began new battles for change across a range of social, economic, political and cultural issues. Two pressing items would be: what would happen to the women at work once the troops returned home from the war? When would Parliament extend the voting system to permit women to vote? On both these issues, the fate of women's post-war lives would be decided by male attitudes.

Many men, including the Prime Minister Lloyd George, had been impressed by women's war work. But it became clear from laws passed straight after the war that the authorities wanted women to be pushed back into their traditional roles (see Source 81). These laws reserved many jobs for men, even though many women had done these jobs.

An all-party committee of MPs eventually passed 'The Representation of the People Act' in 1918. This permitted women over 30, subject to certain conditions, to vote. Only 6 million women were allowed the vote. Many millions of women in their twenties who had contributed to the war effort still found themselves without the right to vote.

'Any rule, practice or custom departed from during the war is to be restored. . . . Where new branches have been established within an industry, pre-war practices are to apply to it.'

SOURCE 81
Clauses 1 and 2 from 'The Restoration of Pre-war Practices Act' which was passed in August 1919.

attainment target

1 How did women's jobs change:
   in offices?
   in factories?
   on farms?
   Which showed the biggest change?

2 How did men's attitudes towards women at work change: during the Great War? After the Great War?

3 Did women like the changes brought about by the War? Explain your answer.

4 Women contributed a great deal to the war effort. How did the changes at work affect women's attitudes to other parts of their lives?

5 How much of a turning point in the role of women was the Great War?

Women and the Second World War

As you saw earlier (pages 138 to 151), the Second World War demanded that women become much more involved in the war effort than they had been in the Great War. Once again, millions balanced the difficult wartime roles of maintaining homes and working in what was still seen as male territory. These pages look at the wartime roles of women at home and at work.

Women at home

Women often had to fulfil the dual roles of providers for their families and contributors to the war effort, as Source 82 shows. This source also suggests that this man's attitude to the domestic role of wife had remained the same, despite the changed circumstances of the war.

Food and rationing

The effects of war caused disruption to every aspect of women's lives. The government had to act to counter the threat to food supplies from overseas posed by German U-boats, and to ensure that the armed forces received priority in what was available.

More crops were grown, often through labour provided by the Women's Land Army. As Source 83 shows, women were encouraged to grow more vegetables as part of a 'Dig For Victory' campaign at home.

SOURCE 82
Newspaper advertisement for 'Mrs Peek's Puddings'.

SOURCE 83
Ministry of Information 'Dig for Victory' poster.

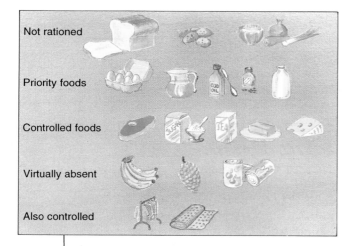

SOURCE 84
Items rationed and those freely available.

SOURCE 86
Helen Parker describes her work at Peek Freans.

When the war broke out, the firm wrote to me and asked me if I wanted to go back. I had two children at school and had a woman who could look after them, so I said, "yes".

I started doing my normal job. Peek Freans were still making biscuits but they were soldiers' biscuits. I also then did other jobs as well, like soldering linings for gas masks. I don't know what you call them, they have a special name, but they were panels for aeroplanes. They'd have the instruments and I'd have to solder them on. All those bits of wire I could take as long as I liked, as long as it was done properly. It was people's lives after all.

I used to work from 7.30 in the morning till about 6 pm at night, and if they wanted you to work overtime, you worked till 8 o'clock. If you went in on Saturday you got time and a half. I shouldn't think we were getting paid as much as the men. It wasn't much money we got I remember. It wasn't a union firm, so you couldn't go on strike.

We had to wear an overall and they supplied that, and we had to tie our hair back. We were supposed to have a pint of milk a day, but we never got it. If you swore you'd be sent to the manager and you'd be suspended.

I had to leave Peeks after two years, because the bombing got so bad and I went with my kids to Nottingham.

After the war some women stayed on at Peeks, but the men did get their jobs back. During the war we were needed; afterwards it was different.

'Rationing was terrible, but we managed somehow. I used to make my kids bananas out of parsnips. I used to boil them and put banana essence in them. My kids used to think they had bananas. We did a lot of things like that.'

SOURCE 85
Helen Parker recalls cooking during the war.

Rationing was introduced to share out the food more fairly. The quantities allowed per person provided an average daily intake of around 3,000 calories, although many people's diets were neither nutritious or varied. Source 84 shows how although basic 'fillers' were outside the rationing scheme, most items were either strictly rationed on a points system, or virtually unobtainable (unless the temptations of 'the black market' became too strong). Lengthy queues for scarce items were a common feature of shopping.

All women became skilled in preparing recipes using substitute ingredients as Helen Parker recalls in Source 85.

Women at work

The Mrs Peek's puddings used by 'Mrs X' shown in Source 82 were made at Peek Freans' London factory. Helen Parker, whose views on rationing you read in Source 85 worked for the same firm. Her pre-war job was to solder biscuit tins together.

Using her story (Source 86) we can learn about how one group of women, in one factory: were recruited; felt about their war effort; faced dangers and disruption to their lives; were treated during and after the War; were switched from making peacetime products to working in wartime production tasks.

1 What attitudes to women lie behind the advertisement in Source 82?

2 In pairs, discuss Source 86 in relation to the prompts within the text.

3 Imagine that, by chance, 'Mrs X' and Helen Parker meet up long after the war. Suggest how their conversation might develop as they compare the changes that the war brought to their lives.

4 In which ways were the roles of women in the Second World War: similar; different; to those in the First World War?

Why have women's roles changed during this century?

Many women saw the changes to their lives brought about by the Great War as very important (Source 87). But we have seen that many changes at work were purely temporary (see Source 81 on page 155). Did their war work, and gaining the vote in 1918 and 1928, mark a turning-point for women?

In the 1920s and 30s, some middle-class women were determined to retain their new found independence, and to live their lives with greater personal freedom (Source 88).

For the majority of married working-class women, life went on as before. If anything it was worse because of the effects of the Great Depression. With many men out of work, some saw women as having no right to be taking jobs. Often they were exploited as a cheap source of labour. To such women, the view of society offered in Source 89 would seem a remote prospect.

Although there were women in all the jobs mentioned, they were few in number. Women mostly gave up their jobs if they got married. This was partly the norm, as Source 90 suggests. It was also partly because of how men expected women to live (Source 91).

> . . . the historian of 100 years ago would be confounded if he could return and see the world of women today! He would find women engineers, architects, lawyers, doctors, dentists, vets, librarians, journalists, scientists and tax inspectors.

SOURCE 89
Woman writer in the *Daily Telegraph* describing women's jobs in the 1930s.

> 'We introduce ourselves and our new weekly for the modern young wife who loves her home.
> *Woman's Own* will be a paper with a purpose – a paper thoroughly alive to the altered conditions of the present day. The home paper that makes any girl worth her salt want to be the best housewife ever.'

SOURCE 90
Woman's Own, 15 October 1932.

> 'It (the War) allowed women to stand on their own feet. It was the turning point for women.'

SOURCE 87
Elsie Farlow, in an interview recorded in 1976.

SOURCE 88
Women smoking in a restaurant in 1920.

> 'I'm afraid I'm old fashioned enough to want a whole-time wife, whose main interest in life will be in her home, her children and me.
> I want a wife whose first and only interest is me – and then, our home. Later on there ought to be children. A wife who is earning will not be at all keen to have them . . . so let me do the earning. Let her stick to the whole-time job of being my wife'.

SOURCE 91
A letter in *Woman's Own*, 1938.

Changes since 1945

After the Second World War, women once again returned to their traditional roles. Yet, looking at women today there have clearly been dramatic changes. Why? Here are some of the reasons.

Improvements in education for girls

In schools since the 1970s subjects are no longer thought of as ones for either 'girls' or 'boys' (Source 92). All mixed sex schools have equal opportunities policies that state that both sexes must be given equal and fair chances to succeed at school.

SOURCE 92
Many girls now study science at school and go on to successful careers in science, industry and engineering.

Organised campaigns by women

The campaign for women's rights did really not surface again in Britain until the late 1960s and 1970s. Supporters of women's groups such as the Women's Liberation Movement organised marches and rallies and published magazines, newspapers and feminist novels. They also tried to put pressure on MPs to change laws affecting women in employment, abortion and discrimination. They publicised a wide range of issues such as sexual discrimination at work, sexist language and campaigned against nuclear weapons, especially at the US base at Greenham Common.

Improved contraception

The figures in Source 93 show the dramatic effect on family size brought about by the widespread use of more reliable forms of contraception. Since the 1960s the contraceptive pill has been widely used and, since 1974, it has been available on the NHS. This has given many women control over their sex lives. This has allowed them to make their own decisions about pregnancy, motherhood and family size. As a result some women choose to follow careers first, then have children. Sometimes, sooner or later, women return to work. Women such as Paula Yates act as important role models to show that in modern Britain it is quite possible to juggle the twin roles of career woman and carer.

Labour-saving machines

At the turn of the century, women were expected to perform the endless drudgery of housework. Today, there is a wide range of easy to operate, efficient, machinery. Housework can be done more quickly – by both sexes – thereby freeing up time for other activities.

New laws to protect women's rights

Among the most important changes have been a series of laws giving women the same legal rights as men. In 1970 the Equal Pay Act stated that men and women doing the same job should get the same pay. After 1975, the Sex Discrimination Act meant that all jobs were open to both sexes on the same basis. Some employers have found ways of getting round these laws. The Equal Opportunities Commission was set up to monitor cases of inequality at work. Women, or men, who feel cheated can ask for their case to be heard in court.

Women in politics

Although women have had legal equality in politics since 1928, in reality the number of female MPs has always been relatively small. Nevertheless, among their number, important individuals have risen to positions of power, none more so than Margaret Thatcher who was Britain's first woman Prime Minister from 1979 until 1990.

SOURCE 93
Average size of family, 1961 to 1991.

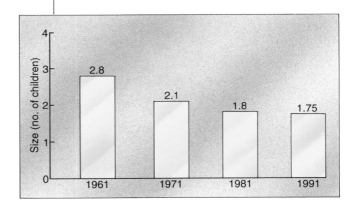

1. Can you name any examples from your own school of equal opportunities for girls and boys?

2. What are the main effects of the Women's Movement in trying to achieve equality?

3. Explain the link between contraception and: family size; improved options for women.

4. How important do you think the Equal Opportunity Laws were?

5. Do you think laws can change attitudes?

6. How important in accepting the changing roles of women have been men's attitudes?

Britain in the post-war world

In this overview we shall look at the legacy of the war on Britain, Europe, the superpowers (USA and USSR) and the European empires. Source 94 shows that one of the major consequences of the war was a death toll of 43.7 million (in the First World War it was 17 million). The huge economies of the USA and USSR, and the success of their armies during the war, meant that they dominated the world after 1945. Other countries, such as Britain and France, continued to be important European countries.

Europe

The deaths, destruction and cost of the war (see Sources 94, 95 and 96) left all European countries weak and facing serious problems in rebuilding. This led leaders in France, Germany, Italy, the Netherlands, Belgium and Luxembourg to seek to bury centuries of hostility and work together. Economic co-operation came first: heavy industries in different countries depended on each other, so the European Coal and Steel Community was set up in 1952. The success of this led in 1957 to the Common Market.

War deaths			Expenditure of the war	
Country	war deaths (millions)		Country	Expenditure (millions)
			Allies	
USSR	21.0		USA	£84.5
Poland	7.3		USSR	£48
Germany	4.4		Britain	£28
China	2.2		Others	£11
Yugoslavia	2.0		*Axis powers*	
Japan	1.2		Germany	£68
France	0.7		Italy	£28.5
Rumania	1.0		Japan	£14
Hungary	0.6			
Italy	0.5			
USA	0.4			
Britain	0.4			
Others	2.0			
TOTAL	43.7			

SOURCE 94
Numbers of people killed and expenditure of each country during the Second World War.

SOURCE 95
Dresden in ruins, 1946.

SOURCE 96
German refugees moving from their homes in what was Germany but had become part of Poland.

Britain

An election was called in Britain in July 1945. Everyone expected Churchill, the great war leader, to win. But although he was very popular, people were not sure of him or the Conservative party in peace. There was less of the mistrust of Labour than there had been between the wars. Labour politicians and trade unionists had played an important part in the war effort. As you may have seen in the depth study on pages 138 to 151, there were also widespread hopes for a better Britain after the war, expressed particularly in support for the Beveridge Report. Labour seemed more likely to deliver these hopes (see Source 97) and won the election with a majority of over 150 seats.

The Labour government 1945–50

In Attlee's words, the country was in a mess. Factories and houses were in ruins; the country was £3,300 million in debt. In spite of this, the Labour government was committed to radical change and spending money in building a welfare state. However, the legacy of war was not all bad. There were new technologies developed in wartime, such as electronics, which could be applied to peacetime uses. Further, people had got used to controls on their lives.

SOURCE 97
Labour Party poster, 1945.

Labour directed industrial effort towards export (see Source 98). Several industries were nationalised: coal, electricity, gas, rail, road and air transport, iron and steel. A National Health Service began in 1948 and the government was proud of its welfare state provisions 'from the cradle to the grave'.

However, life was not all that easy for the British people for many years. There was a housing shortage and rationing only ended in the 1950s. It took time for British governments of both parties to realise that the power situation in the world had changed. Many still saw Britain as a great power, an imperial power. Efforts to involve Britain in the experiment in co-operation going on in Europe all failed (see Source 99).

SOURCE 98
A poster encouraging people to work hard to produce goods for export, 1947.

'Time was slipping by, and my attempt to create a nucleus around which a European Community might be formed met with no response from the one great power in Europe which was then in a position to take such a responsibility (Britain). (From Jean Monnet's *Memoirs*.)

When, on our return we put these proposals to Bevin [Foreign Secretary in the Labour Government], they were immediately rejected, as Bevin felt that they went too far in the direction of a surrender of British sovereignty. (From Edwin Plowden's *Memoirs*.)'

SOURCE 99
Reports of a high-level meeting held in April 1949 between Jean Monnet, French foreign minister, and Edwin Plowden of the British delegation.

A divided Europe

Look at Source 100. It shows people being pulled over the Berlin Wall. The Wall was built in 1963 splitting the city of Berlin in two. It was the most obvious sign of a division which ran right across Europe and was only broken down quite recently, in 1989. How could it happen that Berlin, Germany and Europe were divided like this for so long? The answer lies in the year 1945.

The USA, Britain and the USSR were allies during the war, as you have seen. When their victorious soldiers met, in Germany, or in Korea, they took friendly photos of each other (see Source 101). But the relations between the leaders were not so friendly. In February 1945 they met in Yalta in the USSR (Source 102).

Stalin was suspicious of the motives of Churchill and Roosevelt. The western democracies had been hostile to the Communist rulers of the USSR since the 1917 Revolution. They had failed to join in stopping Hitler in the 1930s. Stalin also felt that the Allies had been slow in opening up a second Front in western Europe to relieve German pressure on the USSR.

Churchill was no friend of the USSR but realised that their success in defeating Hitler gave them great power. He was prepared to make deals with Stalin.

Roosevelt wanted peace to be based not on deals, but on open, democratic decisions of all countries in the United Nations (see pages 166 and 167). He was critical of imperial countries, such as Britain, and assumed Stalin was too. He also assumed that he and Stalin felt the same about democracy. However, many Americans were far more hostile to Stalin than Roosevelt was.

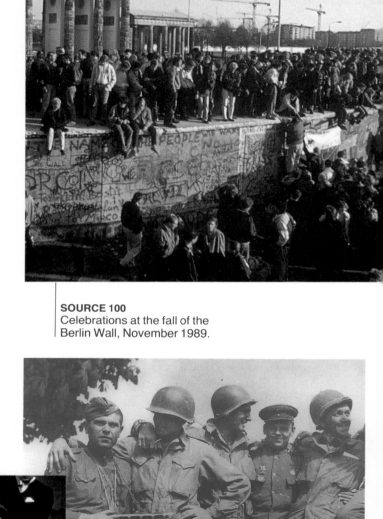

SOURCE 100
Celebrations at the fall of the Berlin Wall, November 1989.

SOURCE 102
Churchill, Roosevelt and Stalin at the Yalta Conference, February 1945.

SOURCE 101
Russian and US troops meeting in Germany, 1945.

The Allies fall out

The main aim of the meeting at Yalta was to agree how Germany, and the countries Germany had conquered, should be dealt with as the war ended. No one felt like being generous to Germany. Wider public knowledge of the Holocaust brought anger on all sides. Stalin wanted Germany to pay 20 billion dollars in reparation, half of which would go to the USSR to help rebuild all they had lost. They agreed that Germany should be divided into occupation zones for each of the Allies. The city of Berlin, inside the Soviet zone, should also be divided. The French were given the same powers later in 1945, making four zones (see Source 103).

Stalin had persuaded the Allies that the borders of the USSR should be moved westwards at the expense of Poland. Now he suggested that Poland should be compensated by taking land from Germany. Roosevelt was not keen on this, but wanted to keep on good terms with Stalin. The Americans needed the Red Army to help defeat Germany. They also hoped the USSR would help them defeat Japan, and work with the Allies in setting up the United Nations. There was little they could do anyway, as Soviet armies occupied all the areas of Poland and Germany in question. They therefore agreed to the boundary changes, even though it meant that 2 million Germans would have to leave their homes.

attainment target

Look at these two interpretations of what Stalin had done in 1945.

A *An American view:* 'The Soviets are aiming to take over the whole of Europe if they can. In the countries of eastern Europe Stalin is setting up governments which do what he tells them. We expected democratic elections in these countries. The one-party states Stalin is setting up are just what we fought the war to prevent. Stalin must be stopped.'

B *A Soviet view:* 'Russia was attacked through Poland in 1914, 1920 and in 1941. We must be able to defend ourselves. The western Allies have set up their own friendly government in Greece. We have just done the same. We have won the right to do this through our sacrifices and victories over the Nazis.'

1 Explain how the authors of both **A** and **B** would use Source 103 to support their case.

2 Which interpretation, **A** or **B**, do you find most accurate? Explain your answer.

3 Why do you think such wide differences of interpretation between the US and the USSR had arisen so quickly?

4 How do the authors of both **A** and **B** make use of history to support their interpretation?

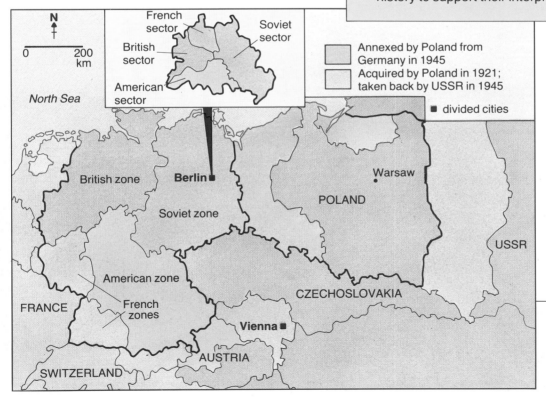

SOURCE 103
Map showing the division of Germany and Berlin between the four Allied powers and changes to the boundaries of Poland.

Potsdam

By the time of the next conference, at Potsdam in July 1945, things were different. Roosevelt had died and his place was taken by Harry Truman. Clement Attlee had taken over from Churchill following the British general election (see page 161). Stalin still ruled supreme over the USSR. Indeed, his power seemed to go further. He had set up a Communist, pro-Soviet government in Poland and arrested several non-Communist Polish leaders. The same thing seemed to be about to happen in Czechoslovakia and Hungary.

Truman was much less friendly towards the USSR than Roosevelt had been. He was angry at what seemed to be happening in eastern Europe. He had expected that people would be allowed to elect their own governments in these countries. Instead, Stalin seemed to be doing as he pleased.

The Potsdam Conference agreed that former Nazis should be sought out and put on trial. Not much else was decided. Within weeks of the end of the war (8 May 1945) relations between the victorious allies had deteriorated.

Superpower rivalry

We saw on page 160 how the USA and the USSR had borne the cost of the war. They emerged from it as superpowers. The USA was clearly the richest and most powerful nation in the world, confident in its way of life (Source 105). It also had the atom bomb.

'You evidently don't agree that the Soviet Union is entitled to seek in Poland a government that would be friendly to it. To put it plainly: you want me to set aside the interests of the security of the Soviet Union; but I cannot proceed against the interests of my own country.'

SOURCE 104
Stalin, writing to President Truman in 1946.

The USSR, though crippled by the war, had huge resources and a powerful, victorious army. It controlled eastern Europe and had an influence across the globe second only to the USA.

Relations between the superpowers were not friendly. As early as March 1946, Winston Churchill, with President Truman at his side, spoke of an Iron Curtain across Europe (see Source 107). Sources 108 and 106 show what this Iron Curtain looked like and where it went. The Cold War between the superpowers was to dominate world politics for 40 years after the end of the war.

SOURCE 105
Poster from the USA.

What is a cold war?

A 'cold war' is a war carried on against an enemy by every means short of actually fighting. In the Cold War between the USA and the USSR, both sides built up their stocks of nuclear weapons in an 'arms race'. They targeted these weapons at each other. Each side built up a network of alliances. If a war broke out anywhere in the world, the USA and the USSR supported opposite sides.

SOURCE 106
The Iron Curtain across Europe by 1948.

'A shadow has fallen upon the scenes so lately lighted by the Allied victory. From…the Baltic to…the Adriatic an iron curtain has descended across the continent. Behind that line lie all the capitals of the ancient states of central and eastern Europe…
Whatever conclusions may be drawn from these facts, this is not the liberated Europe we fought to build up.'

SOURCE 107
From Winston Churchill's 'Iron Curtain' speech at Fulton, Missouri, USA, March 1946.

The peoples of the great Soviet state have won the right to be respected as one of the Great Powers in the world. The glorious Red Army, advancing on the Fascist beast saved the world from the bloodthirsty Hitlerite regime. The victorious liberating Red Army led by the genius of its great Commander, Comrade Stalin, completely cleared the German invaders from the soil of the Soviet Union, Poland, Romania, Bulgaria, Finland and most of Czechoslovakia and Hungary. We have no ambition towards anyone's territory. We only want to advance the happiness of our socialist country.

SOURCE 109
From Soviet newspapers, 1947.

'Looking towards Europe from Moscow, Soviet Russia was expansively stabbing westwards, knifing into nations left empty by war, with misery and chaos as allies.'

SOURCE 110
From US newsreel commentary, 1947.

SOURCE 108
The Iron Curtain.

attainment target

Read Sources 109 and 110.

1 Explain how useful these sources are for describing the events of the war?

2 Explain how useful these sources are in telling us how the USSR and the USA felt about the events of the war?

3 Use these sources to explain why the Cold War took place.

The United Nations

The war aims of the Allies were set out in the Declaration of the United Nations, signed on 1 January 1942. They had agreed to use all their resources to fight Germany, Italy and Japan until all three had surrendered. So much for the fighting, but what were they fighting for?

The first task was to try to remove the grievances which cause wars. In August 1941, Roosevelt and Churchill met and drew up the Atlantic Charter (see Source 111). This formed part of the Declaration of the United Nations. The principles were summarised as 'The Four Freedoms': Freedom of Speech, Freedom of Worship, Freedom from Want and Freedom from Fear (see Source 112).

No more wars?

The Allies agreed that an international peace-keeping organisation was needed. The plan for the United Nations was developed at Dumbarton Oaks, in the USA, in August 1944 and put to the Allied leaders at Yalta in February 1945 (see Source 102, page 162).

We saw in unit 2 that the League of Nations failed to prevent the outbreak of the Second World War. Look back at the section on the League of Nations on page 106. How could the new organisation learn from the mistakes of the League?

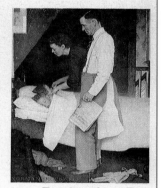

Freedom of Speech · Freedom of Worship · Freedom from Want · Freedom from Fear

SOURCE 112
Poster showing 'The Four Freedoms' of the Atlantic Charter.

1 No part of a country can be taken away from it without the free consent of its people.

2 All citizens have a right to choose the form of government under which they live.

3 All countries have equal right of access to world trade and raw materials.

4 All countries should co-operate fully in running the world economy, and strive to eliminate poverty.

5 All countries and people should be able to live peacefully together and travel wherever they want.

6 Worldwide disarmament is a realistic and attainable goal.

SOURCE 111
Principles of the Atlantic Charter, August 1941. These were later included in the Declaration of the United Nations, January 1942 and the Charter of the United Nations, June 1945.

The UN Charter

The nations of the world meet in the General Assembly. They have one vote each. As we saw on page 106, one of the problems of the League was that some powerful nations were not in it, or by-passed it. The UN tried to recognise the importance of the powerful nations by giving them permanent seats on the Security Council. These were the USA, the USSR and Britain plus China and France. Further, the Security Council, unlike the Council of the League of Nations, is always meeting, so can act quickly. The Security Council has the right to impose sanctions such as trade boycotts, in the same way that the League could. It can also put together a UN armed force to send to a trouble-spot, something the League could not do (see Source 113).

The Charter was signed at a conference in San Francisco in 1945 by the first 51 nations. Over the years, many other nations have also joined. There are now over 180, and the UN has permanent headquarters in New York.

Universal Declaration of Human Rights

Look at Source 114. How can the UN protect individuals against cruel governments? If people lead lives which are unhappy, or fearful, the peace and prosperity outlined in the Atlantic Charter (Source 111) cannot be achieved. Poverty and injustice are often the roots of wars.

In the same way that the Atlantic Charter was drawn up to protect countries, the Declaration of Human Rights was drawn up in 1948 to protect individuals (see Source 115). It says that everyone has the right not to be tortured, imprisoned without trial, enslaved or discriminated against on the grounds of race, religion or sex. It lays down the right of everyone to work, travel, worship, marry, vote and hold peaceful political meetings or demonstrations. It also says that everyone has the right to an education, a reasonable wage and a reasonable standard of living. Every nation in the UN has signed the Universal Declaration. In fact, though, many nations break its terms quite regularly.

SOURCE 114
Mothers in Argentina carrying portraits of their children who had 'disappeared', probably killed by the police on the instructions of the government, 1983.

'All human beings are born free and equal in dignity and rights.
Everyone is entitled to all the freedoms set forth in the Declaration without distinction of any kind.
Everyone has the right to life, liberty and security of person.

SOURCE 115
From the Universal Declaration of Human Rights, agreed by the UN in 1948.

SOURCE 113
UN forces in Yugoslavia, 1992.

ACTIVITY

1 Look at the TV news or the Foreign News pages of a newspaper for a week. Is the UN mentioned? What is it doing?

   Are there any stories where the UN could act to keep the peace, but is not doing so? Why isn't it involved?

2 Compare the Atlantic Charter with the Universal Declaration of Human Rights. Which do you think are the most important: the rights of countries or the rights of individuals?

3 Why do governments break the Human Rights Declaration? What examples do you know about from the last few months?

The end of empires

The Second World War meant the end of European empires around the world. It was most obvious in the Far East. The Japanese had shown the peoples of Asia that the white colonial rulers could be beaten. French Indo-China and the Dutch East Indies fell to the Japanese. The great British fortress of Singapore also fell, and the French, Dutch and British went off into captivity.

The colonies were freed from Japanese rule, not by their former colonial rulers, but by the Americans. Burma was the only colony freed by its colonial rulers, in this case the British. Britain did not want to be in the undignified position of ruling their colony with American permission.

Some nationalists, such as Subhas Chandra Bose in India, decided to accept Japanese rule, preferring it to their European rulers. Most, however, soon realised that Japanese rule was no better and struggled against it. Having fought against the Japanese, they were in no mood to succumb to European rule again. The Dutch returned to find an armed nationalist movement in Indonesia as did the French in Indo-China (see Source 116).

The European countries, weakened by war, could no longer afford the costs of Empire either. India became independent from the British in 1947, under Prime Minister Nehru (see Sources 117 and 118).

The fine words of the Atlantic Charter (see Source 111, page 166) had a powerful meaning all over the world. Why shouldn't all the people in the world have the right to rule themselves? From Asia to Africa and the Caribbean, the days of colonial rule were numbered.

SOURCE 117
British troops march past the British Governor of Bombay and the Indian Prime Minister before handing over power to India, August 1947.

SOURCE 116
Vietnamese soldiers celebrate independence from France, 1952.

SOURCE 118
Nehru, first Prime Minister of independent India, 1947.

Glossary

Allotment
Small piece of land which people rent to grow crops for their own use, mainly vegetables.

Anti-Semitism
Hatred of Jews.

Armistice
An agreement between countries at war to stop fighting for a time to discuss a peace settlement.

Assassinate
To murder a public figure or important person.

Attrition
Wearing down the enemy by attacking over a long period, causing regular losses.

Blockade
The military stopping of supplies to the enemy, for example by stopping or sinking ships.

Celibate
Remaining unmarried.

Census
Counting the number of people in the country. A population census has been carried out by the British government every 10 years since 1801 (except for 1941).

Democracy
System of government where the people choose their rulers by voting for them in regular elections.

Dictator
A leader whose rule is not restricted by a constitution, laws or a recognised opposition.

Domestic system
The system of making cloth, or any other product, in people's homes.

Duckboards
Wooden boards laid over a muddy trench floor.

Dugout
A shelter in the wall of a trench.

Emigrate
To leave your own country permanently.

Empire
Many lands and people under one ruler.

Epidemic
Disease affecting a large number of people.

Evangelicals
Members of the Christian church who place a strong emphasis on converting others to Christianity.

Factory
Building where products are made by machines, usually powered machines.

Fatigues
Duties carried out by soldiers.

Fire step
The ledge in a trench the sentry stands on.

Ghettoes
Areas of cities, often run-down and over-crowded, where Jews were made to live.

Guerrilla
Armed resistance fighter, often attacking the enemy in small groups in surprise attacks.

Haberdashery
Items used for sewing, such as buttons, zips and ribbons.

Horse-power
Way of measuring the strength of power.

Illegitimate
Referring to a child whose parents are not married.

Incendiary bombs
Bomb designed to cause a fire when it explodes.

Indoctrination
Efforts to persuade people to believe something by repeating it often.

Industrial Revolution
Inventions causing a change in the way goods are produced. These technological developments are usually accompanied by social changes.

Industrialised
Place or country where industry is the most important economic activity.

Infant mortality
Annual number of deaths of children under age one year per 1,000 live births.

Infantry
Troops on foot.

Ironfounder
Someone who runs an ironworks.

Isolationist
Being reluctant to become involved in other countries or international affairs.

Justice of the Peace (JP)
Magistrate who is not a lawyer but is given powers to act as a judge in a local court.

Laissez-faire
The policy of not interfering in social and economic affairs.

Looms
Apparatus – worked by hand or mechanically – for weaving yarn into cloth.

Magistrate
Official who acts as a judge in law courts which deal with less serious crimes or disputes.

Manufacturing
Making products for sale.

Maroons
Runaway slaves.

Media
Methods of transmitting information.

Mobilise
To prepare armed forces for war.

Monopoly
Having exclusive control over a market.

Municipal
To do with towns and cities (*see also* under socialism).

Mutiny
When soldiers (or sailors) disobey their officers and turn against them.

Nabob
Rich East India Company merchant, living like an Indian prince.

No-man's land
The zone between enemy trenches.

Obeah men
Leaders of a cult which originated in West Africa and was also used in the Caribbean.

Offensive
A large-scale planned attack.

Paddle-steamer
Steam-powered boat in which the engine drives large paddles to make the boat move.

Pamphlet
Small booklet or newsletter.

Patent
A grant given to an inventor by the government.

Patriotism
Being proud of your country.

Pawnshop
Shop of a moneylender who lends money in return for goods. You claim your goods back when you can repay the money with interest.

Plantations
Very large farms on which crops such as sugar-cane, tobacco, rice and cotton were grown. Plantations used slave labour.

Plebiscite
A vote by all the people of a country.

Platoon
A section of an army regiment of about 30 men.

Propaganda
Information put out by a government or organisation to influence public opinion.

Radical
Someone who works for a big change in the way the country is governed.

Reform
Change: in particular, changing the way Parliament was elected, who could vote and who could be an MP.

Reparations
Payments of money made by the loser of a war to the victor.

Royalty
A sum of money paid for the permission to use a patented invention.

Sanctions
A penalty (often refusing to sell oil or other goods) imposed on a country or group to persuade them to obey certain rules.

Sentry
A soldier who keeps watch for enemy attack.

Sewage
Waste products from people and households.

Socialism
Belief that, because the difference between rich and poor is so great, the government should intervene to achieve more equality by helping poor people. 'Municipal socialism' is where town or city governments raise money by local taxes (rates) and use it to improve conditions.

Spin
To make wool or cotton into thread.

Sterilised
Operated on so that they could never have children.

Strategy
The overall plan for a war or battle.

Subscription
The money paid to join an organisation.

Suburbs
Areas of housing built around a city.

Suffragettes
Those who campaigned for the right of women to have the vote.

Temperance
Not drinking alcohol.

Terrace
Row of houses, joined together.

Testimonies
Spoken or written reports of events.

Trade union
Organisation of all the workers of a particular trade. They combine together so as to be stronger in pressing for what they each want.

Transported
Form of punishment in which people were forcibly taken to live and work in a colony, usually Australia.

Ultimatum
A final offer or warning issued during negotiations.

Urban
To do with towns or cities: opposite of rural.

Weaver
The person who makes cloth by weaving the YARN on a machine called a loom.

Welfare state
A system where the government provides benefits for those in need in society, such as the old or the unemployed, by a scheme into which all pay contributions.

Yarn
Continuous thread made by spinning fibres or wool and cotton together.

Yeomanry
A cavalry force, formed in 1761, made up of local volunteers.

Every effort has been made to contact the holders of copyright material but if any have been inadvertently overlooked the publishers will be pleased to make the necessary arrangements at the first opportunity.

Photographs The publishers would like to thank the following for permission to reproduce photographs on these pages:

T = top, B = bottom, C = centre, L = left, R = right

After the Battle 96; AKG, London 115T, 115B, 131R; Barbados National Trust 36T; Barnaby's Picture Library 102BL, 158; Beamish Open Air Museum 63; Bildarchiv Preussischer Kulturbesitz 160L; Birmingham City Museums and Art Gallery 45L; Courtesy Bolton Metro 23TR; Bridgeman Art Library/Manchester City Art Gallery 4R; City of Bristol Museum and Art Gallery 27; The British Library 5L, 36B; Reproduced by courtesy of the Trustees of the British Museum 29B; British Waterways 10-11; Bundesarchiv Koblenz 112C, 116B, 117TR; Cambridge University Library 7B; Camera Press 107C, 168BR; Centre for the Study of Cartoons and Caricature, Canterbury/Trustees of the Evening Standard 103CR and 113, David Low, 137B Vicky; Cheltenham Art Gallery and Museum 21B; Chicago Historical Society 29T; Commonwealth War Graves Commission 98; Communist Party Library 52; Courtesy of the Co-operative Union Ltd 54B; Crown copyright/Cambridge University Collection of Air Photographs 15R; Robin Dengate 19B; Derby Local Studies Library 7T; E.T. Archive 33L, 77; Edifice/Darley 8, 24T; Peter Fisher 79T, 79C, 79BR, 96, 97; Courtesy of the Foreign and Commonwealth Office Library 33R; Fotomas Index 37B; Courtesy Gladstone Pottery Museum 21C; Glasgow Museums/The People's Palace 66; John Gorman Collection 55, 57R; Greater London Photograph Library 25T, 69B, 73L; Guildhall Library 32; Helmshore, Lancashire County Museums 6; Henry Moore Foundation 143C; David Hey 5R; Hulton Deutsch Collection, 20T, 22, 60B, 62T, 64, 68T, 71L, 72, 73R, 74TL, 74TC, 74TR, 81, 140L, 143T, 144TR, 148R, 150, 165, 168C, 168BL; Illustrated London News 152; Imperial War Museum 84, 85, 86, 87, 88, 92, 93, 95, 100T, 100B. 101, 106, 108T, 109, 125, 126BL, 127T, 127B, 128, 129 139L, 142TR, 144TL, 147, 148L, 149, 151, 154, 155, 162BR, 166; Iona Antiques 15L; Jacob's Bakery 156; Oscar and Peter Johnson 26; Library of Congress, Washington, D.C. 164; ©Jeremy Lowe, 'Welsh Industrial Workers Housing 1775-1875', Cardiff 1989 17; Manchester Central Library 13, 50, 58R; The Mander and Mitchenson Collection 25B; Mansell Collection 9B, 12, 35R, 38, 39R, 40, 43B, 45R, 46T, 49B, 54T, 57L, 58L, 62B, 69T, 74BL, 74BC, 75T, 75B, 76B, 107T; Mary Evans Picture Library 91, 117TL, 146; Military Archive and Research Services 136; Philip Mould 18; Musée Carnavalet 43T; Museum of London 46B; National Library of Jamaica 39L; The Board of Trustees of NMGM 24B; The National Museum of Labour History 56, 68B; Courtesy of the New York Historical Society, New York City 37T; Peter Newark's Historical Pictures 11; Collection Newport Museum and Art Gallery, Gwent 53; O.I.O.C, British Library 31B; A. J. Peacock, 'A Rendevous with Death', Gunfire no. 5 90; Edward Piper 23TL; Popperfoto 103T, 111, 116C, 133TR, 134T, 138L, 138R, 140R, 142B, 144B, 145; Private Collection 19T; The Punch Library 65; Rex Features 76T, 78, 132T, 159, 162T, 167T, 167B; RGS 31T; Robert Opie 139R; Robert Hunt Library 108B, 133TL, 133B, 137T, 162BL; Courtesy Rochdale Metro 23B; Royal Albert Memorial Museum 34; The Royal Archives © 1995 Her Majesty the Queen 44; Reproduced by permission of the Trustees of the Science Museum 3, 9T; Sheffield Industrial Museum 16T; Society for Co-operation in Russian and Soviet Studies 131L; Staatliche Museen zu Berlin, Preussischer Kulturbesitz Nationalgalerie 99; Süddeutscher Verlag 112B, 114, 118B, 160R; Syndication International 102BR; The Tate Gallery, London 4L; Tolson Museum/Kirklees Metropolitan Council 48; Topham Picture Source 79BL, 82, 103CL, 118T, 134B, 147T, 161; The Master and Fellows of Trinity College, Cambridge 61; TUC LIbrary 74BR; Ullstein Bilderdienst 120, 121, 126BR, 130, 135; Victoria and Albert Museum 21T; The Victorian Society 20B; Harland Walshaw/Dorothy Girouard 16B; Courtesy Josiah Wedgwood and Sons Ltd 41; Weimar Archive 119; Weiner Library 122, 124T, 124B; Welsh Industrial and Maritime Museum 60T; Wilberforce House, Hull City Museums, Art Galleries and Archives 35L; Windsor Castle Royal Library © 1995 Her Majesty the Queen 51; Yale University Library 42.

Cover photographs Reproduced by permission of the Trustees of the Science Museum R; Hulton Deutsch Collection L.

The authors and publishers gratefully acknowledge the following publications from which written sources in this book are drawn:

After the Battle for an extract from Rose E.B. Coombs, *Before Endeavours Fade*; Cambridge University Press for an extract from Gill Thomas, *Life on All Fronts*, 1989; Jonathan Cape for extracts from Angus Calder and Dorothy Sheridan, *Mass Observation – Speak for Yourselves*; Leo Cooper for an extract from H. Sulzbach, *With the German Guns*, 1973; André Deutsch Ltd for an extract from John Ellis, *Brute Force*; Faber and Faber Ltd for extracts from Siegfried Sassoon, *Memoirs of an Infantry Officer,* 1930; Robert Hale Limited for an extract from Nigel Jones, *The War Walk*, 1983; The Controller of Her Majesty's Stationery Office for an extract from Crown copyright material held in the Public Record Office (WO 95/2308, *Newfoundland Regiment War Diary*) and for an extract from *The Strategic Air Offensive Against Germany, 1939–1945*;

ACKNOWLEDGEMENTS

The Imperial War Museum for captions from the film *The Battle of the Somme*, 1916 (captions 8, 41 and 37), preserved in the film archive of the Imperial War Museum, Lambeth Road, London, from whom copies of the film may be purchased on video-cassette or rented; Michael Joseph for an extract from T.E.B. Clarke, *This Is Where I Came In*; extract from Sir Charles Webster and Noble Frankland; Thomas Nelson for an extract from Stuart Sillars, *Women in World War I*, 1987; Oxford University Press for extracts from James Munson (ed), *Echoes of the Great War: The Diary of the Reverend Andrew Clark 1914-1919* © James Munson, 1985; Dr A.J. Peacock for extracts from 'A Rendezvous with Death', *Gun Fire* issue number 5, 1986; George Sassoon for poems by Siegfried Sassoon: 'The Hero' and 'The General'; Sidgwick and Jackson for extracts from Malcolm Brown, *The First World War*, 1991; Trentham Books Ltd for extracts from Carrie Supple, *The Holocaust;* Virago Press for an extract from Vera Brittain, *Testament of Youth*, © Paul Berry, The Literary Executor of Vera Brittain, 1970; A.P. Watt Ltd on behalf of The Executors of the Estate of Lord Beveridge for a short extract from *Beveridge and his Plan*; Weidenfeld and Nicolson Ltd for an extract from Konrad Adenauer, *Memoirs 1945–1953* and Joachim Fest *Hitler*.

First published in 1995 by Collins Educational
An imprint of Harper Collins *Publishers*
77-85 Fulham Palace Road
Hammersmith
London W6 8JB

ISBN 000 327280 X

The publishers would like to thank Fiona Macdonald for writing the depth study 'Women's lives' (pages 66–75).

Series planned by Nicole Lagneau
Edited by Helen Mortimer and Lorimer Poultney
Cover designed by Glynis Edwards
Book designed by Sally Boothroyd and Derek Lee
Picture research by Celia Dearing and Diana Morris
Artwork by John Booth, Gay Galsworthy, Julia Osorno, Linda Rogers Associates/Peter Dennis
Production by Mandy Inness
Printed and bound by Rotolito Lombarda, Italy